EDITED BY CONNIE CULPEPPER

The Same River Twice:

Reminiscences from a Century of Learning at Peabody Demonstration School-University School of Nashville

1915-2015

Edited by Connie Culpepper

Printed in the United States of America

ISBN 978-161522-471-5

University School of Nashville
2000 Edgehill Avenue
Nashville, Tennessee 37212

www.usn.org

ACKNOWLEDGMENTS FROM THE EDITOR

We are grateful to the alumni and others who wrote essays for this book, taking time from already busy schedules to take on this project. We are also grateful to those who found time to be interviewed by the writers or to contribute their recollections in writing. Thanks also go to Susan Pearlman, assistant to Vince Durnan, who typed the selections from The Past Is Prologue *that appear in this book; to Lorie Hoover, who proofed each chapter; to Jenny Winston and Jeff Goold for finding the photos we needed; to everyone who offered advice and support no matter how many times I asked for them.*

—CONNIE CULPEPPER

CONTENTS

This Centennial book was conceived as a celebration of whatever it is in the "Peabody spirit" that provides the energy, determination, and optimism required to carry University School of Nashville to its 100th birthday. Despite, and maybe because of, what were long odds at crucial junctures, we have reached this milestone.

When we first thought about writing a book to celebrate the Centennial, we knew that the book should contain more than one voice. We asked some writers who are members of the PDS and USN family to contribute their views of the school's history, whether formed as a student, a teacher, or an administrator. And we asked them to share their stories.

This book was never intended to be a comprehensive history of a school with more tales and legends than most. It's a collection of essays bound together only by their chief subject: Peabody Demonstration School or University School of Nashville. No two voices are alike, but each expresses a truth.

We hope you will hear echoes of your own experience if you were a student or teacher here or if your family shares a connection with the Peabody Demonstration School-University School of Nashville narrative. We offer this volume in gratitude for all the effort that has brought us this far, and we look forward, as our predecessors seem always to have done, to a bright future.

DAVID EWING
Class of 1985

Before We Arrived

In 1915 Nashville was a growing city. Fifty years after the end of the Civil War, the capital of Tennessee was rapidly expanding.

After the Civil War, many Northern religious institutions and philanthropists decided that Nashville, after being occupied for three years by the Federal Army, needed institutions for the education of former slaves, women, and other citizens.

THE AFRICAN-AMERICAN AND WOMEN'S ATHENS OF THE SOUTH

In the 1860s, three new colleges were started for the education of African-Americans: Fisk University, Central Tennessee College (later Walden University), and Roger Williams University. That same decade, two schools, St. Cecilia Academy and Ward Seminary (later Ward-Belmont, now Harpeth Hall), were established to educate girls.

After the Civil War, Nashville grew as an education center. By the turn of the century, Nashville was a leading city for schools and colleges for women, including Price's College for Women, Radnor College for Women, Belmont College for Women, Buford College, and Boscobel College. Nashville was popularly known as "The Athens of The South," but it also had a great reputation for the education of African-Americans and women.

Others benefited as well. In 1873 railroad and shipping magnate Cornelius Vanderbilt agreed to give what would amount to a million dollar gift to establish a university in Nashville. Religious colleges also found a good home in Nashville. In 1891 Nashville Bible School (now Lipscomb University) was established on the outskirts of Nashville. Another religious school, Trevecca Nazarene University, was started in 1901 and is now on the old campus of Walden University on Murfreesboro Road. In 1928 the Dominican Sisters started St. Cecilia Normal School, which in 1961 became Aquinas Junior College (now Aquinas College).

One of the oldest schools in Nashville was Roger Williams University, which was started for former slaves. Its first site was in downtown Nashville, but the college purchased land south of Edgehill Avenue in order to expand. The American Baptist Home Mission Society, the Northeastern white religious group which started the school, purchased the Gordon estate (now the current site of Peabody College) in 1874, the year after Vanderbilt was founded. Roger Williams University's two main academic buildings and a dorm were built on the highest point of the property along Hillsboro Road, just across the street from Vanderbilt University.

Roger Williams University thrived and was an important place where many African-Americans, including John Hope, a future President of Morehouse College, graduated. In 1905 two separate mysterious fires started in the two main buildings, Centennial Hall and the Mansion House, completely destroying them. The students and faculty wished to rebuild on the site, but the Baptist Mission Society kept the insurance money and sold the land out from under the school. The society built a new, smaller, and inferior campus in the Whites Creek area near Nashville. The college struggled in their new location and closed in 1929. That campus is the current site of American Baptist College.

THE FIRST SCHOOL IN THE ATHENS OF THE SOUTH

Nashville's commitment to education goes back to its very beginnings. Its oldest educational institution was the University of Nashville. Its roots can be traced back to December 1785, when the state of North Carolina gave James Robertson, the co-founder of Nashville, a 240-acre land grant and approved the charter for Davidson Academy. In 1786 this small preparatory school for boys opened its doors six miles northeast of Nashville on Gallatin Road in a small rural stone church. In 1805 the school moved downtown near the area of Nashville that James Robertson and John Donelson had originally settled.

The land grant included 240 acres of the Broadway area and south up to Rutledge Hill. With no bridges built to cross the Cumberland River, trustees of Davidson Academy operated a ferry from the east bank to the area where Riverfront Park is today to make it easier for students to attend this new school. The school would later donate three acres of land for the construction of the street called Broadway. Other land was eventually sold, and the school kept just seven acres at the highest point where Davidson Academy built their campus. In 1806 the school changed its name to Cumberland College. In 1824 Phillip Lindsley, acting President of the College of New Jersey (now Princeton University), was hired as President, turning down New Jersey's offer of a permanent job. The school had good leadership, with Presidents Andrew Jackson, James K. Polk, and Andrew Johnson each serving as trustees at one time.

Two years later, the Tennessee state legislature changed the name and charter to "The University of Nashville." During the 25 years of Phillip Lindsley's leadership, the school enrolled 1,059 students and awarded 432 degrees. It was during Lindsley's tenure that Nashville was first called the Athens of the West, later changed to the South. In 1850 the university and city faced a huge cholera outbreak. Many students died from the disease, and funeral processions to the nearby City Cemetery became a common sight. In the spring of 1850, Phillip Lindsley resigned as president, and the university temporarily closed.

NASHVILLE'S FIRST MEDICAL SCHOOL

In October of 1850, Lindsley's son Dr. John Berrien Lindsley reopened the school as a medical school. The success of the medical school allowed the University of Nashville to reopen its literary department. Lindsley needed to build a new building for the academic department. The Tennessee State Capitol had just been completed on the highest point in the city, and Lindsley wanted the second highest point to have a Gothic stone building to educate his students. In October 1854 classes were first held in Lindsley Hall, but the school continued to struggle.

Though the university closed during the Civil War, Lindsley was allowed by the Union Army who occupied Nashville to keep the medical school in operation. From 1875 to 1895, Vanderbilt University and the University of Nashville jointly operated the medical school, and the diplomas bore both schools' names. In 1895 after Vanderbilt's prestige grew, Vanderbilt severed their ties and opened up their own medical school. Without Vanderbilt, the University of Nashville struggled to keep the medical school and eventually merged it with the University of Tennessee medical department.

The University of Nashville reopened after the Civil War and in 1867 used money from a bequest to establish on their downtown campus an all boys' school, Montgomery Bell Academy, named after the benefactor. The state legislature acted again, in 1875 amending its charter to establish a state normal school at the University of Nashville. The Peabody Fund to educate teachers supported this program, which held classes in Lindsley Hall. The support continued to grow, and in 1889 the school was renamed Peabody Normal College. A new University of Nashville board was formed to oversee the operations of Peabody College, while the original board kept oversight of MBA and the medical department. In 1911, facing competition from Vanderbilt and a declining enrollment, the University of Nashville closed its doors.

This stone, once displayed on the University of Nashville's Gate Keeper's Lodge on Second Avenue, now lies on the ground at Peabody College near the Mayborn Building.

The medical school graduated its last student in 1911. Though the trustees attempted to give the medical properties to the University of Tennessee, this move was blocked by the Tennessee legislature, whose members were urged by Vanderbilt to prevent the state school from having a large foothold in Nashville, according to Ridley Wills' *History of MBA*. The University of Tennessee kept the medical department and as a compromise moved it to Memphis, where it would not directly compete with Vanderbilt. During this period the state legislature started a normal school in 1911, now known as Middle Tennessee State University, and in 1912 a normal school for African-American teachers which is now known as Tennessee State University.

University School's surviving tie to the old University of Nashville is that when Peabody Demonstration School opened, it used the school colors of the University of Nashville: garnet and Columbia blue. When PDS was reincorporated in 1975, its new name "University School of Nashville" also suggested a tie to the past institution. Today the only building remaining from the old University of Nashville campus on 2nd Avenue is Lindsley Hall, now a Metro office building.

One of the final acts of the University of Nashville board was to decide where Montgomery Bell Academy would be located. The board of the new Peabody College for Teachers wanted to take over the remaining assets of the University of Nashville including MBA. The proposal would have relocated MBA south of Capers Avenue, making MBA the model school of Peabody College. This idea did have some support among the University of Nashville trustees, but in December 1912 a proposal to convey the assets of the University of Nashville (including MBA) to Peabody College was rejected 7-4. Four months later, the same proposal was rejected again 6-4 by the board. After both unsuccessful votes, Peabody College President Dr. Bruce Payne moved ahead with plans to develop his new campus without MBA, deciding to create a new model school called "Peabody Demonstration School" on the new campus which was about to open. In 1915 MBA moved from downtown Nashville to their current location on Harding Road.

The newly established Peabody College also searched for a new home, with its board divided on whether to stay on its historic hilltop site overlooking downtown Nashville and the Cumberland River or move outside the then city limits across from Vanderbilt on Hillsboro Pike. It was a time when most schools and colleges were fleeing downtown for more land in less urban settings. After the Roger Williams fire, rumors spread about Peabody's interest in its suburban site. There was even talk that the two universities would trade locations, and Roger Williams would move downtown. In 1906 newspapers reported that the former site of Roger Williams was being developed by local construction firm Foster and Creighton, who promised

13,000 yards of excavation, 3,800 feet of new streets, and 3,000 feet of sidewalk. This project never happened, and years later the vacant campus was still on the market.

NEW NEIGHBORS IN EDGEHILL

At the turn of the century, the area around Edgehill Avenue had great promise for development even before Peabody College moved to the area. One of the first neighborhood groups of the area, called "Belmont Civic Federation," presented a lengthy report urging the city to improve the area and establish guidelines for future residential development. The group endorsed the "City Beautiful" campaign of the recently formed Centennial Club, which lobbied for a clean city with safe streets and more trees and parks. The Belmont group abolished the "front fences" in the neighborhood and set a goal to remove back fences of homes as well. The 1909 report said, "with back fences go the ugly coal sheds and chicken coops." The group went on to pass a resolution to depart "the medieval days of wandering stock including chickens. None of them have a place in a city." The report concludes that back fences are "hideous" and "hedges make a fine substitute." These improvements in the area attracted more families and developers.

In 1909 business leader Percy Warner proposed a new Hillsboro Pike streetcar line to extend from Broadway down Hillsboro Road to Acklen Avenue. The line helped drive the residential growth of the area and made it a more attractive location for Peabody College to move to in 1911.

After new streetcar service brought more people to the area, the city of Nashville improved water and sewer service to the neighborhood. In 1913 Nashville started work on a new $16,000 water main down Edgehill, reaching Hillsboro with 6,715 feet of iron pipe. Years before, the Nashville city council had approved $3,000 to connect the Edgehill area to the West End sewer line. The Edgehill Avenue neighborhood now had water, sewer, and new sidewalks, and houses were rapidly being built in the area.

PEABODY COLLEGE'S NEW HOME

In 1910 the Peabody College Board of Trustees made a deal to purchase the 27-acre Roger Williams site for $172,000. The George Peabody Fund had given $1,000,000 for a new campus, but none of the money could be used for buildings or the site. The million dollars was for endowment only, so the city, county and state leaders worked together to help close the deal. The city of Nashville contributed $100,000 while Davidson County gave another $200,000, and the state of Tennessee added $250,000. With this money in hand, the board closed on the deal and made plans to build a new campus.

The first home of PDS as it appears today.

In 1912 work began on six of the thirty-three campus buildings designed by the New York architecture firm of Ludlow and Peabody, where architect Henry C. Hibbs worked. Hibbs' work included the President's House, Women's Dormitory, Domestic Economy building, the powerhouse, manual training building, and the Psychology Building. When Peabody College opened the Demonstration School, it was housed in the Jesup Psychology Building, where it remained until 1925. (In 1916 Hibbs would leave the firm, move to Nashville, and continue to design buildings for local colleges.)

South of the future site of Peabody College was the most significant and historic home in the area, "Belmont," built in 1853 as the summer home for Adelicia and Joseph Acklen. During the Civil War the mansion was briefly taken over by the Union Army. It served as headquarters for General Thomas Wood on December 1, 1864, two weeks prior to the Battle of Nashville. It was inside Belmont Mansion that General Wood and 122 of his soldiers planned their strategy. On December 15 they ordered the 13,000 troops that were stationed behind the mansion to go into battle during the Battle of Nashville's first day.

After Acklen's death, the mansion was sold, and in 1890 a new women's college called Belmont College for Women began to hold classes in the mansion. This women's school merged with Ward Seminary in 1913 to become Ward-Belmont, which it remained until 1951. Then the Tennessee Baptist Convention purchased the land and the school to start a new four-year Baptist college called Belmont College (now Belmont University).

When Commodore Cornelius Vanderbilt gave $1,000,000 to start a college, the site selected was outside the city limits of Nashville in an area which was largely undeveloped. In fact, the first line of Vanderbilt's Alma Mater is "On the city's western border, reared against the sky." But that area quickly experienced a real estate boom too, with the new streetcar lines one factor. Another factor was the Centennial Exposition.

GREATEST SHOW IN TENNESSEE

When Vanderbilt opened in 1873, West Side Park was the largest nearby landmark. West Side Park, a racetrack on West End Avenue, was the home of the 19th century version of the Tennessee State Fair. The neighborhood was transformed and greatly improved after the site was selected in 1897 for the Tennessee Centennial Exposition.

The Exposition, led by John W. Thomas, president of the Nashville, Chattanooga and St. Louis Railroad, started May 1, 1897 and lasted six months. Modeled after Chicago's famous Columbian Exposition known as "The White City," it attracted people from every state, including 21 governors who visited the biggest event the state of Tennessee had ever seen. On October 31, 1897 when the fair closed, over 1.8 million people had attended, including President William McKinley, Booker T. Washington, and Susan B. Anthony. Its success meant many Nashville citizens and visitors saw this choice area of Davidson County for the first time.

ON HILLSBORO PIKE

In 1903 another school was eyeing the area near the future home of PDS as an excellent location. The Sisters of Mercy, who first opened a school for Catholic girls in 1866, purchased the home of the late George Sterling Bolling, moving St. Bernard Academy to its current location off Hillsboro Pike in 1905.

Hillsboro Pike was a main thoroughfare out of Nashville on the way to Franklin. In the 1920s a bustling shopping district was formed along it, with two significant movie houses. The Hillsboro Theatre (now The Belcourt Theatre) started as a movie house after the silent movie era. At its original entrance on Hillsboro, where the Villager pub is today, the name "Hillsboro" is still visible above the door. The Hillsboro soon had a big competitor at the end of the block, "the Belmont," owned by the South's largest theatre owner, Tony Sudekum. Its Southwest Spanish style architecture set the Belmont apart from the big Art Deco marquee theatres of the era.

Unable to compete against the Sudekum theatre empire, the Hillsboro's owners turned their house to live performances and plays. While the Belmont was showing first run movies in the 30s, the Hillsboro became the second home of the Grand Ole Opry and where it had its first stage. The Opry, which had outgrown its home on the fifth floor of National Life Insurance Company in downtown, invited the public officially to watch the show for the first time on Hillsboro Pike.

ON EDGEHILL

The name for Edgehill Avenue came from the name of Charles A. R. Thompson's Victorian home Edgehill on that street. This 75-acre estate near the corner of Edgehill and Hillsboro included the land where PDS was later built and where Scarritt-Bennett is located today. (The house Edgehill was later moved to Bowling Avenue.)

Where USN stands today, in 1896 Vanderbilt student Thomas Webb, Jr. and three of his friends built a crude nine-hole golf course, according to Ridley Wills' *History of Belle Meade Country Club*. This course, believed to be the first in Nashville, was made with empty tomato cans pushed into the ground for each hole and broomsticks serving as pins. The cattle grazing the land kept the grass low for ideal golfing, and the course's proximity to Vanderbilt meant students could play when not in class. The nine-hole course enticed other men to try this game, including those who a few years later founded Belle Meade Country Club.

The area around Peabody Demonstration School soon became a thriving middle class neighborhood with close access to Nashville. Edgehill Avenue starts at Hillsboro Pike and extends to 8th Avenue. Though it's less than two miles long, Edgehill has had more major schools than any street in Nashville except West End Avenue. Across from University School of Nashville today is the campus of Peabody College of Vanderbilt University, then around 12th Avenue Carter Lawrence School, then Rose Park Middle School, The W.O. Smith School of Music, and, at the corner of Edgehill Avenue and 8th Avenue, the Fall School building, the oldest Nashville public school building still standing today.

In 1897 the city of Nashville constructed this modern two story, perfectly square brick building with a short tower at the cost of $20,000. The Fall School was named after Phillip Fall, who was the father of one of the first school teachers in Nashville. This school enrolled 275 children from first through eighth grades. Its state-of-the-art building was the first in Nashville to use venetian blinds, which regulated daylight better than shades. Every classroom was situated so sunlight would come over each student's left shoulder from the rear. It was the first school to capitalize on an expanding population south of Nashville and outside of the district where Hume School was located.

Former postmaster and mayor of Nashville Brownlee Currey lived at the highest point of Edgehill in the early 19th century. The land was considered as the site for Nashville's reservoir because of its height before the present nearby location off of 8th Avenue was picked. When Currey's home stood there, the hill was much higher than it is today. Currey Hill later served as a rock quarry until the 1960s, with its rock used for the reservoir. Today the Currey land is Metro's Rose Park, which has a community center and sports fields used by Belmont University and the neighborhood.

TENNESSEE WILLIAMS' FIRST EDUCATION?

From 1914-1916 when he was a child, the famous playwright Tennessee Williams lived a few blocks away from the current site of University School. Four-year-old Williams lived with his grandmother and grandfather, the Rev. Walter E. Dakin, rector of The Episcopal Church of the Advent on the corner of Edgehill and 17th Avenue in a brick rectory next to the church. In an interview years later, Tennessee fondly remembered taking trips to Centennial Park with his African-American Nurse Ozie, who would read ghost stories to him and make up some others.

"Tom," as he was called as a child, also recalled crying when his mother dropped him off at kindergarten for the first time. The city of Nashville did not offer kindergarten classes in this era, and it is very likely Tennessee Williams attended PDS for one year when he lived two blocks away. Sadly, no PDS kindergarten records from the early years exist. It was in Nashville that Tennessee said he rode his first streetcar. (When Tennessee Williams died in 1983, he left his estate to The University of the South in honor of his grandfather, who graduated from Sewanee.)

Edgehill Avenue was a diverse neighborhood, especially in the area near Fort Negley and 12th Avenue, with African-Americans moving there from downtown around the turn of the century. Before the Civil War, the area around the current site of Schermerhorn Symphony Center was home to many stables, feed stores, and other agriculture supply stores. It was also the site of slave auctions. After the Civil War, many African-Americans lived in the area south of Broadway referred to as "Black Bottom." (The Wallace University School for Boys was founded in 1886 and was located in this area at the current site of the Music City Center. Later Wallace also joined the exodus of downtown schools to the Hillsboro area, moving to West End and 20th Avenue.)

Starting in the 1870s, city leaders wanted to move the African-American population out of this part of downtown. After decades of being pressured to leave this area so the city could "clean it up," many residents of Black Bottom moved to the Edgehill Avenue Area. The areas around Wedgewood-Houston and Fort Negley became African-American neighborhoods.

WILLIAM EDMONDSON ON CAMPUS

One famous African-American Edgehill area resident was William Edmondson. The son of slaves, Edmondson lacked a formal education and worked menial jobs before he said he was called by God to be a sculptor. His primitive limestone carvings of animals, birds, and historic figures were displayed in the front yard of his home on 14th Avenue South near Edgehill, attracting the attention of numerous art patrons. In 1937 this attention allowed him to become the first American-American to have a solo show at the Museum of Modern Art in New York.

According to an interview, Katherine Reed, a sixth grader at PDS in 1915 (its first year) remembers meeting Edmondson at school. Reed said that from the fall of 1916 until 1918, William Edmondson worked at PDS as a janitor in the Psychology Building, where she took classes before the 1925 PDS building opening.

A tragic event occurred near Peabody's campus before PDS had its own building. In 1916 after school one day, a nine-year-old student, Norman Wilson Griswold, Jr., went with two friends to play football on Vanderbilt's campus. After crossing Hillsboro at Edgehill and climbing a fence to reach Vanderbilt, the three boys finished their game and climbed back over the fence to cross Hillsboro. The outbound streetcar passed the boys on their way back toward Peabody campus with Norman leading the way. He did not see the inbound street car, which struck Norman. The child suffered massive head injuries and died at the hospital. A few weeks later, on the same spot, a streetcar struck a horse and wagon and injured both driver and passenger.

While the Peabody Demonstration School building at 2000 Edgehill Avenue was going up, across the street on 19th Avenue Peabody College architect Henry Hibbs was working on another big educational project. In 1924 Hibbs was hired to design buildings for a college moving to Nashville from Kansas City, Scarritt College for Christian Workers (now Scarritt-Bennett Center). His use of light-colored Crab Orchard stone in the Gothic style buildings of Scarritt immediately gained Hibbs more awards and national attention. The buildings included Scarritt Hall, Bennett Hall, The Tower, and Wightman Chapel, where Dr. Martin Luther King, Jr. spoke in 1957, just across the street from PDS during the dawn of the Civil Rights Movement. Hibbs would use similar Gothic style in 1930 when he designed the library at Fisk University with another tall, looming tower made of red brick with Indiana limestone.

Today the Edgehill neighborhood includes a mix of artists, educators, young families, and older African-American families who grew up in the neighborhood. In the 1950s singers, songwriters, producers, and publishing companies flocked to the area, and since then, with its famous recording studios, it has been known as "Music Row." As Nashville and the Vanderbilt campus have grown, the Edgehill area still feels local and welcoming to those who live there and visit.

Peabody Demonstration School's long journey from its downtown roots in the earliest days of Nashville was aided by Nashville's growth of population to the western suburbs. As streetcar lines and automobiles made this area more accessible, its popularity grew. Peabody President Payne's vision of a large campus anchored by the new Demonstration School across the street on Edgehill Avenue was complete in 1925.

DAVID EWING

David Ewing '85 is a ninth-generation Nashvillian, lawyer, and historian. He graduated from Connecticut College and Vanderbilt School of Law. He frequently speaks, writes, and gives tours on Nashville history. He started the Facebook site "The Nashville I Wish I Knew," which was voted the "Best Facebook Page" in the 2013 Readers and Editors Poll of the *Nashville Scene*. He is the past President of the Old Oak Club. David is married to Alice Randall, and his step-daughter Caroline Randall Williams attended USN from kindergarten to eighth grade.

A shorter version of this chapter appeared in *2000 Edgehill, the Alumni Magazine of Peabody Demonstration School and University School of Nashville*, Issue 1, 2014.

CONNIE CULPEPPER
Communications Director, 1995-Present
University School of Nashville

How it Began:
The First Quarter Century

It's a miracle that we are celebrating a century of exemplary education on this corner. More than once, even long before anyone thought of Peabody Demonstration School, the failure of the whole enterprise seemed inevitable.

The struggle that ultimately resulted in today's peaceful neighborhood group of Vanderbilt University, its Peabody College, and University School of Nashville was long and, metaphorically speaking, bloody. At first it pitted light against darkness, North against South, youth against age, man against worm. And it grew from an attempt to heal the wounds from the nation's greatest struggle.

Before University School came Peabody Demonstration School, founded in 1915 by Peabody College. We can trace the story of Peabody College to its nineteenth century beginnings on the campus of the University of Nashville. *That* school was founded in 1826 as the successor to Davidson Academy and Cumberland College, which began in 1785 despite the fact that no Nashville existed, nor even Tennessee, for that matter. Cherokees, who had yet to concede their land to the settlers, attacked the school.

By 1875, the University of Nashville had relinquished its briefly-realized claims to being a great university. Indeed, nothing remained but its South Nashville campus and Montgomery Bell Academy. So began the State Normal College, the ancestor of George Peabody College for Teachers, the parent of the Winthrop School, and thus the grandparent of University School of Nashville. (A "normal" school trained teachers, with less rigorous academic requirements than those of a college. Nashville's was considered the best in the South.)

THE OLD VS. THE NEW

Paul Conkin's *Peabody College: From a Frontier Academy to the Frontiers of Teaching and Learning* describes the struggle over the fate of the George Peabody Normal College more than a century ago.

On one side were the mostly young, mostly Northern men holding the purse-strings of the Peabody and Rockefeller education funds which the George Peabody College for Teachers required. On the other side were students, faculty, alumni, and neighbors of the University of Nashville, led by septuagenarian President James Porter, former governor of Tennessee.

Since the Peabody Education Fund had promised to endow the new Peabody College with $1,000,000, the men in charge of that money would dictate the future of the college. Would it remain a recognizable version of the old Normal School in its familiar if shabby home? Or would it desert the old neighborhood for a heretofore undeveloped part of town out on the Hillsboro Road and become an all-new institution run by outsiders from up north?

Porter and his allies wanted and fully expected to keep Peabody College on the old campus on what is now Second Avenue. The other group, which numbered among its key members Chancellor Kirkland of the young Vanderbilt University, was determined to improve Peabody by making it part of Vanderbilt.

This group, as Conkin says, "envisioned a new Peabody that . . . was qualitatively so far above the old Peabody as to mark a difference in kind, not of degree. They knew firsthand the limited size of the old campus, the inadequacy of its buildings, and the overall mediocrity of its faculty. The Peabody of their dreams could not be grafted onto the old Peabody. The problem with Porter and the local supporters of the old institution is that they simply could not conceive of what a quality graduate institution required" (p. 167).

Another difficulty was squeezing money for education out of the Tennessee General Assembly while trying to square George Peabody's wishes with an Assembly that described the new college as being for white teachers. Though until 1954 the college would in fact be for whites only, the trustees of the Peabody Fund did not want to put in writing a disregard for Mr. Peabody's known desire to help all the people of the South.[1] This new complication seems to have made Porter's struggle to get financing that much more difficult.

You know how it turned out. If only we had space to tell the whole story: how Governor Porter was deceived, with his employee Wickliffe Rose in constant correspondence with Wallace Buttrick, executive secretary of the Rockefeller General Education Board, scheming in secret with Chancellor Kirkland and Daniel Gilman of Johns Hopkins to guarantee that the new college would be part of Vanderbilt. Certain it would be his choice to make, Kirkland was ready to name Gilman the first president of the new Peabody.

Instead the presidency was first offered to Wickliffe Rose, who turned it down. (Rose went to work for the Rockefeller Foundation in their campaign to rid the South of hookworms, later becoming the chief executive of the General Education Board.) Porter resigned. In what was described by one of the participants as the "skirmish in Nashville between the old generation and the coming one," the old generation lost.

But in the end Vanderbilt had to settle for getting the old South Nashville campus for its medical and dental schools, postponing for sixty years its dream of taking over Peabody. The long struggle left the two institutions neighbors but hardly the best of friends. Though Kirkland came to regret swapping precious Vanderbilt land for Peabody's South Nashville campus, when he tried to buy back the land, for several years Peabody refused. In 1914, when those negotiations finally ended, Peabody received the land on which the Demonstration School would be built a decade later. But, Conkin says, "This exchange of land left hard feelings, particularly at Vanderbilt. Chancellor Kirkland, who felt betrayed, later admitted that the end of his dream of a Vanderbilt-Peabody connection had been the greatest disappointment of his career" (p. 196).

---

[1] A report in the October 2, 1879 *New York Times* of the annual meeting of the Trustees of the Peabody Fund says, "The suggestion was made that the Federal Government should extend some aid to the Southern States in their efforts to educate the ignorant classes, particularly the colored people. Trained teachers are greatly needed."

MODEL OR PRACTICE?

No one learns to teach by simply listening to lectures on pedagogy. But where and how should beginning teachers learn their art? In the late nineteenth century, some argued that students should merely observe in a "model school." Others claimed that students had to practice their teaching in real classrooms. Some said that a model school failed to prepare teachers for the real world. Others argued that learning to teach under ideal conditions constituted the best preparation for creating excellent schools.

In the State Normal College 1878 *Annual Report*, president Eben Stearns said that he had arranged for the nearby Howard School and other city schools "to take the place of a smaller and less representative model school" and that Normal College students would "teach in them as substitutes from time to time."

But the college's next president, William H. Payne, started a model school which *forbade* student teaching. In 1891 he said, "It has not been my purpose to organize an experimental school—that is a school in which children are taught by pupil teachers—but rather a school which is taught and governed by an accomplished teacher, who is able to produce results worthy of imitation and study. An experimental school cannot at the same time be a model school."

That pronouncement formed the basis of the Winthrop Model School, founded on the college campus in 1888 and housed in a handsome new building with funds provided by J.P. Morgan. The Normal College described Winthrop in its 1895 catalogue as "ideal in its environment, its appointments for lighting, heating, and ventilation, its furniture, its apparatus, its discipline, its mode of instruction . . . ." Those studying to be teachers could learn the most, it was argued, from observing education under ideal conditions. President W. H. Payne called it "a school in which our pupils may observe in actual use the most approved modern methods of instruction" which could be "reproduced wherever our students become teachers."

In 1901, in his last report to the Board of Trustees, just before he was forced to resign for reasons unrelated to his educational philosophy, Payne said the Model School was "not a 'laboratory,' where callous youths make experiments on trusting and helpless children, but a plain school in which students may observe the work done by efficient teachers."

Governor Porter, who succeeded him as president, had such an opposing view that he determined to close the Model School and open "a school of practice," which he claimed "commands approval of the most enlightened directors and instructors in modern schools for teachers."

So the Winthrop School added upper grades, ultimately abolishing the primary ones. When school opened in 1908, Winthrop enrolled 167 students, of whom more than fifty came from surrounding states. One student recalled being driven there by her brother, who went to MBA "across from the Winthrop School," in a two-seated pony cart. They drove down "Chicken Pike," now Elm Hill Pike, just as the school song claims: "From town and hill and dale we come/To swell old Winthrop's name."

As its successor Peabody Demonstration School would be in 1975, the Winthrop School was abandoned by its parent college in 1911. No group of committed parents appeared to save Winthrop, however, and it dwindled away on the old South Nashville campus.

But even then its rebirth was envisioned. "The connection of Winthrop with Peabody has been intimate and the closing of the two comes simultaneously. After a period of two or three years, when the time for reopening arrives, there will, no doubt, be a number of Winthrop graduates ready to take up their abode again under the care of **The George Peabody College for Teachers**. None will have a right to feel more at home nor will be made to feel more welcome." *(Advertisement in the back of the 1911* Surf, *its last year.)*

Bruce Ryburn Payne, first president of Peabody College.

INVENTING THE DEMONSTRATION SCHOOL

In 1911 Bruce Ryburn Payne became the first president of Peabody College. For twenty-six years, until his death, he gave his life to the college, supervising its rapid construction, raising the money needed for it to survive. He and Mrs. Payne lived in the Social Religious Building (now the Wyatt Center).

From the beginning, a demonstration school was an important part of Payne's vision. But it couldn't be just any demonstration school. Peabody was intended to train better teachers for rural schools. In its last days, University of Nashville trustees had offered to surrender the college's remaining assets to its successor, the new Peabody College, but only if they could keep MBA on or near the Peabody Campus. They wanted to maintain some control of the new college, and they wanted Peabody to support MBA.

Payne wasn't buying. The demonstration school he had in mind would be the perfect tool for transforming education in the little farm towns across the South. Future teachers in those schools, many of them women, would learn their craft from his hand-picked master educators in their own classrooms. Filling those rooms with nothing but boys must have seemed foolish to Payne.

A 1912 article in *The New York Times* quotes Payne, who often traveled to the Northeast in his quest to raise money. "More than 80 percent of the population of the South is in the country districts, but the present rural school is only a poorly equipped and poorly taught city school located in the country. The Peabody College proposes to establish strong departments of rural education, agriculture, domestic sciences, applied art and design, home decoration and home gardening and manual training."

Therefore the first two buildings to arise on the new campus were the beautiful manual training building and the home economics building, designed by the New York architects Ludlow and Peabody. Note that despite their being considered of primary importance a century ago, these two departments no longer exist. (Someone at Columbia decided that "industrial arts" was a better term than "manual training," so Peabody College named it the Industrial Arts Building. Now it's the Mayborn Building, which Paul Conkin calls "the most pleasing building on the Peabody campus, or for that matter on the present Vanderbilt campus.")

At first Peabody Demonstration School was intended to include both a model and a practice school, as explained in the 1916 *Bulletin, George Peabody College for Teachers*. "Two parallel divisions" for the elementary school with "a six-grade observation division, taught by the very best teachers" would be matched by a "practice division of the elementary school" similarly organized. The difference would lie in the "teaching corps," with "students specializing in education" teaching in the practice division.

It's not clear that such a structure was ever put in place. In any case, the two divisions of the school soon blurred. Nor was this the only way that the school diverged from early plans for it.

WHY ARE WE HERE?

Schools are meant to prepare students for life and often for college; some have a form of the word "prepare" in their very names. But a hundred years ago, Bruce Payne knew he was standing on shifting educational sand. "It is an extremely difficult thing to say just what the curriculum of a twentieth century school should be," according to the *Bulletin*.

Payne's first task was finding someone who could help form his demonstration school vision. He recruited a young disciple of educational reformer John Dewey, who founded the University of Chicago Lab Schools. Thomas Alexander, "Father of Peabody Demonstration School," came to Peabody in 1914.

Payne's and Alexander's foundational ideas for the Demonstration School include, beyond the college preparatory course that we recognize, several we do not. Since after seventh grade "there should be some differentiation in the course to meet the varying needs of the children," we find a course for "those children who do not intend to attend school beyond the seventh, eighth, or ninth grade."

They envisioned tracks for girls who would face only "the duties of home life" and boys who might want a "commercial course" to prepare for business, not college. Payne wanted an agricultural course, with practice work no doubt at the college's Knapp Farm. Behind all of these plans was the idea "that a boy can be educated from a study of those things which are going to serve some real purpose in his life."

Plans for the new school seem radical. "A large part of the mathematics, classical languages, college entrance requirements in English, and certain forms of science which are nothing more than a list of symbols and definitions, are going to be put aside." Instead, "subjects which enable a child to interpret, appreciate and feel himself at home with his environments are the subjects which must be included in the curricula of the modern school."

These words fail to describe the school that had its beginnings that summer of 1915 at Peabody College. Yes, it was "only a beginning" and "nothing definite has been done." For decades yet to come, girls would sign up for classes in home economics. But few if any Peabody students seem to have dropped out of school after seventh grade or studied only the science needed by a storekeeper. That "list of symbols and definitions" remained in the classroom after all, as generations of PDS alumni can attest.

These were the goals: "The organization of a school along the latest, most improved lines which shall meet the need of a teachers college for demonstration and practice purposes; the assembling of a highly-trained teaching staff; and the marking out of that course of study which shall be most adequately suited to present-day problems." Had Bruce Payne and Thomas Alexander not succeeded, we wouldn't have this book.

EARLIEST DAYS OF PDS

In the summer of 1915, the embryonic Demonstration School, kindergarten through seventh grades, began to meet in the brand-new Jesup Psychological Laboratory. So did the psychology, modern languages, elementary education, and economics departments, which must have been small indeed.

That first elementary school, "eight grades organized in four rooms," drew a hundred children from Nashville's public schools. Thirty came to kindergarten. Miss Marion Hanckel and Miss Amelia McLester, stars of the kindergarten world with impressive Teachers College credentials, signed on for that inaugural summer. Through those four rooms in Jesup, which still smelled of paint and varnish, traipsed 3,000 visitors that first summer, teachers from all over the South.

Alexander, also a professor in the elementary education department, kept his office there. "Dr. McMurry, Mr. Thomas Alexander, and Miss Frances Jenkins used classes from the demonstration school to illustrate the principles which had been developed in the courses they were offering" and to show Peabody students "how good teaching should be done."

Thomas Alexander,
"Father of the Demonstration School."

Summer school at Peabody College seems to have been a chautauqua for the benefit of the entire neighborhood. In summer evenings the "twilight play hour" drew neighbors of all ages, who "entered into the spirit of the playground with hearty abandon."

That first summer, the fifth and sixth graders performed an outdoor play on campus, "the children's own dramatization of the story of King Alfred." Even in 1915, Demonstration School principles were in effect: "the small playwrights and actors were allowed full freedom and initiative in working out their own ideas in shaping the play, conducting rehearsals, and staging the scenes. The members of the demonstration rural school were the invited guests composing the appreciative audience."

"QUIET FREEDOM AND HAPPY EASE OF ATMOSPHERE"

Somehow, word of this new and promising school spread across Nashville. In fall 1916, children from kindergarten through the ninth grade made their way to the Jesup Psychology Lab. They walked or rode the streetcar that went down the Hillsboro Road. Their parents paid tuition of forty dollars for a thirty-six week term. ("The first installment, twenty dollars, must be paid on the day of entrance.")

Sending your child to this new school meant embracing the new: new neighborhood, new college, new ideas. Thomas Alexander's vision for the Demonstration School promised "to insure a happier and richer childhood and youth and a more truly efficient manhood and womanhood."

Farewell to the old ways. "Traditional education concerned itself too largely with mental training at the expense of body training, heart training, and hand training," Alexander says in the 1916 *Bulletin of Peabody College.*

"Our aim is to have our pupils grow power, power in every direction; power to think, to feel, to do, to be," he writes a century ago. "School life should be through all its years a happy earnest living through which there may be happy, earnest learning. Boys and girls who care whole-heartedly for school do not work with less interest and effort but surely with more."

Such is the philosophical foundation of the institution that for a century has taught children to love learning and love coming to school. All that has set PDS and USN apart from other schools can be found in Thomas Alexander's vision. "Wherever possible, responsibility is thrown upon the pupils for the general outcome of conduct," he writes. "Good discipline is not external control. It is classroom atmosphere and spirit determined in large measure through sympathetic insight on the part of the teacher and mutual understanding."

"Good learning and good teaching" mean "quiet freedom and happy ease of atmosphere in which pupils feel fully encouraged toward self-expression and achievement." The teachers' relationship with their students "shows helpfulness, kindliness, consideration, and natural friendliness."

Other tenets of "Dr. Alex's" educational philosophy:

- Our greatest concern must be for what the child is and is becoming from day to day rather than in what he just knows.

- If we succeed in giving the love of learning, the learning itself is sure to follow.

- To do a mechanical or artistic piece of work thoroughly is much more than the material operation. It is a moral achievement.

- The ability to do a thing well is the basis of all active morality.

THE LIFE OF A DEMONSTRATION SCHOOL STUDENT

In our archives we find clues to what the 1920s were like for those first PDS students. A class history for the third class to graduate, 1922, mentions what was memorable to high school students looking back on their early schooling. The gardens they made in sixth grade, field day in seventh. They recall the opera *Pinafore* in 1917 and *The Mikado* the following year.

In 1919, ROTC began, and the boys "have soldier uniforms." With its oldest boys now juniors, PDS got its first football team. The popular English teacher Miss Flemma Snidow starts a school paper, *The Peabody Volunteer*. "We are all interested in it." The school's first Commencement took place in 1920. (More than sixty years later, Amelia Appleton Atkinson '20 recalled Miss Snidow as "one of the greatest inspirations and influences of my life.")

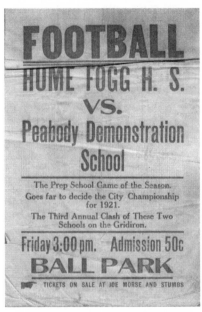

FOOTBALL
HUME FOGG H. S.
VS.
Peabody Demonstration
School

The Prep School Game of the Season.
Goes far to decide the City Championship
for 1921.
The Third Annual Clash of These Two
Schools on the Gridiron.

Friday 3:00 pm. Admission 50c
BALL PARK
TICKETS ON SALE AT JOE MORSE AND STUMBS

From the scrapbook of Elinor Berger, class of 1924.

In November 1921, "We won the city championship in football! Before the game with Wallace we had a big auto parade, five blocks long, and circled all through town. The team is to get little gold footballs and red sweaters." (In those days the school color was called red, not maroon.)

"We juniors are to break into society this year with a progressive dinner for the Seniors, school dances, Easter breakfast for the officers, ushers on Class Night and Commencement, etc." "Society" is the word. Scrapbooks assembled by two girls who graduated in those years are a window into that world of constant parties. Elinor Berger '24 was among that first group of children who came to the new Demonstration School in 1915, when she was in fourth grade.

Eleanor Brown '21, "Brownie" to her friends, also kept a scrapbook. It holds newspaper clippings about her classmates, dance cards, invitations, photographs, programs, even a scrap of fabric. She recorded what she wore to a few of these dances (organdy seems to have been her favorite dress material).

From her description of the progressive dinner that the juniors gave the seniors: " . . . we had the dessert, a dandy ice. The Dixie Melody Boys furnished the music and we danced until twelve. . . . It was an awfully 'peppy' dance. I wore pink organdy— the first time I wore pink in my life. Laurence Polk and Tyler Calhoun brought me home." This may be the place to note that Eleanor had red hair, often mentioned by those who autographed her scrapbook. One called it "Florida orange colored."

"On January 7 we played Franklin. Father, Mother, Bess, Annie, Ellen Rion Caldwell and I went in our car. We went after the interurban but passed it and met them there. It was so exciting." (The "interurban" was the streetcar.)

One of the last Peabody social events for the Class of 1921 was the banquet given them by the P.T.A. at the Centennial Club just before Commencement. Brownie had been asked to give a talk on "Parents" as part of their class history. Other topics were Eats, Actions, Badness, Obedience, and Daydreams. Eleanor's scrapbook reveals that she knew she was losing something when she left P.D.S. behind.

"This was some banquet. I went with Johnnie and for once we went thru a nite without having a really fuss. We sat at the head table and felt so big 'neverything. I wore my orchid organdy and carried my feather fan. My talk was a joke. Extemporaneous sure is the word for it. Buddy was so disappointed. The 'chaps' were Miss McMurray & Mr. Tipp & Dr. and Mrs. Alexander at the tables Mrs. Parkes, Cain, Crandall, Orr, Hardcastle and Brown not seated and it was the last time the crowd would ever be together just by ourselves as the Senior Class. Horrible—but it sure was a dandy banquet."

THE BUTTRICK DEMONSTRATION SCHOOL

Meanwhile, Bruce Payne was working with missionary zeal to establish Peabody College on a firm financial foundation. His chief goal was convincing the General Education Board of the Rockefeller Foundation to give the money to build the Demonstration School and other campus buildings.

The Rockefeller Archive Center contains letter after letter from Payne to one Rockefeller purse-string holder after another. Wallace Buttrick, secretary (1902-1917), president (1917-1923), and chairman (1923-1926) of the General Education Board, was the man Payne asked most often for money.

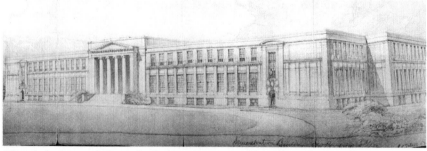

This early drawing reveals the grand scale of Bruce Payne's plans for the Demonstration School.

In May of 1922 he wrote a long letter to Anson Phelps Stokes, GEB member. "By all that's right and holy," Payne said, "this demonstration school building ought to be called the Wallace Buttrick Demonstration School." He'd been brooding over this idea since Buttrick's farewell visit to Tennessee a few weeks earlier. Buttrick had "sat on our front porch and talked to our faculty longer than usual and more affectionately than usual. [His] farewell . . . has brought a distinct cloud over our community and one that does not seem to pass."

"He has, of course, been the one great patron of our work here; and we will lick any man or combination of men who question the sincerity of our affection for him whom we call the father of Peabody in the same breath in which we call George Peabody the founder of Peabody."

Stokes' reply was in a much cooler vein. "It is quite clear that the work of the George Peabody College would be greatly advanced by a modern demonstration school. The question is, to get the money."

The correspondence reveals the board's pattern of attempting to rein in Payne's grand ambitions for his new school building. Forwarding Payne's letter to Abraham Flexner, General Secretary of the General Education Board (remembered today for the *Flexner Report*, which reformed medical education), Stokes adds, "whether this particular project would be a suitable one for the Board to enter into, I am not in a position to say."

An April 13, 1923 memo from Flexner, who had just met with the demonstration school building architect Mr. Fenner of McKim, Mead and White and with Mr. Hagman the builder, says, "$500,000 would be needed instead of the $400,000 contemplated in our gift."

"I said frankly to them that I would not be willing to present that to our Board. After considerable conversation it was suggested that one wing of the building might be omitted for the present, and the cost of the remaining part of the structure not exceed $400,000. It was agreed that this was the wisest thing to do."

When Flexner and H.J. Thorkelson, another GEB officer, visited Nashville a few days later, they went over with Payne the preliminary plans from McKim, Mead and White. The plans did not seem "the most economical construction" and thus "the architect can profitably make a further study of this problem."

Buttrick, who had no interest in seeing his name plastered across the front of this school in Nashville wrote that "greater economy may be secured if the floor plan is altered to an E form instead of the I form presented." It was a bitter disappointment to Payne.

But he was not one to give up easily. In September he wrote yet another GEB officer, Wickliffe Rose, the former University of Nashville professor who was once offered the presidency of Peabody College. "Dr. Little and I have been sitting out on the steps of this old shack in which our office is, wondering how we are going to run Peabody College much longer in these kitchens and cellars that are a part of this building," the letter opens. With the "final plans" for the $400,000 Demonstration School in hand, Payne now felt able to try to secure money for his new administration building to replace the "old shack."

In fact, though construction continued, the Demonstration School question was far from settled. On the very last day of 1923, Dr. Flexner reported that Mr. Thorkelson was "a little uneasy," having heard "that a school accommodating 1,000 to 1,200 children was contemplated." The tireless Dr. Payne was working toward "obtaining a considerably larger sum" than the $400,000 agreed upon.

Flexner, Thorkelson, and Bachman called Payne on the carpet. Dr. Payne said the "plans had been worked out by a committee of his faculty in conjunction with the architects and builders." Despite cuts already made, the cost of building the school was 50% more than "the amount in hand to build with."

Flexner was concerned that "it appeared that no account had been taken of the considerable sum that would be required to pay for the upkeep of an elaborate modern building equipped with every convenience." For his part, Payne claimed that he could double tuition without reducing the number of his pupils.

Before he left the hours-long meeting early to attend to other matters, Flexner told Payne "that the scale and elaborateness of the proposed school exceeded anything anywhere else in the United States and I raised the question whether this was the best way in which to serve southern needs at this time."

Immediately Payne asked Thomas Alexander to justify the "elaborateness of the proposed school." Dr. Alex's letter, written with help from his faculty committee, claims that the Demonstration School is the "center of organization for the entire work of the college." Alexander shared Payne's ambitions: far from being too large, the school is "much too small for our development as we conceive it."

One reason is that they need extra pupils so they can have control groups for experiments, or as he puts it "experimentation purposes." He explains the plan for foreign language instruction, number of classes needed, etc. ("It is very easily seen, then, that the Latin room will be occupied all the time.") The room for "commercial work," filled with mysterious equipment, can be used for nothing else. Other proposed rooms include a school museum, school store, even a school bank. One section of the building would be devoted to printing, mechanic arts, and woodworking. Another room would accommodate large groups of observers.

Next, the projected numbers: 420 children K-6, 420 children 7-12. (The current enrollment was only 505.) Dr. Alex was confident that they could snag the additional pupils, Peabody's tuition being $25 lower than that of Nashville's other preparatory schools. Budget concerns are dismissed: "It might be noted here that our light bill is practically nothing."

"We know we can succeed. The public of Nashville have shown their increasing confidence in this school even when their children were housed in cellars and garrets for eight years."

THE LEGEND COMES TRUE

Yes, the students were busy with their parties and such, but they also found time to wonder if the new building they had been promised would ever become a reality. Writing in *The Volunteer* literary magazine in 1924, Robert Ross talks about the "vague rumor that Peabody was to have a new building, a building all her own, for the Demonstration School, where the college might not penetrate."

Students had caught wind of the machinations going on around them. "Soon after however there was shortage of funds; it looked as tho the new building was still to be a thing of the future. But money was raised, the work continued, and next year, they tell us, the building will be finished and ready for occupation."

Ross writes, "No more were we to be inconvenienced by the college and in turn disturb them. We could swim, eat, and play at our pleasure. Nor should we receive lectures weekly at assembly for taking up more than half the walk, or otherwise

Dignitaries on their way to the dedication of the new Demonstration School building, February 19, 1925.

misbehaving toward college students."

Swim at their pleasure? Despite the enforced cost-cutting, PDS got its swimming pool, thanks to the Peabody Woman's Club's Auxiliary ("girl graduates of the Demonstration School"). This group committed to raise the $7,000 needed by holding the Mardi Gras ball, "one of the outstanding social events of the winter season in Nashville," at the Hermitage Hotel. Tickets cost $1, and Francis Craig's Orchestra played, as it would not be an "outstanding social event" otherwise.

In 1925 Peabody College celebrated its semi-centennial with alumni, "the British ambassador, various professors and Supreme Court officials, and other celebrities." Though the role of Demonstration School students in all this glory was "to stand off and respectfully admire," they were a key part of one event in the panoply: "the dedication of the new Peabody Demonstration School Building, with a speech by Dr. Thomas Alexander," who was visiting from his new job back at Teachers College, Columbia University.

It was Thursday, February 19 at 2:00. Sam Caldwell '25 writes that the "beautiful new auditorium, seating over six hundred people, overflowed" and that the "fine, large stage held two or three hundred P.D.S. students and alumni." Payne presided over a program of music and speeches that heightened audience anticipation of Alexander's address.

"There was the same old Dr. Alex, just as he used to be in the classroom—perfectly at home, speaking with snap—frank, plain, ironic, almost sarcastic when he wished, and withal almost as humorous as a sensible man might possibly be." Alexander said he had been preparing the speech for ten years.

"He told of the dark days when classes were held in basements, when College people complained of the 'noisy Demonstration School bunch,' and when 'Keep off the Grass' signs frowned forbiddingly from every green spot. He repeated the old 'New Building' legend, which for a while had been relied upon by some, then cast aside by all . . . ."

Afterwards seniors, alumni, and former teachers went to the big new gymnasium, where the principal "Mr. Yarbrough industriously wended his way about, spreading free ice cream and much satisfaction in his wake. Then, after a few tours about the building to see how truly fine it was, the party broke up."

STUDENT RESPONSIBILITY FLOWERS

In 1925, when Peabody Demonstration School had just moved into its palatial new building on Edgehill Avenue, everything seemed possible.

The students, particularly the seniors, believed that PDS was their school as much as the faculty's. They managed to convince their principal W.H. Yarbrough that they should have a voice in its governance. Thus the "Cooperative Student Council" was born, with one boy and one girl from each of the upper grades entrusted to "arbitrate" between students, between students and teachers, and even "*between members of the aforesaid faculty*, which shall involve the interest of the said student body." (Italics mine.)

One charter member of the Council described it as "another milestone in the upward climb toward a general acceptance of some form of student responsibility." This attitude was fundamental. Here is a description of PDS from a 1926 equivalent of what we call an admissions viewbook, with "freedom" the first adjective chosen:

> The school seeks to develop an atmosphere characterized by freedom, good habits of work, proper use of leisure, self control, courtesy and cooperation. Because of the emphasis on individual responsibility, the formal rules and regulations of the school are few and simple, and the children are given the largest opportunities possible for the development of self-government and self-directed conduct.

> The attitude of the pupils of Peabody Demonstration School is
> characterized by a cheerfulness, an interest and an enthusiasm rarely
> found. The school has been peculiarly fortunate in the loyalty and
> devotion of patrons and children.

The Cooperative Student Council first met December 16, 1925. "The feature of the meeting was a talk by Mr. Yarbrough." Not for the last time, he listed the problems he wanted them to address:

- Talking before and during assembly, which seems to have consisted of a lecture by Mr. Yarbrough or a guest speaker

- "Slipping up" in the cafeteria line

- Conduct in the halls
  (parents had complained of the noise, he said, unconvincingly)

- Smoking

One student reminded Mr. Yarbrough of "the improvement already effected in the cafeteria line. The senior and junior boy representatives asserted that they personally had seen no smoking since the occupation of the new building."

Such were the concerns and duties of the Cooperative Student Council for the next several years. A pattern established itself, with Yarbrough ever hopeful that the Council could help him get people to listen in assembly, wait patiently in line, and wipe their feet before entering the library.

The Student Council also dealt with issues of theft, exam scheduling, physical education requirements, and girls immodestly appearing in the halls in their gym clothes. They heard cases of students about to be kicked out of school for poor grades or for skipping class or assembly. One student was falsely accused of putting an anonymous letter that mentioned a girl's knee in the Council's complaint box.

But as years passed, the students ceased to discuss whether a classmate should resign from the Student Council for sneaking off campus to the Dog Wagon at lunch. They began to concern themselves mainly with dance planning. At the last meeting recorded, April 5, 1934, we learn: "Punch was decided upon as the refreshment. It was suggested that the floors be waxed but it was decided that this would be too expensive."

GOOD-NATURED TEACHERS

That collegial relationship with teachers was never limited to the Cooperative Student Council. Dillard Jacobs '28 credited the success of the Peabody Cinema Club, which made Nashville's first feature-length films in 1927 and 1928, to having "good natured teachers and a Physics lab handy." (English teacher Miss Lucille Heath seems to have devoted much time to chaperoning the student actors used by Jacobs and Walter Sharp '28 in their pioneering movie making.)

Some of the teachers who would make their mark on PDS for decades had found their way to the school by this time. Miss Snidow had gone, as had the tiny Miss Meribah Clark, remembered by Elizabeth Bogle Street '28 as having "such small shoes that they turned up at the toes. Her introduction to a new period began, 'Now I'll tell you a story' and made history fascinating." These new teachers included:

- French teacher Helen Lacy (later Mrs. Shane), called "Aunt Helen" by students who took her class year after year. "One observer from the college complimented her on having 'so many nice nieces and nephews.'"

- Mrs. Carrie Parsons made Latin "interesting and at times even exciting," teaching it in "a way to make us love it" and becoming "almost everyone's favorite teacher."

- "Mr. Beauchamp managed to make chemistry seem one of the most exciting and interesting subjects."

- Miss Foust "made history seem like an unfolding tale of adventure . . . so fascinating that you didn't have to study it. You could learn all that you needed to know in the class discussion, but you could also go home and read some more about it because it was so interesting."

Other unforgettable teachers beginning long careers at PDS around this time included Miss Pitts, Mr. Holden, Miss Hodgson, Miss McMullan, Miss Parkinson, Mr. Bridges, and "Teach" Huggins.

Guided by these dedicated teachers and by Yarbrough and his successor J. E. Windrow, in the 1930s Peabody Demonstration School was fulfilling the vision of Payne and Alexander. No doubt some families were struggling to pay tuition as the

Depression gripped Nashville, but only the faintest hints of those struggles survive in the records we have. And no one seemed to be thinking about what would come at the end of the decade, though many of the boys graduating from PDS that decade would enter the war, and some would die in it.[2]

SYNECDOCHE OF PDS

Mr. Beauchamp (whose influence can never be overstated) and his science classes presented the assembly program, "The Beelzebub Assembly," in which "two boys who did not believe in science" were "lured to the lower regions [by two flapper devils]. There, Satan called on his court to make experiments to convince the boys." The program ended with a song, "I Believe in Science."

When a silver dirigible flew over Peabody, "students dashed madly to the classroom windows. Few of us had ever seen a real dirigible before, and maybe the faculty had not seen many in their day, for they let us watch it out of sight."

Such details tell us what we need to know about Peabody Demonstration School in the 1930s. Toss in the airplane that the shop class somehow got from the Nashville Flying Service so they could overhaul and rebuild it. Toss in the debate team, which drew "two cars of rooters" to Murfreesboro to hear future Nobel laureate Stanford Moore '31 and Bruce Henderson '32 argue unsuccessfully against the topic "Resolved: That Installment Buying is Socially and Economically Desired."

It's easy to imagine a Peabody with "rooters" for its debate team. It's harder to imagine a school dismissed at noon so students could decorate their cars ("whether Packard or Ford"), drive in a parade, and celebrate a football victory. But that happened after the PDS/Central High game. "Believe it or not—Peabody won the game! The score being 7 to 0! Oh!" one student wrote.

An elaborate banquet followed in the cafeteria, with a "huge cake, decorated as a football field and all fitted out with yarn players." Speeches followed. Everyone liked Coach Bridges, who was also their math teacher and their basketball and baseball coach. The grateful team gave him a leather suitcase.

---

[2] A typewritten list in our archives with the title "Gold Stars" bears these names: Lt. Ralph Adkins '29, Lt. Anderson Austin '30, Capt. Henry Cain '27, Lt. Dan Cockrill '29, Staff Sgt. Jackson Hardeman '38, Conrad Jamison, Jr. '40, and Ensign John Manchester '40.

Which he soon packed. (As the football coach, that is. He would teach math at PDS for years to come.)

WHAT HAPPENED TO FOOTBALL

According to Jim Coddington's chapter in *The Past Is Prologue, Peabody Demonstration School 1915-1970*, in 1933, President Payne hired Vanderbilt star Bill Schwartz to coach the football team in order to dispel the Demonstration School's "sissy" image.

It worked. The team's record improved from 1933's 0-6-1 to 9-0 in 1934. And in 1934, opposing teams scored nary a point against Peabody: the season's cumulative score was 190-0. No one called the PDS boys eggheads then. But Peabody would pay a price for this instant success.

How did it happen? As recollected in a 1998 PDS/USN alumni magazine interview with two starters on the 1934 PDS "Murderer's Row," the story begins with that "sissy" image. In the memory of Dick Henderson '35, every year a group of boys left Peabody for high school at boys' schools Wallace or Duncan. "Peabody had a small student body, two thirds of them girls. I don't think we had but 17 senior boys."

According to Henderson, the losing 1933 PDS football squad had a total of 13 men. Eight of those would form the core of the next year's winning team, with "about 3 or 4 players that were recruited. That's where Bill Schwartz came in. He knew a good football player when he saw one."

Not only that, Schwartz was a good coach. Roy "Red" Huggins '37 called him "the smartest coach I've ever seen," adding that his next coaches, at Vanderbilt, "didn't teach me anything. I taught *them* things."

But Schwartz relied on more than his coaching skills to turn around the Peabody team. When the 1935 season ended with a scorecard of PDS 255, Opponents 6, the TSSAA had heard enough. To quote a November letter from the head of the TSSAA to the college's Dr. Roemer: "It is reported that your coach has been heard to say that he was going out to get him some athletes. The Board also believes that friends of the school are paying the tuition of some of your boys . . . ." The letter goes on to say that Peabody Demonstration School could not renew its TSSAA membership.

Eager to avert this catastrophe, Yarbrough appointed faculty committees to come up with a solution. In January 1936, the college's Demonstration School Committee received their unanimous report. The teachers wanted to continue interscholastic athletics, but not as they had been. "We recommend a moderate interscholastic program. By a moderate program we mean not too many contests and not too much emphasis on winning a championship."

That month Peabody was reinstated to the TSSAA, but with conditions: the end of athletic scholarships and the development of an intramural program. PDS teachers must have been pleased—they must have wanted moderation all along. The following fall, after struggling to find schools willing to play them, the PDS football team compiled an 8-1 record, winning another city championship.

That was the last one. In spring 1937, three football stars graduated: Red Huggins, Ed Hiestand, and Jack Irby. Switching to intramural competition, Peabody would not play other schools again until 1944.

Thus ended for a time an era of pep rallies, parades of decorated Fords and Packards, crowds of "rooters." The twenties and early thirties were the days when the whole thriving neighborhood came to the PDS field out back to watch the games. President Payne joined the crowd too, proud of what his demonstration school had become in just twenty years, cheering on the Maroon and Blue.

In April 1937, soon after all this bad news and just as the irises were coming into bloom on the college campus, Bruce Payne died suddenly. He was sixty-three years old. He had been at Peabody College, which he had called into being, since 1911. Challenges he could not have imagined lay in the future, and not far. But Peabody Demonstration School was ready.

CONNIE CULPEPPER

Connie Culpepper is Communications Director at University School of Nashville. As editor of *2000 Edgehill*, the alumni magazine, she has developed an interest in the school's history. As a high school English teacher in the late seventies and early eighties, she developed a lasting appreciation for USN students. She is married to a PDS alumnus, Tom Brittingham, and they are parents of three thirteen-year USN alumni: Charlie Brittingham '04, Margaret Brittingham '05, and Jane Brittingham '08.

Parts of this chapter appeared in other form in *2000 Edgehill, the Alumni Magazine of Peabody Demonstration School and University School of Nashville*.

ROBERT K. MASSIE
Class of 1946

Fighting the Second World War at Peabody Demonstration School

My family and I arrived in Nashville from Lexington, Kentucky in September 1939 when I was ten. Before that, I had learned that Hitler was evil and that war, when planes began dropping bombs on people in houses, would destroy civilization.

The Second World War began just as we arrived, and, as I had feared, violence broke out immediately. My brother, Kim, and I were sent to Woodmont School on Estes Road. And there, I was wounded . . . and not by an aerial bomb. I was in the Boys Bathroom with my new friends and we were "horsing around." Water was involved. The school principal arrived outside the door and shouted for us to come out. I was the one she caught by the ear. I was wearing knickers. She began whacking me on my bare legs with a metal-edged yardstick. No adult had ever hit me before and, reflexively, I hit back.

I was marched to the office; my mother was called; my behavior reported. Molly (everyone called her Molly) looked at my legs, saw red welts, and took Kim and me home. In the twinkling of an eye (the next day, it seemed) we were enrolled at Peabody, where I spent six years and Kim seven. It was the right place for us. I don't think I've ever been happier.

Decades later, I took my children to see Woodmont School. It had vanished. Where the school had been, there was nothing but a grass field with a beautiful children's playground. While my children climbed on the jungle gym, swung on the swings, and rode the seesaw, I wondered what had happened. Had Woodmont School become a twentieth-century Carthage—plowed under, seeded with salt? Because of the beating of a small boy throwing water and wearing knickers?

Later I learned that it had survived and that all four children of my life-long best friend Jack May had gone to Woodmont. And that its subsequent disappearance was not a form of punitive retribution; merely a routine administrative decision.

Up this unconventional entry path, Kim and I were guided into the Peabody classrooms of remarkable teachers. I can still see and hear them: Dr. Holden (History), Dr. Beauchamp (Chemistry and Physics), Mrs. Parsons (Latin), Miss McMullan (English), Professor Lancaster (English). Later, at Yale and Oxford, I had other teachers who helped me move forward, but they were building on the foundations laid at Peabody.

And through those six years I also kept close track of the war. I felt personally involved because I knew that if Adolf Hitler won the war in Europe, it would mean a different life for Bobby Massie. For a long time, this outcome seemed possible. When I was in sixth grade, Poland was crushed; Polish cavalry fared badly against German tanks. In the spring of 1940, Denmark, Norway, Holland, and Belgium were swallowed up. France collapsed, and only Winston Churchill remained to rumble defiance at the Conqueror across the Channel.

Every morning, Dr. Turner, on his way to Meharry Medical College, drove us to school in his black Buick with his car radio tuned to Edward R. Murrow describing the great air battles swirling over Kent and the mouth of the Thames. Later, on the same radio, we followed the ebb and flow of desert battle as British, German, and Italian tanks churned the sand around sun-baked North African towns named Tobruk and Sidi Barani. In June 1941, I was drinking cocoa from an enamel cup in the dining hall of a Boy Scout camp on the Harpeth River when I learned that Hitler had invaded Russia. I followed the black arrows on maps as they moved inexorably past Kiev towards Leningrad, towards Moscow. I studied the thin ascetic faces of the German field marshals, von Leeb, von Bock, and von Runstedt, staring coldly out from the covers of *Time Magazine*.

History came closer on a December afternoon, bursting into our living room, thrusting aside the symphony coming from the old radio beside my mother's armchair. Suddenly the music stopped. "We interrupt this program," said a voice, declaring that there were reports of a Japanese air attack on the American Pacific Fleet at Pearl Harbor. I rushed to the telephone to call my friends. Next day, sitting in Miss McMullan's eighth grade English class, we all looked at each other solemnly and listened to President Roosevelt tell Congress that December 7, 1941 was "a date which will live in infamy." And that America was going to war.

After that, the senior boys went straight into the service, reappearing briefly at school in their new uniforms before going off to North Africa or the Solomon Islands. The early years were bad, but then, slowly, things began to improve. On June 6, 1944, my brother and I were asleep in a tent in our back yard when my mother came out on the back porch and told us that American paratroops were landing in Northern France. We dashed into the kitchen to listen to the first day of the liberation of Western Europe.

Meanwhile, in the fall of 1944, Peabody had reentered interscholastic football competition. I played on two of those teams. In my senior year I was the quarterback and a co-captain and we lost only one game. I wasn't very good, and most of us weren't very good, but we had three superlative players, Joe Naron, Bill Tanksley, and Bobby Goodman, who made certain that we usually won. My brother Kim later described Bobby Goodman as the best football player, pound for pound, on any team, anywhere, ever. Bobby weighed 140 pounds.

On April 12, 1945, an afternoon of spring football practice on the dusty field behind the school was interrupted. A group of us, helmeted, adolescent gladiators, were butting heads when someone came out and told us that Franklin D. Roosevelt, the great war leader, the only president that any of us had ever known, was dead. I looked away. And then I saw that it was all right: some of the other boys had tears in their eyes too.

Franklin Roosevelt almost lived to see the end of the war. On a sunny day in August 1945, I was sitting on a bunk at a boys' camp in the Smoky Mountains of North Carolina when I learned that America had dropped an atomic bomb on Japan. A week later, the war was over. We had won. I rejoiced. I was sixteen years old.

I left Nashville the following year, 1946, to go to college, then to England, to the Navy, to journalism, and then to write books. Now I've lived in the same Hudson River village for fifty years. But always, when people ask me, "Is Irvington your hometown?" I say, unthinkingly, "No, Nashville is my hometown." And the center of my life in Nashville was Peabody Demonstration School.

A footnote to close: My only regret is that in transforming its name from PDS to University School, it was obviously necessary to set aside the old school song, perhaps the worst—both as to lyrics and music—in the whole vast field of secondary school self-celebratory hymns. The tune is a sickly, wobbling wail. The words are worse:

> "Why do I long for It-a-ly?
>
> Why do I dream of Greece?
>
> Here where the pillars of Pea-bo-dy
>
> Lift to their glad release?
>
> *Forgotten lines, then back to the pillars . . .*
>
> Why do I ever, who love them so,
>
> Sigh for an alien place?"

ROBERT K. MASSIE
Robert K. Massie is the author of *Nicholas and Alexandra*, the basis of an Academy Award-winning film of the same name, and of *Peter the Great: His Life and World*, which won the Pulitzer Prize for Biography in 1981. His most recent book, *Catherine the Great: Portrait of a Woman*, was awarded the 2012 Andrew Carnegie Medal for Excellence in Nonfiction and the 2012 PEN/Jacqueline Bograd Weld Award for Biography. He lives in Irvington, New York.

JON VAN TIL *Class of 1957*
WITH MARY LEE MCCHAREN DI SPIRITO *Class of 1956*
AND A CAST OF DOZENS

PDS Forever:
The School in the Fifties

The school stood on one side of Edgehill Avenue, facing the uphill green lawns of the college. Both were named for George Peabody, a name easily ridiculed in the teenage vernacular that prevailed among clever youths of the duller sort. Later on, the School was reborn as University School of Nashville, but that's a story for another chapter. This chapter is about the Peabody Demonstration School. As was sung in solemn occasions of assembly or athletic combat: "PDS Forever." (Put aside for the moment the following lines: "Our boys tonight: Eager for battle, ready for the fight . . . .")

FROM GEORGE PEABODY TO PHIL EVERLY: THE FIFTIES

George Peabody was a great American philanthropist, but was his life ever explored at this namesake school? Perhaps in a graduate talk now and then, but this septuagenarian cannot recall, even in those few editorials he penned for *The Paw Print*, ever urging upon his peers the adoption of Peabody's values of supporting arts, culture and education, or dedicating wealth to social causes rather than willing it to one's descendants. These were the fifties, after all, and we were young. And in the eyes of our younger brothers, we were giants. Twelve-year-old Roy Van Til watched us come of age:

To my hero-worshipping pre-adolescent eyes, John LeCornu was the impossible embodiment of cool. Our resident Elvis. The dominant recollection of how this force of nature affected me is that I still aspire, with limited success, to emulate some of his patented but wildly spontaneous dance moves he used to bust after lunch when Whispering Knox McCharen would permit a half hour of frenetic terpsichorean sock-hopping in the auditorium in the spring of '57, when the real Elvis dominated the airwaves and fired the imaginations and awakened the nascent hormones of young girls and guys.

Recall that the King had his third and final appearance on the Ed Sullivan show on January 6, 1957, two days before his 22nd birthday. Elvis was shown from the waist up that Sunday evening, singing 'Hound Dog,' 'Love Me Tender,' 'Heartbreak Hotel,' 'Don't Be Cruel,' and ironically, 'Peace in the Valley.' But on those afternoons in our youth, our 18-year-old LeCornu let fly, as he turned the sedate Dem School into a sweaty, lurching, spasmodic, but brilliantly hoofed scene out of Dante.

Oozing preternatural charm and self-confidence, Big John would adjust the spit curl leading his righteously slicked back and jet black DA, and then stroll over to grab Lycrecia Williams (Hank's step-daughter, who drove to school in the blue Caddy convertible) with the 4-4 beat pounding out primal rhythms through everyone's adolescent confusion and Brylcreemed pompadours. When the music reached a crescendo, there was the Great One tucking his ankle behind his knee in mid-gyration, backing the supple Lycrecia toward the wall, to throw some pelvic twists and thrusts in the direction of the country goddess performing her own seductive rendition of the dirty bop before his killer eyes. To my unblinking twelve-year old pre-libido, this was akin to witnessing the act of creation itself. Though 56 years have come and gone since that incredible display of the pinnacle of rock and roll dancing, the smoldering after-image remains seared on my grateful retinas.

John LeCornu '57 played guitar for the Green Hill Boys, the mainly-PDS "hillbilly" band that won the 1954 Nashville talent contest for the Ted Mack Amateur Hour. Charlie Smith '56, Ken Born '56, and Michael Born '55 were the others in the group, joined at various times by Harry Height '55, Hugh Binkley of Bellevue and Willo Collins of Hillsboro High; on one notable occasion by Don Everly.

PDS in the fifties was a Mecca of music, as Chris Stevenson '56 recalls, with not only LeCornu and the Green Hill Boys, Lycrecia Williams—but Phil Everly as well. When Phil died in 2013, Chris wrote:

I recall not really knowing him very much until my senior year (his junior year). I don't recall how we first met and got into conversation, but I recall being impressed by how bright he was but also shy. We were both on the track team and ran together as a relay team. What I think bonded us was a 3-way meet at Central High School which included Hillsboro HS and PDS. We had only 6 team members, so we felt overwhelmed by the other two big schools. I recall Hillsboro's team arriving on a school bus, and when the players exited the bus they were all wearing green and gold warm-up suits over their track uniforms. Central was also stylishly dressed in what I believe were black and gold uniforms. We were mostly wearing basketball-style white shirts with a blue P and whatever shorts we wore from home. We also traveled in our own cars or family cars.

Phil (and maybe Charlie Mann) rode from the school with me in my '49 Chevrolet convertible. Others I recall on our team were Ben Rowan (high jump), Rick Lindman (pole vault and discus) and José Varona (100 and 220 sprints). Phil ran low hurdles and (I think) the 440-yard run. I ran the half mile and also high jumped.

Anyway, that day each guy on our team won at least one first place and at least one runner-up place, and we compiled enough points to win the meet. It was very exciting. Phil and I plus Ben and someone else (José) won our relay race, and I'm pretty certain it was the only time we had ever run that event as a team. We were so excited that we'd won the meet that we caravanned over to a Howard Johnson's for a celebratory '3-D Burger.' Do you remember those? They were forerunners of a Big Mac, with two layers of meat and a sesame seed bun. From that day forward I felt like Phil was truly one of us, and he enjoyed the cutting up and celebrating as much as the rest of us.

A short time later on a Saturday morning Phil and I drove downtown to a radio studio, perhaps WSM, and he brought his guitar. I knew only vaguely that his family was a gospel singing group. Don showed up on his own, and then the two of them joined Chet Atkins. I was impressed that Phil knew Chet, and I was flattered to be introduced. I think I mentioned the Green Hill Boys, whom he knew. Then for a couple of hours I sat in a folding chair and watched Phil and Don and Chet practice/jam. Don and Phil seemed to me to be very good players, but Chet was unbelievably good. He wrapped his lanky frame around a steel folding chair and played all the time I was there, often discussing what he was doing with Phil and Don and showing them some techniques.

Mary Lee McCharen Di Spirito '56, Knox McCharen's daughter, remembers what her father thought of having rock and roll stars at the school:

> On the Everly brothers . . . Dad always said he would be very tolerant of their absences, etc. because at some point when he might need a loan, he would know where to start to get one. He must have had a good idea of where they were headed. (And for those of you who took summer school classes, 'Little Suzy' was in class with me, and it was either general science or biology.)

Music formed an important part of the PDS curriculum too. As Eileen Harap Drath '56 remembers, it was a "major part of high school life. We sang madrigals before school and had chorus and band throughout the day. I can still smell that band room vault with its moist felt and velvet odor of the linings of the instrument cases!"

Among the most notable of music teachers at PDS in those days was Charles F. Bryan, one of the people responsible for making American folk music acceptable in the classroom and the concert hall long before its 1960s popularity.

REMARKABLE TEACHING

PDS in the fifties was not all rock and roll, to be sure. It was a place of serious teaching, some traditional and conventional, some innovative and even experimental. But all of it was taken very seriously, and teachers taught, and students learned. A healthy mix of faculty combined long-term teachers, often beloved over decades or even generations, with younger ones.

Helen "Brownie" Morgan Williams '51 recalls four teachers in particular:

> Mrs. Lundberg in Geometry (whom I would gladly canonize) for her compassion to us—especially for those like myself with difficulties in math. She would take the little bits of success and make them into a lot more.
>
> Doc Holden (History) with his witty and dry humor.
>
> Miss Mac and her incredible manner of teaching English. Once she described seeing the original *Blue Boy* painted by Gainesborough. To this day I remember that you could hear a pin drop from only her description.
>
> Mr. Charles Bryan and music. Fantastic. Such a gentle, kindly person.

Mary Lee McCharen Di Spirito adds:

> Miss Mac . . . her spelling list of 100 words.
> To this day, the 'learnings' of those 100 words
> come back regularly as I hear some misused
> or otherwise not correct. Being able to
> successfully complete that spelling list (given
> weekly) was a requirement to get a passing
> grade at the end of the year. *Too, to, two*;
> *weather* and *whether*; *their* and *there*, *its* or *it's*;
> *I* or *me*? I bet others can add to the list.

Miss McMullan, who loved picnics.

Eileen Harap Drath '56, whose father Henry
Harap taught at Peabody College from 1937
until 1960, says, "We grew up surrounded by
interesting people and ideas, influenced by our
parents and by the excellent faculty at PDS."

She remembers her teachers well:

> We were automatically academic, by nature of the courses we took. Mrs.
> Shane taught us French and Spanish, and her students excelled always. To
> this day I know my grammar from those languages because of her and Miss
> Mac, our English teacher, who had us parse sentences in ninth grade into
> the wee hours of many nights. I have engraved in my mind the words, 'The
> word xxxxx is used to,' and then we were to write out the part of speech
> and use of every word in the sentences she gave us.

Joining the faculty, often for only a year or two, were the best and the brightest of
doctoral students from George Peabody College for Teachers, themselves studying
with a faculty that cornered the market of the luminaries in the education discipline
by recruiting the "four horsemen": Willard Goslin, Harold Benjamin, Nicholas
Hobbs, and William Van Til. Two students of the last-mentioned professor, who
also was my father, were named Ruffin and Vars and were my seventh and eighth
grade teachers, respectively. After the first day of seventh grade, fresh myself from
our move from Illinois, my father asked how the day had gone. I responded, in true
PDS style: "Is Ruffin ready?" He was indeed, and so was Gordon Vars, as Chris
Stevenson '56 recalls:

> Gordon became a wonderful friend first because of professional overlaps.
> He was a co-creator and preserver of the concept of 'Core Curriculum,'

and he was a longtime professor at Kent State U. I did a research study with a doctoral student in Vermont into an application of Gordon's work that we referred to as 'Integrated Studies.' My student and I subsequently published a book about our research we called *Dancing through Walls* that was well-received. Gordon decided to will his scholarly papers to the archives in the Bailey-Howe Library at U. of Vermont, where they are now located. Two years ago Gordon was tragically struck and killed by an out of control speeder while walking home one night after choir practice.

Chris Stevenson, who became a distinguished education professor himself, reflected on the quality of teaching PDS was able to attract:

> The teacher who replaced Doc Holden when he retired was a young man named Paul George. Paul was at PDS for 5-6 years until he finished his doctorate at the College and took a position at U. of Florida. He still talks about how much he enjoyed being at PDS. In the late '80s Paul and I met and found some common scholarly interests. We co-authored a couple of research articles and later wrote a book together. We were friends for quite a long time before discovering serendipitously that we shared a PDS connection. Both Paul and Gordon are wonderful representatives of Peabody Dem School, and they both loved their years of teaching there.

Presiding over the affairs of the school was the remarkable figure of W. Knox McCharen, its principal. His daughter Mary Lee recalls:

> I think it was the first graduating class after Dad arrived at PDS when Gareth Griffin '52 (his father was also on the college faculty) arrived for the graduation ceremony wearing white buck shoes. Dad took one look at him (fellows all wore white formal jackets) and sent him home to get his black shoes.
>
> Dad was also one to be sure folks did follow directions. That was just one of his teaching moments he thought all should learn: follow the directions given. They are given for a reason.
>
> So, it was fortunate Gareth lived very close by, and everyone waited for him to return with proper attire for the graduation ceremonies. We all sat on stage with the girls in long white dresses and the fellows in summer tux attire. I think that the Class of '56 was the last to dress in this type of attire for the graduation event.

Dr. McCharen was not an easy man to shake from his beliefs. As a rising ninth grader, I decided I would select a course in Typing instead of Biology, which I planned to take in my sophomore year. McCharen called me and my father into his office (my father recalls, was a leading international figure in progressive education) and explained the foolishness of my choice, predicting that it would ruin my chances for eventual college admission and success in life. With Dad's support, I held to my choice, and later, carrying a College Board score of 1600, was admitted to Harvard, Yale, Oberlin, Carleton, and Swarthmore. My PDS transcript consisted of 47 As and one B—of course in typing, a skill which stood me in good stead for a career as a scholar and writer—just take a look at this chapter and remember where I learned to "keyboard."

Dr. McCharen with a friend.

Mary Lee recalls about her father:

> One year for Algebra I there were just too many students. Looking for a way to split the class and keep the learning environment, Dr. McCharen divided the class in half. I do not recall the teacher of the other half of the class, but my teacher was Dr. McCharen. Now, how would anyone know he was not only a Latin and Greek scholar but also a math major? And he did know his algebra. I was not really sure how having Dad as the algebra teacher would go, but it worked out well.

> Reading about some of the students entering PDS at odd times of the year brought back memories of how Dr. McCharen just had a way not only with the students, but also parents.

> I recall one student who arrived at PDS in about October. He was a bright child but very small. His age indicated he should be in fourth grade, but his intellect said seventh grade or higher. Dad worked out a different pattern for him, and he went on to be quite a success in the computer world, always making a visit to our home when he was in town.

> Then you have the first grader who would arrive each morning and stop in the office. If Dr. McCharen was at his desk, the boy would proceed to his

classroom. If Dad was not in the office, the child would go in, sit down, and just wait for him to arrive back at the desk. Only then would the child quietly move out of the office and to his classroom. His security blanket!

Morris (Moshe) Werthan '55 recounts what it was like to come to Peabody as a new high school student:

I attended Montgomery Bell Academy for my freshman and sophomore years, then transferred to Peabody as a junior. MBA was known to be academically the hardest school in Nashville, and I guess you could say I came to Peabody with an attitude. In my family, achieving anything less than an A was totally unacceptable, and since I had made As at MBA, Peabody should be a cinch.

Dr. Holden was my American History teacher, and for the first six weeks report, he gave me a C. To say I was shocked would be a gross understatement. Needless to say, I got off my high horse and really hit the books. When our final 12 week grades were received, Dr. Holden had given me an A-. That sure helped my standing at home.

Twenty years or so later, I ran into Dr. Holden at a get-together and we started talking about old times. He said, "I really got your attention with that C, didn't I?" He continued, "You know, you really didn't make a C, but I wanted to teach you a lesson that was more important than the grade."

He was right about one thing—he taught me a good lesson, He was wrong about the other, I thought I really deserved a C. I wonder if teachers play such tricks these days.

Miss Mac had her own bag of teacher's tricks, too, ranging from her sometimes just a bit over the top announcement of a "little chance to make 100" just when we felt like an 85 was probably the best we could muster, to her joy in seeing Bruce Stratvert '57 and David Nicholls '57 team up in a song-and-guitar rendition of Herrick's "To the Virgins, to Make Much of Time." 57 years later, the tones and words still echo in this head:

That age is best which is the first,
When youth and blood are warmer;
But being spent, the worse and worst
Times still succeed the former.

NASHVILLE IN THE FIFTIES

Nashville surrounded the school with its politics, at least from time to time. Mary Lee recalls when Estes Kefauver sought the Presidential nomination. His coonskin hat had become a trademark for him.

> Mrs. Tibbott and her art students fashioned a coonskin hat and put it on the dome of the State Capitol in Nashville. I remember helping to make the tail that would hang down from the cap over the dome. He was VP candidate on the ticket with Adlai Stevenson in 1956.

Nashville in the '50s was a Southern city with old-fashioned charm, as Brownie Williams (Helen Winfred Morgan '51) recalls:

> All the old stores: Castner-Knott's, Harvey's, Chester's, Cain-Sloan, Mill's, Zibart's. Fifth Avenue and all the dime stores. Going downtown Saturday for lunch and shopping.

> The *Banner-Tennessean* and the Society sections for items such as engagements and club meetings. The attire of ladies still included white gloves on Sunday.

> And the houses! Belmont Mansion—we lived for about four years a few blocks from there, 1219 16th Avenue South, originally owned by my great-grandfather, Judge Warren B. Ballard. Belle Meade—I'm a descendant of Sally Harding (married Robert Page) whose brother John was the first builder of that mansion. Harding Place, Harding Road, Page Road, and Old Harding Pike were named for these families.

Nashville in the '50, like PDS within it, was a thoroughly segregated Southern city. *Brown v. Board of Education* called for school integration, and activists in Nashville (including my father) worked bravely for its schools to follow the law of the land. But by my graduation in 1957, PDS had not yet integrated. My final editorial in *The Paw Print* warned of a possible PDS future as a private school: Would it remain segregated and become "A Haven for Bigots?"

The first black student was not enrolled until 1964, and by the end of the 1950s Nashville was the scene of sit-ins at its lunch counters, placing it squarely in the center of the national struggle for civil rights.

LATER LIFE

A remarkable number of PDS grads from the fifties made their mark in life. One example is lawyer McNeil Stokes '56, who reflects on what he learned there and how it affected him:

> I have recently dedicated my new book *Missing Links to Jesus: Evidence in the Dead Sea Scrolls* to my third grade teacher at Peabody Demonstration School, Mrs. Eloise McKnight. This book, which is a comparative study of the Dead Sea Scrolls and the teachings of Jesus using pattern evidence techniques, would not have been written if it were not for her. She diagnosed that the reason I could not read in the third grade was that I probably had dyslexia, and she arranged for me as well as Charlie Appleton '56 to receive special education help at Peabody College. It gave me remedial extracurricular help and instilled putting the maximum effort into being successful in reading. This book and eight previous hardbacks are a direct result of her efforts to help and inspire me to achieve reading proficiency. Charlie Appleton had a similar literary result, as he was a reporter for the *Nashville Banner* for fifty years and Press Secretary to the Governor of Tennessee. I just hope that every student will find a Mrs. McKnight to set him or her on the right course for achievement in life.

Mac Stokes recalls another

> . . . indelible event at Peabody, which occurred in 1955 in chemistry laboratory our junior year when each member of the class was making chlorine with a lab partner. Because the entire class was creating chlorine gas at the same time without proper exhaust, we all breathed in large doses of the chlorine gas. Fortunately we all escaped to the second floor balcony coughing and gasping for air. It must have been similar to being gassed in the trenches in World War I.

SOCIAL LIFE AT PDS IN THE FIFTIES

The PDS chemistry within the student body was almost as complex as that chlorine experiment. Like all school cohorts, it was a system of differing ranks and preferences. At the top were the "big men"—the athletes who were also smart and who had that élan of leadership. The aforementioned LeCornu, who went on to an outstanding military and legal career, was quintessential.

Then there were the "faculty brats," a few of whom were "big men and women,"[1] but most of whom contented themselves to serve as the candidate for vice-president who was slated to lose, or editor of *The Paw Print*, or mainstays of the Debate Team, or set-up guys on the basketball team (to describe my own yearbook-type accomplishments). Faculty brats tended to be very successful at college admission and often found their ways into academic careers, with publications and other achievements.

Faculty brats did not corner the whole market of academic success at PDS. They were probably outnumbered by mainstream achievers, who often found themselves in military or law school, or both, and built successful careers for themselves in those competitive lines of endeavor.

I don't remember there being very many ordinary hangers-on in my class of 40 or so, but I do recall a kind of revolving-door segment of kids who seemed to have gotten into some sort of difficulty in their previous school and suddenly entered PDS, often in the middle of term. I suspect I was too much of an insider to pay much attention to these folks, which was surely more my loss than theirs.

Some students at PDS were what we called "boys," and others were "girls." Students learned about gender roles when school dance times came along, even for seventh and eighth graders who were not yet ready to see boys "ask and lead" and girls "respond and follow." As a newly transplanted seventh grader from Illinois, I not only needed to learn how to play "Yankees and Rebels" at recess, but I also needed to catch my breath and respond when I was invited by a classmate to be her date at an upcoming school dance.

Such invitations seemed to require the asker for a direct explanation of her query. For me, the seventh grade invitation was prefaced by the observation that I was the "only boy left," and the eighth grade version came with the notation that I was the "shortest boy not yet asked." Perhaps it is not surprising that when I finally reached high school and was able to generate my own invitations, I found another classmate to be my "high school girl."

So what was it like to be a "PDS girl" in the fifties? Gail Cosman Patton '57 reminds us that "social life at PDS may always be reviewed in a copy of the *Volunteer*, the school yearbook, which recaptures the faculty, classes, clubs, sports and other annual events."

---

[1] Jim Ward was one such. He was to co-author this chapter when an untimely death removed him late in 2013.

Gail, a cheerleader for three years, recalls that the late '50s were "full of excitement, especially when promoting Tiger school spirit at pep rallies on game days, when the Auditorium brought the entire student body together."

Gail continues:

> The girls had an intramural sports program of four teams comprised of 7th-12th graders, directed by "Teach" Huggins. Competition abounded in volleyball, soccer, basketball, swimming, tennis and softball. Obesity wasn't in our vocabulary then. As seniors we had the privilege of leaving school on Fridays for lunch, though maybe just once a month! Thinking of food, there was a Sadie Hawkins Day event in the Auditorium. Girls made box lunches that were bid on by the boys. Proceeds went to the Athletic Department.

> The social highlight each year was the Senior Prom. "Tea House of the August Moon" was the theme of the Class of '57. The most elaborate set was designed by Chris Tibbott and the Art Department. The stage and auditorium were magical that night, a memorable event at the end of my PDS years.

PDS was a school of small classes, and it was not difficult to know most of the students in one's own and adjacent classes. Close personal and working relations emerged from working together on the Yearbook staff or *The Paw Print* or from belonging to one of the many clubs: Audio-Visual, Library, Forensics, Debate Team, Music, Band, Orchestra, Chorus, and Madrigals.

Eileen Harap Drath recalls:

> My longtime friends were supportive in so many ways, and in the summer days, we gathered to carry on those friendships. There were student council conferences and class projects, and proms to decorate for, and many causes to celebrate, plus all the discussions and conversations about what we were reading or doing.

Betty Lee Weinstein Rosen '58 attended PDS from nursery school through the sixth grade. She writes:

> I have wonderful, warm memories of my years at PDS—from Nell Parkinson waving her handkerchief to gather us in from the playground in second grade to a year filled with play productions in the fourth

grade. The swimming pool always seemed a bit creepy—perhaps due to its dungeon-like location. PDS always seemed to be a happy, safe and loving environment.

Betty's three sons graduated from USN, and three of her grandchildren are either graduates or current students. When her husband, Howard, retired from medicine in 2002, he became [and remains] a volunteer eighth grade science teacher.

Eileen Harap Drath sums it up:

Being at PDS was a rich experience. The teachers trusted us and gave us freedom to make decisions and find our voices. From high school we entered the world of college or jobs with good solid backgrounds to continue our lives. We left PDS with a feeling of pride and accomplishment.

ATHLETICS

Drath recalls the way all sports, not just football, permeated the PDS experience:

For me, sports were primary. In fourth grade, Miss Bernice Hay Huggins, better known as "'Teach," entered my life when I began to learn tennis at school. As the years progressed I played tennis year-round, riding with Daddy to his office on early summer mornings and going straight over to school to play tennis with others there.

Teach kept us challenged by giving us lessons and even entering me in city tournaments to get experience in competition. All four years of high school I played interscholastic tennis, loving every moment of the hard work she stressed. She would say to us, "If you want to talk about boys, then go down to the drug store and drink Cokes. If you want to work on your tennis, stay here." We loved Teach and her philosophy of life; she held court from an armchair in the front of the locker room.

The other big part of sports for girls was intramural sports. There were four teams, and we rotated sports from soccer to basketball to softball all year long. We looked up to the older captains and eventually became them ourselves. One winter the floor of the gym was refinished, and Teach ordered roller skates for us to use indoors. We raced around the gym floor and learned to turn around, cross over, start and stop, and do tricks on skates. What a wonderful opportunity.

An early photo of the class of 1956, with these names written on the back: Jane Chapman, Eileen Harris, Carolyn Williams, Sandra Williams, Wallace Wolfe, Ben Rowan, Bobby Vaughn, Steve Riven, and Sam Dillard.

THE FIFTIES MARKED THE END OF ONE SPORT AT PDS

In the fifties, PDS still had a football team. In 1952, the Tigers started practice that fall with a mere 14 boys on the high school team, just three more than the number required to field a team. So lean was the program that the coach drafted four or five players off the eighth grade team to dress out for Friday's high school games.

The eighth grade team played its games on Thursday afternoons, and then the selected group would dress out for the high school games on Fridays. Steve Riven '56 was the eighth grade team's quarterback. Ben Rowan '56 was its running back. Sam Dillard '56 played center, and Charlie Appleton '56 was the fullback. None of them ever played a down in a high school game, but they gave the team the impression of depth when they did pre-game warm ups and then took their place on the bench with the three other subs.

In one game, the PDS varsity football team actually led 6-0, but then its star player, Ed Davis '52, got hurt and the wheels came off. The final score was something like 76-6.

"As I recall," writes Charlie Appleton, "the girls in our class thought we were pretty cool."

But by the eighth game, injuries had so depleted the Maroon and Blue that school administrators decided to pull the plug on the team.

Such was the last season that PDS would field a football team.

Morris (Moshe) Werthan tells a story about TSSAA tennis, circa 1956:

> MBA was top dog in the State of Tennessee when it came to high school tennis. It turned out, however, that Steve Riven '56 and I made it to the doubles finals in 1956 and were playing for the championship against Jerry Averbuch and Jerry Mehlman of West High. The match was held on the Vanderbilt varsity courts and we even had supporters cheering for both teams.
>
> Steve and I won the first set 6-2, but then lost the second and were down 5-0, 40-0, triple match point in the third. Somehow we fought back and won the match 6-2, 3-6, 7-5. Needless to say it was extremely exciting for us and for our coach, Dr. B. S. Holden. I guess it was newsy enough that Bobby Teitlebaum '57, who did a sports column for *The Tennessean*, put our picture in the paper with a big write-up about the match. Even today Steve can show you that article.

Peabody Demonstration School became University School of Nashville in 1975. One would have to read another chapter in this book to learn if "PDS Forever" still is sung in the Edgehill Avenue sporting venues. But to those who were there in that decade, the words still echo: "Our boys tonight, eager for battle and ready for the fight."

There comes, however, a time to call it a day. Charlie Appleton recalls of that last football season: "I had bought a new pair of cleats at the start of that season and the decision was so sudden that I never had an opportunity to retrieve them from the locker room."

Maybe, in some dark corner, they remain. Or at least we can hear a faint echo of those many other feet that walked and ran and danced in these halls. Indeed, PDS Forever, or at least for long enough.

JON VAN TIL

Jon Van Til is Professor Emeritus of Urban Studies and Community Planning at Rutgers University. His twelve authored or co-edited books include *Resolving Community Conflicts and Problems* (2011), *Breaching Derry's Walls* (2008), *Growing Civil Society* (2008, 2000), and *Mapping the Third Sector* (1988). He served as Fulbright Specialist in Northern Ireland in 2006 and Hungary in 2010-2011, and is the past president of ARNOVA and the recipient of its career award for distinguished research and service.

MARY LEE MCCHAREN DI SPIRITO

Mary Lee McCharen Di Spirito claims both classes of 1956 and '57. (Yes, she is Dr. McCharen's daughter.) With a degree in Business Education from Peabody College, she worked in the Office of Senator Albert Gore, Sr. She also did marketing for two resort hotels, substitute taught in Fairfax County, and edited the *Digest of Motor Laws for AAA*. Now retired, she coordinates a meals on wheels program and a furniture program for a local non-profit. Helping with this section of the publication was a joy because of reconnection with so many PDS folks.

HEBER ROGERS

History Teacher, Assistant Director and Interim Director, 1959-1995
University School of Nashville

Integration at PDS, 1964

On June 5, 1964, the following letter was sent by Knox McCharen, Director of Peabody Demonstration School, to all patrons:

Dear Patrons:

We have just finished another good year at PDS and are now busy getting ready for the summer session which will begin on 8 June. Some outstanding honors came to the school in Mathematics, English, and Foreign Languages, and a Merit Scholarship was earned by one of our seniors. Seventy-four students graduated on 28 May.

The school enrollment was up slightly and many more could have been added if we had had room for them. We anticipate a heavy enrollment for summer school.

We look forward with enthusiasm to the next school year, which will begin on 8 September. The faculty is practically complete and details of the program will be worked out during the summer.

The general announcement of next year with the calendar of events is enclosed for your information. The postal card on which you can express your wishes about enrolling your children for next year is enclosed also. Please fill out the card and return it to us immediately—certainly not later than 15 July. After that date we shall fill the vacancies with new students.

A year ago, in May 1963, the Peabody College Board of Trustees adopted the policy of taking qualified students without regard to race, color, or creed. The policy was put into full operation at the college last September.

It will be put into operation from the Nursery School through the ninth grade at the Dem School in September of this year.

We appreciate the fine cooperation you have given us and solicit your support and good will in the future.

Very truly yours,

(Signed)
W.K. McCharen
Director

Integration was coming to the Dem School. It is important to put this historic moment in perspective by reviewing what was happening in Nashville and in other parts of the country.

Here in Nashville, the University Center's Scarritt College was integrated in 1950. In 1954 the U.S. Supreme Court, voting 9-0 in *Brown v. Board of Education* in Topeka, Kansas, struck down the "separate but equal" doctrine set forth in the 1896 *Plessy v. Ferguson* case. In 1957, Nashville City Schools (note that metropolitan government was not launched until 1963) adopted a one-grade-a-year integration plan. During that first year, a bomb was exploded at Hattie Cotton Elementary School, where one African-American pupil was enrolled. Fortunately, no one was hurt.

Also in 1957, desegregation took place at Little Rock Central High School. Nine black pupils entered the school under the protection of 1,000 federal troops after Governor Orval Faubus had summoned the Arkansas National Guard to prevent the black students' attendance. One result locally of the Nashville City Schools plan was the formation of the "Parents' Voluntary Plan." In its pamphlet directed to Nashville parents, the first sentence states, "This plan will prevent forced integration in Nashville."

Further in the pamphlet is a section titled "What the Parents' Voluntary Plan Does": "It allows a parent, whether White or Negro, to say which you honestly prefer—a segregated school or an integrated school."

It provides three classes of schools.

1. Negro schools for Negroes who wish to have their own schools
2. White schools for Whites who wish to have their own schools

3. Mixed schools for those Negroes and Whites who wish to go to school together.

The pamphlet's summary states:

> The Parents' Voluntary Plan is the only plan that meets the desires of each and every citizen and also meets the requirements of the Constitution and the United States Supreme Court. It is democratic, moral, and practical and will preserve peace, prosperity, and harmony between the races. Russia is forging ahead in science and education. This is no time for us to allow Communist influences to breed strife in our schools. Urge your school board to adopt the PVP—an American plan—and save Nashville from the strife and tragedy of Little Rock.

In early 1960, "sit-ins" by African-American students took place in Southern cities. In Nashville, these actions occurred along "5 & 10 cent store row" on 5th Avenue North, where Woolworth's, McClellan's, and Kresge's were located. In April of that same year, the house of the prominent African-American attorney Z. Alexander Looby was fire-bombed. This act presumably was directed at Looby because he had represented the students arrested in the sit-ins.

Shortly after the bombing, thousands of students and others marched downtown to City Hall to confront Nashville Mayor Ben West. A leader of the protest movement, Diane Nash, asked Mayor West whether segregation was morally right. His response was negative, and Nashville became the first Southern city to integrate lunch counters.

Atlanta's public schools began integrating in 1961, and one year later Vanderbilt University's board of trust adopted a policy of integration at all levels. The fall of 1962 brought renewed tension and strife in the issue of integration. In October federal troops were used to force the admission of African-American student James Meredith at the University of Mississippi.

In the summer of 1963, civil rights protest proliferated—especially in Birmingham. Nightly TV news reports showed scenes of police dogs attacking protesters, police clubbings, and the use of fire hoses to disperse the crowds. A Birmingham church was bombed, killing four young African-American girls.

In August of the same year, the famous civil rights march on Washington took place, attended by a quarter-million people. Fearing violence, President John F. Kennedy had tried to convince the leaders of the march to cancel the plan. Large numbers of federal troops were held in readiness outside the city.

CLOSER TO HOME

And now some specifics about integration at PDS. The reader should keep in mind that the Dem School was an arm of the Department of Education at George Peabody College and was ultimately responsible to its board of trustees.

In 1953, by action of its board of trustees, George Peabody College substantially integrated at the graduate level. This policy was enacted without outside coercion and prior to *Brown v. Board of Education* in 1954. In a written statement from the Peabody College board ten years later, in 1963, it was established that:

> Now it is important that we take voluntary action to prepare George Peabody College at all levels, including the Demonstration School, for a destiny of national leadership. It is therefore recommended that the Board of Trustees at George Peabody College adopt a policy of admission at all levels, including PDS, without discrimination because of race, color, or creed and that a policy of desegregation be implemented at a time and manner to be determined by the administration.

For the Dem School this meant the Director, Knox McCharen.

In the same board report under the heading "Other Considerations," it is relevant to note the following:

> The admissions officer at Peabody, other members of the administration, and the faculty at large are in support of a change to admit qualified applicants without regard to race at both undergraduate and graduate levels and in the Dem School.

> A basic and important advantage of the private university is its tax exempt status. Eventually it is probable that any institution receiving funds directly or indirectly from governmental sources will need to be desegregated in order to qualify for participation.

> The growing contingent of foreign students, many of whom are dark-skinned, are surprised to discover that Peabody extends to them without question or reservation privileges and facilities which it denies to American citizens who are Negroes.

In the board action to make these changes, there was one dissenting vote.

The foregoing paragraphs detail what was going on at the Peabody College board level in 1963. Actually, the issue had already surfaced at the Dem School in 1960. In the PDS/USN archives, a document of unknown authorship indicates the evolution of thought regarding integration at the school. Some comments from that document appear below.

In 1960 Bernie Schweid, a local bookstore owner and a PDS parent, got together with two other parents, Eunice Orr and Jenny Grantham, to discuss this revolutionary idea of desegregation at PDS. Their first step toward making Dr. McCharen aware of parental interest in this issue was to approach him with a petition signed by many parents. The fact that "more people signed it than wouldn't" proved that, although there was some opposition, "a lot of people wanted it [desegregation]."

PREPARING THE WAY

Before submitting his proposal to integrate PDS to the George Peabody College board of trustees, McCharen wisely sought the support of students, parents, and teachers. He succeeded in gaining the approval of the student council, which represented all pupils. He received the majority vote of the PTA. Although there was some mild protest, no parents threatened to remove their children from the school.

The president of the PTA actually did not support the idea, but the majority ruled and she was forced to back McCharen.

Next McCharen had to gain the support of the teachers. He managed to talk privately with each faculty member. A questionnaire was sent to all teachers, and the results revealed no great opposition to the plan, there being but "one teacher who was violently opposed" to the idea. McCharen was advised by the board not to accept "too many" blacks in the first year, then only "top notch" blacks. In the same document noted in the two previous paragraphs, the writer stated that Felix Robb, President of George Peabody College, was "afraid of integration at PDS."

Three weeks before notifying parents of his intention to integrate PDS, McCharen wrote to Dr. Robb and assured him that systematic preparation had been made for this important policy change. He stated that he believed all the constituencies of the school were as "nearly ready for it" as they ever would be.

In order to keep the integration "routine," McCharen kept the story "away from anyone who would publish it." The first day "went smoothly" because there were no photographers or reporters on the scene. On that first day of school in 1964, only a few blacks including Luther Harrell, Harold Stinson, Cassandra Teague, and Kay Roberts entered the high school. (This writer has no information regarding black pupils who may have entered other levels.)

The desegregation of Peabody Demonstration School was taking place at around the same time as the nation's Civil Rights Act, signed into law by President Johnson on July 2, 1964. The Civil Rights Act ended segregation in public places and banned employment discrimination on the basis of race, color, religion, sex or national origin.

Kay Roberts, voted "Most Talented," and Luther Harrell, voted "Most Athletic." Photos are from The Volunteer.

It was not until five years later, in 1969, that the first African-American teacher would come to PDS. That was Dolores Nicholson, elementary music teacher. Two years later, in the spring of 1971, the prominent black Nashville attorney Avon Williams, Sr. wrote McCharen questioning "only token hiring of black faculty." Also at this time Kelley Miller Smith, a black minister and member of Vanderbilt's Theology Department, notified McCharen that he was withdrawing his children from the Dem School for the same reason stated by Avon Williams.

The Dem School community's reactions to integration were muted. But one would be naïve to think that racism was totally absent.

In conclusion, it is important to view integration at PDS in 1964 as a beginning toward the diversity that exists today in our school community. As Director Vince Durnan stated in 2005 in the alumni magazine, *2000 Edgehill*: "Embracing cultural difference is not an after-thought for us: it is a guiding strategic principle. Our by-laws articulate a commitment to societally broad representation in USN's governance structure, 'proposing an ethnically, racially, religiously, and economically diversified institution with a Board of Trustees that should reflect that same diversity.'"

HEBER ROGERS
Heber Rogers first came to Peabody Demonstration School to teach summer school in 1954. He retired from University School of Nashville in 1995, having taught history in middle and high school and served as both assistant and interim director, among other roles. He also took countless high school students on trips to Europe. After his retirement from USN, he supervised student teachers at Peabody College.

JULIE REICHMAN, WITH CONTRIBUTORS
Class of 1970

Happy the land where men hold dear
Myth that is truest memory
Prophesy that is poetry.

— DONALD DAVIDSON

The Penultimate PDS

It has been said of the 1960s, "If you remember them, you probably weren't really there." So it is with some trepidation that I commit to the page impressions of Peabody Demonstration School from the perspective of students whose high school careers encompassed the 1960s.

We were really there . . . energetic, engaged, and excited. This was a period of challenge and change for our school, our community, and our country. Besides our own adolescence, we were confronting conflicts surrounding the Vietnam War, the environmental movement, the Civil Rights movement, a musical revolution, and the availability and proliferation of drugs. With this backdrop, PDS offered a uniquely stimulating and safe context for processing these forces and a superior academic and social education to advance our own transition from adolescence to adulthood. We were largely and blissfully unaware of the impending fiscal crises facing the PDS and George Peabody College communities, challenges that, four years later, culminated in the school's changing its administration, affiliation, and name.

Thanks to the 12 members of the class of 1969-1970 and one faculty member who shared vivid, insightful, and touching recollections of their time at "The Dem School." I sent a letter of inquiry by e-mail or through the post to every 1969-1970 classmate whose contact information was available through the USN website.

Where names had no contact information, I searched the Internet for addresses and added to my list those who were located. I apologize to classmates who did not receive a request but would like to have had the opportunity to contribute.

Neuroscientists warn us of memory's lack of reliability and malleability for details of specific events. Nonetheless, I found among my classmates a remarkable convergence of thought with regard to the imprint left by the Peabody years and the educational legacy that continues to be carried forward. Their reflections served to inform this chapter and provide witness to the power of the PDS experience.

THE PAST IS PROLOGUE

In the fall of 1969, 12 students from the 1969-1970 senior class enrolled in an elective social studies course entitled *American Problems* taught by Leland Johnson (later Dr. Leland Johnson). The initial goal of the course was to investigate political and social problems of the day. We stood in the midst of a turbulent period in our country's history and were presented no shortage of compelling topics to study. Yet, under the able guidance of our mentor, we received the encouragement and freedom to pursue multiple options. Ultimately, we opted to investigate the history of our own high school, possibly a more formidable task because of the necessity of unearthing primary historical resources. These included faded and fragile newspapers and documents located in various repositories on the PDS and Peabody College campuses. The class's collaborative research and writing culminated in the publication of a book, *The Past Is Prologue: Peabody Demonstration School 1915-1970. (Excerpts from* The Past Is Prologue *are included in the appendix.)*

In the spirit of constructivist learning theory, authentic engagement, and student ownership, the dozen of us reimagined and reconstructed the course, its processes and outcomes. We had assumed ownership of our learning, yet we were aware then, as now, that it would not have been possible without the visionary guidance of Leland Johnson, our teacher, who at the time was also a Vanderbilt PhD student in history and engineering.

This research for the development of *The Past Is Prologue* required the exploration of primary historical sources. The task was accomplished without benefit of scanner or photocopy machine for duplicating text materials for further study; nor did Mr. Johnson's young researchers have access to digital resources or a computer to assist in organizing notes and materials for analysis and development of the written text. This seemingly cumbersome process that might present an obstacle to today's scholar was ultimately transformative for at least one of the book's co-authors, Jim Coddington '70. Coddington, the 2003 recipient of the PDS-USN Distinguished Alumnus award, today serves as Chief Conservator of the Museum of Modern Art in New York. In reflecting upon the collaborative experience of researching and writing *The Past Is Prologue*, Jim reveals:

> The class's impact has been broad, deep and constant. It was my first intellectual experience with primary historical materials, the very stuff of history, material that I have come to live with and work with every day. But this was also a sensual experience for me—the vague smell of must filling my lungs as incandescently yellowed newsprint slid, and maybe even crackled, across my fingers in libraries. An aesthetic experience, too, as I studied the neat, orderly hands that filled columns of records of athletics at PDS across many years. Clearly, I was immersed and simultaneously captivated well beyond the classroom.

Jim's chapter for the book focused on the history of athletics at PDS. The 1969-1970 school year, during which the book was researched and written, predated Title IX of the Civil Rights Act by more than two years. Although girls at PDS participated in a large intramural program and a tennis team, options for interscholastic and competitive sports teams for women were quite limited. In fact, most of the outstanding alumni highlighted in another chapter of the *The Past Is Prologue* were men. Jim comments about this limitation:

> That the materials I studied were an incomplete account of student life at the time, largely excluding women, has been another slowly learned lesson that applies altogether too readily to most historical inquiry. While such questions were not, as I recall, an explicit part of Dr. Johnson's guidance, the fully open-minded principles he asked us to apply were surely of importance to such realizations about historical studies.

In reflecting on the research and development of *The Past Is Prologue,* Jim added:

> There was another facet of *The Past Is Prologue* that has taken me even more years to understand but now is very ingrained in my understanding of historical inquiry. The class introduced me to not just the data of history but the real people, in this case, students and faculty whose hopes and toil populated those records. The young men, now adults, that I wrote about in my chapter on sports were there to be interviewed, their personal

perspectives overlaying a far greater complexity, and thus interest, onto the safe recitation of wins and losses.

The real people of PDS were both the subjects and the sources for another chapter in *The Past is Prologue*. Chapter IX focused on student body and alumni. Among these were alumni whose outstanding careers in education, science, and the arts produced enduring contributions to society. In researching Chapter IX, I corresponded with such luminaries as Robert Massie '46, Pulitzer Prize-winning author; legendary television and movie director and producer Fred Coe '33; and Nobel Prize-winning chemist Stanford Moore '31. The exploration of the lives and impact of PDS graduates was both humbling and inspiring. More systematic follow-up to track outcomes of PDS and USN graduates would, no doubt, reveal a continuing legacy of outstanding contributions. Such an investigation could further uncover the critical supporting features of the PDS/USN experience.

EDUCATIONAL INNOVATION AND EXCELLENCE

Dr. Knox McCharen served as the head administrator for most of our years at PDS. No compelling operational philosophy or curriculum guidelines were apparent in previous research on the McCharen years (1951-1968), as reported in *The Past Is Prologue*. Progressive and traditional teaching approaches were evident among the methods of the diverse and talented faculty.

Although Dr. Mac was remembered as having measured and monitored the distance between dance partners at school-supervised parties, he was not known for heavy-handed, top-down leadership mandates in matters of curriculum, teaching style, or innovation. Trust in the individual teacher and a knack for locating, recruiting, and retaining outstanding faculty proved to be a winning formula for excellence and innovation. A few alumni recollections of memorable faculty members, highlighted here, serve as examples of the exceptional educators gracing the halls of PDS during the 1960s.

THE EARLY YEARS

PDS was recognized by the community as an extraordinary school. The nursery school/kindergarten through grade 12 program was unusual in private and public schools. It offered a sense of continuity and reflected long-term involvement of students and parents.

A number of students attending PDS in the 1960s began their educational journey at age four in the 1950s at the Peabody nursery school located in a building a block east of the current USN campus on Edgehill Avenue. Gean Morgan, herself a PDS graduate, and Lela Newman were the early childhood teachers for those of us attending the Peabody preschool in the mid-1950s. We are fortunate that the Peabody educational community of the early 1920s was prescient in establishing an early childhood program long before it was customary in public schools and decades before the current presidential administration advanced preschool as an administrative priority. As one who benefited from the Peabody preschool experience, I learned that play, the authentic "work" of early childhood, forges a foundational love for learning not available in Baby Einstein or technology for toddlers. An extraordinary video[1] filmed 30 years before my own peers and I attended the Peabody nursery and kindergarten programs documents an approach to learning grounded in hands-on experiences that values full participation supported by access to and application of authentic learning approaches.

Remarkably, this video foreshadows education in the PDS upper grades, where students participated in authentic educational explorations (discussed below). These included "active learning," primary research, and writing, as well as lively debates on the most critical issues of the time.

Few memories of those early Peabody years were shared by chapter contributors. However, Carol Norris Brown '70 still recalls the vision of second grade teacher Miss Parkinson standing in the window of the teacher's lounge with outstretched arm waving a scarf to summon her flock back from recess. Also etched in memory, even a half century later, are elementary school lunchtime routines where students could be assigned to the teacher's table if they cleaned their plates every day but disgracefully removed if they failed to finish the meal. PDS elementary students were the fortunate beneficiaries of such delicacies as chess pie, an especially fond (though distant) culinary memory for those of us who have left the South.

THE MIDDLE YEARS

During our seventh and eighth grade years, the Dem School was still organized into elementary, junior high, and high school, although toward the end of our tenure there, a transition was effected to embrace the middle school philosophy

---

[1]"Peabody Demonstration School 1927/1928." *YouTube*, 1927/1928. Web. April 9, 2008.
   http://www.youtube.com/watch?v=p1tAYnegV24.

and organization. Even though our middle years occurred prior to that transition, the school size, physical organization in one building with shared resources, and a cohesive cohort of students moving through the grades together provided much of the context for and benefits of a middle school environment.

Carol Norris Brown recalls sixth grade as a rigorous, challenging direction changer. Mr. Howick, her teacher, was one among many PDS faculty who either had a PhD or was simultaneously pursuing doctoral studies while teaching at the Dem School. Brown clearly remembers the experience of collaborating with peers on a year-long research project which immersed the class in investigations using primary source materials. The project culminated in these eleven and twelve year olds integrating research findings and presenting them in a multi-media format.

Seventh and eighth grade math teacher Jean Burdick appeared to seamlessly handle the transition from traditional to new math in the mid-1960s and challenged our many gifted math students as well as those of us who were less confident in our math skills. Her teaching was characterized as being competent, kind, and rigorous. Many worked especially hard because she expected it and instilled in each of us the confidence and skill to do the job.

During junior high and throughout high school, gender-segregated physical education classes were the norm. Juanita Clement, our PE teacher, employed the unusual practice during roll call of having each girl indicate whether she was having her menstrual cycle by calling out "here, OC," the "OC" standing for "out of condition." The fortunate or unfortunate female student (depending on your perspective) was excused from the introductory calisthenics and any rigorous physical exercise. Miss Clement taught only a short time at PDS and, like several other faculty, left for a teaching position at the college level. Her successor, Gracie Allen, was much beloved and remembered not only for her affability and teaching skills, but also for her singing and acting talents enjoyed by those who attended theatre productions in the Nashville community. Her portrayal of Nellie Forbush in Theatre Nashville's *South Pacific* brought accolades from local theatre crowds in the 1960s.

HIGH SCHOOL YEARS

Besides physical education, other gender-segregated offerings continued during the high school years. Luther Ralph, our art teacher, offered art classes to girls and mechanical drawing classes to boys. Fred Hinze '70 found mechanical drawing class to be "challenging for this hyper kid." He recalls being told that his lines looked like he had "drawn them with a mop." For girls in the art classes, memories linger of Mr. Ralph's staccato tones requesting us to line up "**qu**ickly and **qu**ietly" so we could walk to art exhibits on the Peabody College campus (and stop by the college snack bar on the way back!). Access to Peabody College and Vanderbilt University facilities expanded our academic, social, and cultural opportunities and reinforced the notion that we were engaged in serious scholarship but also responsible and independent enough to explore our own interests and access the larger community resources.

Mark Turner '70 further highlights this critical influence:

> I remember a life of growing maturity at PDS in the midst of Vanderbilt University and Peabody College across the streets and among classmates and faculty who valued learning and intellectual development. What an environment! For one example, the whole country knew about the famous *Scopes* trial of 1925 that pitted the enduring battle between the scientific theory of evolution and the religious belief of creationism, with the Tennessee courtroom dramatics of lawyers Clarence Darrow and William Jennings Bryan. Well, decades later, John Scopes spoke in the auditorium at PDS while I was in high school there. We were riveted. It was one of his last speeches. But it touched PDS students to history, to a debate that remains unresolved.

Paul George, Emeritus Distinguished Professor of Education, University of Florida, and leading international authority on middle schools, was also pursuing his doctoral studies during his years teaching social studies at the Demonstration School. Many remember him as an innovator and change agent. Several alumni elaborated on the impact of his classes and teaching style.

Dr. George's employment came about fortuitously without benefit of search committee or standard human resource department procedures:

> My first acquaintance with PDS came in the autumn of 1964, when I was given a job as lifeguard at the indoor pool in the basement of PDS. I learned of a position in social studies opening as a consequence of the retirement of a long-time revered teacher, Doc Holden. I had a master's degree in history and a year of high school teaching experience . . . .

I was hired on the spot for this position by the school director, Knox McCharen, after I padded up to his office in my swim suit.

Dr. George began teaching at PDS the following January of 1965. What he found in the high school immediately surprised him:

> I was expecting a conventional class of students who had little or no interest in history and lots of behavior issues; I was stunned to discover that the classes were full of adolescents who were incredibly bright, studious, well mannered, cultured, and who loved learning, even history. They were supported by parents who were well educated, professionally and economically secure, and eager for their children to become involved in the life of the mind. Uncommon then, to be sure; rare now.

Paul George

He continues by noting, ". . . that I am still in touch with a few students 50 years later is a testament to the exceptional nature of the school."

Dr. George's classes were legend for their opportunities and requirements to go beyond the memorization of historical facts. Rather, we were encouraged to develop critical thinking. Many of us carried through our college, master's and doctoral programs analytical skills fostered by such activities as learning and applying logical fallacies to critique and respond to oral and written arguments.

Janet Clodfelter '70 remembers Paul George as always encouraging original thought and urging students to question long-held assumptions and beliefs. The content and methods of his instruction provided lifelong lessons about the fundamental value of education and learning:

> I will always remember the moment of my epiphany at PDS! The day Paul George told the class that we could read related articles and write reviews and give presentations to improve our test grade. From that point

forward, I understood that success was not always measured in academia
by a score on a single test. Suddenly, not being a Merit Scholar was not
defining me as a lost cause.

Bruce Davis '70 adds that he remembered Dr. George's seminar class, often held informally in a circle outside, where current social and political issues were discussed. He was impressed with Dr. George's ability to control the class while simultaneously offering the flexibility to "explore, question, even challenge current practices that often were counter to beliefs that our parents may have had . . . . Paul helped push open the door of possibilities."

Challenging current beliefs and practices could be dangerous in some circles during the 1960s. According to Dr. George, PDS offered a safe haven for pushing the envelope of established educational practice and political thought, and during the tenure of school director Dr. Knox McCharen, no criticism or censorship of such practices occurred. Such was the environment of freedom that permitted a political debate focused on one of the most contentious issues of our time, the Vietnam War. The evening event attracted a standing room only crowd of students and their parents and featured Paul George arguing against the war. His opponent, popular WSM broadcaster, *Billboard Magazine* Southern editor and PDS parent Bill Williams, was a former Vietnam war correspondent and a war hawk. As Dr. George recalls:

> The room was full of parents and students. The debate went well, although
> I think the consensus was in favor of Williams. A few years later, Bill
> Williams told me that he then believed that I had been correct about the
> nature of the conflict and that he had been "brainwashed."

Juniors and seniors who had finished the required world history and American history courses were eligible for Dr. George's elective, "Introduction to the Social Sciences," which divided their studies into 5 units: Anthropology, Political Science, Economics, Sociology, and Psychology. In addition to the traditional classroom discussions, readings, and homework, students engaged in "active learning" by participating in an array of community service activities and job shadowing. Some students elected to tutor in a local, largely minority elementary school where Dr. George's wife Reisa taught. Other students served as volunteers in a local soup kitchen downtown. As a participant in this class, I recall that my chosen activity involved working with law enforcement. Several classmates and I alternated between observing police work by riding in the back seat of police cars on night patrols and later observing at night court.

These activities were emblematic of many of the participatory Peabody experiences of the 1960s. We painted our teacher's classroom in the summer, cleaned up our school during Earth/Environmental Awareness Day, and organized Student Curriculum Days, which involved planning, scheduling, and locating speakers for learning seminars focusing on chosen topics of current interest.

Robert Smotherman's summer civics class, funded by the National Defense Education Act, found scholars holed up in the Vanderbilt Law Library, immersed in researching Federal District, Appeals and Supreme Court cases. Dem School freshmen, sophomores, and juniors in the class analyzed primary source materials consisting of case law documentation and then prepared written and oral arguments for simulated high court presentations and debates.

Heber Rogers

Heber Rogers, longtime history teacher whose tenure included the 1960s, might justifiably be remembered as "Mr. PDS/USN." Apart from being a steady presence at the school for four decades and Interim Head during the difficult transition years, Mr. Rogers also led many student groups on overseas trips to experience history and culture firsthand. More recently, he and his wife established the Fran and Heber Rogers Endowed Scholarship Fund. Besides recalling Mr. Rogers as an exceptional mentor and administrator, many of us have fond recollections of the comfortable sight of his old rusted-out car as we made our way to and from the parking lot each day.

Our English faculty during this period included Betty Kammerud, Nell Ballentine Beazley, Eleanor Hitchcock, Eleanora Tyler, Jim Stelling, and John Offutt. They instilled a love of the written word and skill for developing fiction and expository writing through classroom work and a high level of participation in extracurricular activities, which they sponsored. *The Gallery* literary magazine, *The Paw Print* newspaper, and the yearbook, *The Volunteer*, attracted a large group of enthusiastic and committed high school students. The Drama Club, headed by Mr. Stelling, also had a faithful, dedicated and talented following. Leslie Zarker Morgan '70 recalls long rehearsals and preparation sessions for the plays *The Crucible* and *The Madwoman of Chaillot*.

At PDS, traditional and more progressive styles were mixed with happy results. Fred Hinze recalls his PDS years as having innovative educational opportunities as well as "old school teaching techniques." He remembers in particular the English faculty's tradition of weekly vocabulary quizzes from the *Word Wealth* book. That Friday memorization ritual, while a dreaded event, helped Fred and many classmates through the college years and graduate work.

Leslie Zarker Morgan '70, Professor of Italian and French Language and Literature at Loyola University Maryland, especially appreciated the inclusion of classic drama in the curriculum. Studying works such as *No Exit, Waiting for Godot*, and *Tiger at the Gates* provided explorations that she valued and recommends as part of the literary experience for today's high school students.

English teacher Mrs. Tyler was fondly remembered for her love of poetry and encouraging students to memorize and recite classic works. I still remember and broadcast treasured poetry verses from her classes (much to the annoyance of my children). Mrs. Tyler and Mrs. Beazley practiced more traditional teaching methods that provided us a well-rounded and solid grasp of English language and literature. As seniors, we finished our English training with John Offutt, who was new to PDS but proved to be an inspirational and much beloved teacher. He brought to our final year innovative approaches to the study of English including an introduction to the International Phonetic Alphabet, which proved to be useful for seniors whose college studies included linguistics and communication development and disorders.

A number of Class of 1970 graduates made special mention of Eleanor Hitchcock, whose rigorous and skillful instruction left an enduring effect on our abilities in writing and our love for literature. Mark Turner, who spent much of his career in journalism, reflects:

> I was something of a math and science nerd and had little enthusiasm
> for language arts and literature when I moved to PDS in the tenth grade.
> Mrs. Hitchcock changed all of that. She was pivotal. The breadth of my
> education and interests, rather than a narrow one, I can attribute to her
> influence. I ended up, as a result, not only working in the sciences after
> college, but also becoming a newspaper reporter and editor for much of my
> working life. Most of all, she made me want to read and read and read.

College majors and careers in medicine and the sciences were extremely common among graduates of the 1960s, no doubt inspired in part by our faculty in science and math. In spite of this, classmates' most vivid recollections of science faculty included their more quirky characteristics, such as those of Kathleen Metzger, a rigorous and revered teacher, who would not hesitate to hurl a piece of chalk across the room to gain a student's attention or make a point. Lawrence Bradley, a longtime biology teacher, was remembered for his competence as an instructor but his absolute refusal to teach anything related to the theory of evolution.

The math department at PDS was celebrated for its excellence and a stream of math teams placing first in the Tennessee state math contest. Hazel Lundberg taught at PDS for a quarter of a century and during much of the 1960s guided many math teams to victory. She was known for differentiating instruction long before the term had entered the education vernacular. This skill, to teach effectively to students with a range of abilities but still challenge them to the next level, earned her respect and accolades. In fact, the 1967-68 *Volunteer* is dedicated to Mrs. Lundberg, one of Peabody's "most memorable and remembered teachers."

Robert Kammerud, with his quiet, understated style and dry wit, also spent many years as a PDS math teacher and taught geometry to many of us. Rounding out our math faculty during the senior year was newcomer Robert Moser, who taught trigonometry. Senior transfer Steve Goldstein remembered Mr. Moser for his kindness and for being one of the teachers who motivated him to be excited about coming to school. My own fondness for Mr. Moser grew after one of my many inelegant trigonometry proofs was judged to be "one of the most creative" he had ever seen.

During our time at the Dem School, no Advanced Placement or International Baccalaureate classes existed. In fact, our most advanced mathematics class was Trigonometry. (Yet we had exceptionally successful math teams.) The need for more advanced electives was creatively met by enrolling in classes at Vanderbilt University, an exciting option pursued by numerous PDS students.

SOCIAL AND CULTURAL CLIMATE

PDS distinguished itself by a campus climate of openness, inclusiveness, and freedom. This was perhaps more striking to those who entered the Dem School in their last year or two of high school, as these transfer students more often mentioned these qualities. Gaye Johnston, Nashville area physician and senior transfer to PDS, recalls:

> We did not see color, we saw friends. We did not see nerds, we saw genius; we were young women, not girls, and guys could be trusted to keep their word. It was also fine to be GBL (gay, bisexual or lesbian), but we did not name it as something.

Two other 1969-70 senior transfers, Connie Meyer Newman and Steve Goldstein, spoke in particular about the school climate and culture. Both Connie and Steve had transitioned to PDS from large suburban Nashville area public schools. Steve recalled particularly caring teachers and "the freedom each person had to be themselves." Connie echoed similar sentiments. She remembers being struck with the very open and accepting atmosphere of PDS and the welcoming attitude of classmates. She noted an emphasis on individual expression, initially observed by her and several other classmates in the absence of a dress code. Rather strict dress codes were standard in Nashville public, private, and parochial schools during the 1960s. Connie also observed more inclusiveness than at larger schools in terms of student opportunities for participating and experimenting with a variety of extracurricular activities.

Although many native Nashvillians appreciated the relatively more liberal dress code and welcoming atmosphere, California transplant Fred Hinze saw things differently. As a seventh grade transfer from Los Angeles, he experienced culture shock when his California beach boy style of dress clashed with the more conventional tailored pants, brown Weejun loafers, and Gant button-down shirts with back loops considered to be trophies by female classmates.

In spite of what many considered a laid-back climate at PDS, numerous faculty members expected a more formal style. Fred remembers his introduction on his first day of his homeroom in Mrs. Kammerud's class. During roll call he responded by saying "yes" when his name was called:

> "Yes WHAT," Mrs. Kammerud queried.
> "Yes, that's right," Fred responded.
> "Yes WHAT?" she pressed.
> "Yes, my name is Fred Hinze."
> The class broke into laughter as she corrected him, ***"Yes Ma'am."***

"Such was my introduction to Southern etiquette," Fred recalls.

Fortunately, Fred easily adjusted to the various cultures of the Dem School and served us well as 1970 senior class president. In spite of his rather jarring introduction to the South, he has enjoyed a long and successful career in neighboring North Carolina, where he serves as a licensed psychologist for a major state center for individuals with developmental disabilities.

Other experiences contributed to a sense of freedom and community. Among the most vivid recollections shared were scenes of gatherings on Magnolia Lawn at Peabody College, where many spent lazy lunches and hurried breaks, and where fondly remembered faculty convened outdoor classes on balmy Nashville afternoons. Leslie Zarker Morgan was on a fast track three-year plan at PDS during the late sixties but took time to savor the open campus and lunches on the Peabody College lawn. She recalled many friends who shared those moments. Magnolia Lawn was so often frequented by PDS students that the squirrels inhabiting its numerous trees became acclimated to our meetings and nearly always joined us and delighted in a stolen morsel from our lunch sacks.

While soda machines were not found on the Dem School campus, many students quenched their thirst by sneaking over to the Vanderbilt Bill Wilkerson Clinic (then just east of the PDS campus) to buy sodas from their basement soda machine. Eventually, the clinic personnel complained, but for a while we enjoyed what was then considered a bit of an adventure.

Classmates graduating in 1969-70 reveled in another open campus space reserved specifically for senior class members. The Pit, as it was known, was a sub-basement room in a building on the southeast side of campus. No one recalls any adult supervision there. Carol Norris Brown '70 remembers classmate Craig Kellogg smuggling in a slot machine to add to the TV entertainment available in The Pit. Seniors of the class of 1969-70 considered The Pit a radical symbol of freedom and independence. For its time, The Pit was viewed as being quite progressive. Bruce Davis recalls his friends at other schools being incredulous that PDS seniors enjoyed such a privilege.

It is difficult to accurately summarize the impact of the social and cultural climate on the life of the individual, especially among students in a school as diverse as PDS. It would not be hyperbole to state that our school was life changing to many, and their letters to me confirm this characterization. Charles Lutin, PDS junior transfer, shared his own story, and in it he revealed much of what was magical and extraordinary about the culture and climate of our school and the character of those we were fortunate enough to call our classmates:

> I arrived at PDS at the age of fifteen, the new kid from the football school across town . . . . I was a nerdy, bookish, and very shy teenager. I was good at math, not football. My social and political views seemed way off the left side of the road until my arrival at PDS, and I was almost withdrawn due to my almost universal unpopularity at my previous high school.

> At PDS, I found an opportunity to be me without fear of retribution, and even to be liked and considered perhaps even cool. I do not attribute any of this to changes in myself, but rather changes in my environment and the kids I was attending school with.

PERSPECTIVES ON DESEGREGATION AND DIVERSITY AT PDS

While desegregation after the 1954 *Brown v. Board of Education* Supreme Court ruling came painfully slowly to many public and private schools in Nashville, PDS led the way among private schools:

> The City's several Catholic schools did remove their racial barriers
> to admissions at that time, though, under a decree signed by the
> local bishop, *and the demonstration school at George Peabody College
> for Teachers also desegregated promptly, but no other private schools
> followed suit* (italics added).[2]

---

[2] John Egerton,"Walking into History: The Beginning of School Desegregation in Nashville." *Southern Spaces,* May 4, 2009.

Students attending PDS during the 1960s benefited from their administrators' leadership in effecting early desegregation of the school. Reportedly, the desegregation was accomplished with some careful planning by Dr. Mac. Surveys were sent to faculty to assess attitudes, which were nearly unanimously positive. Of course, being on the forefront means no operational manuals or set of procedural steps are available for guidance. Whatever imperfections in the process may have been perceived, the ultimate outcome was extraordinarily positive for the content and culture of the school. The following section does not attempt to represent personal perspectives of African-American students, those pioneers of school integration whose journeys offer unique insight into the history of PDS in the 1960s.

The sentiments of my classmates who contributed to this chapter were ones of extreme pride regarding the general and specific diversity of PDS. In particular, they point to this decision of PDS, its choosing of diversity in the face of the intransigence of many local schools who did not or would not integrate in the wake of the *Brown* decision. Other students saw it as the norm and realized the significance of the school's desegregation only with the passage of time and the opportunity for reflection. Still others in our group navigated this journey on a bumpier road, one that presented conflicts and discomfort, but ultimately allowed emergence with the tools, resolve, and attitude to celebrate and seek out diversity.

Carol Norris Brown noted an understandable sense of pride about the school being a forerunner for school racial integration in Nashville. She remembers this change starting at the high school level when she was in second grade:

> In the '60s we also picked up some new classmates who were
> leaving other Nashville schools for more freedom from regulations
> and prejudices. We were too small and close a student body to be
> exclusionary—we were each "popular" and had our own groups of
> friends, but we were all welcome into the whole.

Mark Turner '70, former journalist and newspaper editor, reflected on this period:

> Segregation never made much sense to me, although all of us in the
> South were at a minimum susceptible to the insidiousness of growing
> up in a society with racial prejudice. But PDS had none of that, as far
> as I remember. We were all there to excel in our academics and our

intellectual growth, and to be teenagers. Race didn't factor in, except as elements of cultural diversity. PDS set a great example in those years.

Former faculty member Paul George also recalls that race did not seem to be an issue at PDS, even in the midst of the civil rights movement.

Senior class officers of the class of 1970: Kenny Pointer, vice president; Julie Reichman, secretary; Sonnye Dixon, treasurer; Fred Hinze, president. (Photo is from The Volunteer.*)*

However, outside of school, PDS students encountered episodes that provided different perspectives and gave context and contrast to the culture of the school. Bruce Davis '70 recalls that attending one of the first integrated schools was "one of the most unique and valuable aspects of PDS." More broadly, he valued developing extensive friendships "across economic, religious, ethnic, and cultural lines." Nonetheless, he became more aware of differing perspectives through associations and friendships with African-American classmates. A particular experience lingered with him through the years. Bruce and his friend Kenny Pointer, our senior class vice-president and an African-American, were riding down West End Avenue headed toward the Belle Meade area. All of a sudden, the police pulled them over, not because they had violated any traffic law but just because the police wanted to know what they were doing in that neighborhood. Though "racial profiling" was not a familiar term at the time, the implications were painfully apparent.

Social events outside of school revealed the more blatant bigotry that was present at the time. For example, some students' parents forbade them to attend class parties where African-American students were in attendance. As the host of one of these parties, I was initially angered at the response from some of my classmates' parents. It flew in the face of my naïveté about the status of racial harmony and inclusiveness within the larger school community.

It is clear that student experiences outside of school were fraught with shades of bias and prejudice. However, teachable moments were in abundance. What may have been most remarkable about the PDS impact on attitudes was its potential to be transformational. The story of Janet Clodfelter '70 demonstrates the ability of an extraordinary student, coupled with an extraordinary school, to change the life cycle of bigotry:

> I came to PDS from the WASP world and entered a world of true diversity … a world of different cultures, languages, and spiritual beliefs. PDS was a haven of socioeconomic, academic and political diversity. Where else would you sit between a student whose father bagged groceries at H.G. Hill and a student whose family owned Coca-Cola?
>
> Ironically, I came to PDS to avoid racial integration in the public schools. My family had no friends of color. My presence at PDS was fear-motivated on the part of my parents. Thankfully, their fears catapulted me into the world where I belonged. At PDS I protested civil injustices and sat and cried with friends of color over the riots and murders of our national leaders. We advocated together for civil and social justice. At PDS I became sensitized to the complexities and opportunities of life. I learned how to walk the talk in small things. I learned to love greatly and see possibilities that before I had never dreamed.

Janet's association with people of color at PDS set the stage for her to pursue graduate doctoral training in dental medicine at Meharry Medical College, one of the nation's oldest traditionally black academic health sciences centers. It also inspired her to years of philanthropic work in Haiti, where she organizes and participates in medical missionary projects and has established LaFond School, a haven where children in Haiti receive a sustaining gift that this PDS graduate has grown to cherish: a quality education.

THE PAST IS PROLOGUE . . . OR IS IT?

The title of the first history of Peabody Demonstration School, written by Leland Johnson's American Problems class, was *The Past Is Prologue*. This title mirrored one of an earlier book written by President John F. Kennedy. The choice of this title reflected our belief in Kennedy's assertion that "a knowledge of the past prepares one for the crises of the present and the challenges of the future." Many challenges, unforeseen by the authors of *The Past Is Prologue*, necessitated a major transformation of PDS a few short years after our graduation.

The sleek, well-equipped, and well-funded USN facilities of today stand in stark contrast to the aging, underfunded, and minimalist classrooms and facilities of PDS of the 1960s. Nonetheless, our educational journey during the late 1950s and 1960s was rich, authentic, engaging, and personally transformational. It equipped us well to assume ownership of our futures and face the challenges of a changing world. Charles Lutin '70 admits that the "letters USN still do not roll easily off the tongue, or off the fingertips."

This sentiment captures the nostalgia that several of my classmates expressed. They wonder, as do I, if the bright light that was PDS still illuminates the halls of USN today. The degree to which the roots and spirit of the Dem School gave birth to and sustain University School of Nashville will be for others to determine. Likewise, whether the title of the school's first history, *The Past Is Prologue*, is judged to be prophesy or simply poetry is a question for future generations of USN scholars.

CONTRIBUTORS

ALUMNI

CAROL NORRIS BROWN

Carol, whose father was on the faculty at George Peabody College, attended PDS for 12 years—only missing junior year in high school when the family lived a year in Washington, D.C. She has since earned degrees from Brown and Marymount Universities and works in the D.C. area as a Program Manager in the Information Technology industry. Carol married her college sweetheart and they have two grown children. She particularly enjoys keeping in touch with friends, travel, and summer sports such as tennis and sailing.

JANET CLODFELTER

Janet completed her bachelor's degree from the University of Tennessee followed by doctoral studies in Dentistry from Meharry Medical College School of Dentistry. She practices dentistry in Nashville, where she focuses on family, cosmetic, and implant services. Janet enjoys living on the lake in Old Hickory, Tennessee and spending time with her two grown daughters. She is involved in outreach services in the Nashville community but has a special passion and commitment for her mission work in Haiti. Somehow, in her busy schedule, she also finds time to pursue hobbies, including biking, swimming, silversmithing, bird-watching and traveling.

JIM CODDINGTON

After Peabody, Jim earned a BS from Reed College and an MA from the University of Delaware in art conservation. Jim was 1969-1970 PDS school president and is the 2003 recipient of the PDS-USN Distinguished Alumnus Award. He is currently the chief conservator at the Museum of Modern Art.

BRUCE DAVIS

After college, Bruce worked for NASA for many years. In 2009, he retired from NASA to work for the Department of Homeland Security, where he has served as a program manager in Science and Technology Directorate. Bruce reports that his children are grown, married, and employed.

STEVE GOLDSTEIN

Steve Goldstein lives in New York and works as a communications consultant. After graduating from the University of Arizona, he worked on Capitol Hill for the first President Bush, then moved to New York, where he served as head of corporate communications for Dow Jones/ *The Wall Street Journal* and as Chief Communications Officer for both TIAA-CREF and AllianceBernstein. Steve is married to Bill Popeleski.

FRED HINZE

After leaving PDS, Fred earned a bachelor's and master's degree and currently serves as a licensed Psychological Associate for the State of North Carolina. He has 41 years of service in the field of developmental disabilities across Tennessee, Hawaii, and North Carolina. Fred currently specializes in severe behavior disorder/autism/developmental disabilities and dual diagnosis at the J. Iverson Riddle Developmental Center in Morganton, North Carolina and maintains a part-time private practice consulting to mental health programs. He is married with four grown children and enjoys traveling in his spare time.

MARGREETE "GAYE" JOHNSTON

After PDS, Gaye graduated from Peabody College and received her MD from Meharry, specialty pediatric training at Tulane University, and a Master's in Public Health from Vanderbilt. She provided medical services to residents of rural areas in Louisiana, then returned to Nashville, where she has practiced pediatrics since 1985. She and her husband have raised two sons, one of whom is a USN graduate. Gaye enjoys traveling, art, photography, and sunshine.

CHARLIE LUTIN

Charles Lutin graduated from Vanderbilt University (1974) and Duke Medical School (1978) after finishing at PDS. He practiced as an Emergency Physician and USAF Flight Surgeon until 2013 and is now retired and living in Atlanta. Two children live in North Carolina and Georgia. A lifelong passion for aviation has led to an aircraft construction project and a book about the process to follow completion of the aircraft.

LESLIE ZARKER MORGAN

Leslie Zarker Morgan has remained in the academic world; she has studied or taught in New England, New York, Italy, Germany and France. She has taught Italian and French for twenty-five years at Loyola University Maryland (in Baltimore) and looks forward to another ten years or so of doing the same, watching the trends of education—in particular the teaching of language, literature and culture, and through it, how ideas of what culture is (and what needs to be taught) change over time.

CONNIE MEYER NEWMAN

Connie Meyer Newman studied speech-language pathology, earning a bachelor's from Northwestern University and a master's from Vanderbilt University. She has practiced speech pathology in private clinics, schools, nursing homes and hospitals. She and her husband Steve, a career dentist for the Coast Guard, have lived all over the country but recently returned to the Nashville area. Connie has three grown children and enjoys travel, art, and movies.

JULIE REICHMAN

After PDS, Julie earned a MS from Vanderbilt University and PhD from the University of Arizona. She has worked as an audiologist in Pennsylvania and Arizona, taught listening and spoken language to deaf and hard-of-hearing children in Arizona, and served for 25 years on the faculty at the University of Arizona College of Education. She has two grown daughters and lives with her husband in Tucson.

MARK TURNER

After the Dem School and earning his degree from Hanover College, Mark worked for many years in Tucson, Arizona as a reporter for the *Arizona Daily Star*. He then moved to Alaska, where he published a newspaper in Homer for about 10 years until he made a career change into the medical field. He has served as a registered nurse for about a decade in the Homer and Anchorage areas and enjoys cycling in his spare time.

FACULTY

PAUL GEORGE

Paul taught social studies at PDS from 1965-1970. He often says that these were the best teaching years of his career. He then spent the next 40 years in higher education, primarily at the University of Florida, focusing on aspects of school organization and management, such as desegregation and middle schools. He has been married for 46 years to Reisa, has three adult children, and four grandchildren. He would love to hear from former PDS students at: pgeorge8@cox.net.

DAVID VISE
Class of 1978

Saving PDS

Betty Werthan answered the phone and listened intently as her father-in-law delivered the shocking news: the board of Peabody College had just voted to close Peabody Demonstration School. With four kids happily attending PDS, Betty felt deflated and devastated.

Across town, Janet Carney (now Schneider) was summoned with other Peabody Demonstration School faculty to leave the auditorium where they were registering students for the new school year and attend an emergency meeting in the library. It was August 19, 1974, Carney's first day on the job, and she had the jitters typical of someone starting a new position. As she walked upstairs to the library and found a seat alongside other faculty members, Carney mostly felt happy to have a good job at a solid school that had been around for 60 years.

"My focus was quickly taken off myself when Ed Pratt, Director of PDS, stood up and made the announcement that PDS would be closing at the end of the school year due to financial reasons at Peabody College," Carney recalled. "The tie with Peabody had been severed and the school would be no more. I didn't know most of the faculty and didn't know how to process this information except selfishly. I quickly found Claudia Thompson, a friend from Vanderbilt. It was her first day on the job as well, and we commiserated about our futures. Our first employer was 'going out of business.'"

Janet Carney, 1975.

Thompson, a 21-year-old rookie PDS English teacher, could hardly believe it. "I hadn't even taught a class yet. It was scary to think that I had lost my job."

Feeling frazzled, Carney scooted out of the meeting to a pay phone in the school lobby (cell phones did not exist) to call her mother, who had been teaching for 37 years. "Her response was calming," Carney recalled. "She said, 'Learn as much as you can, get a year of experience, and then you can find another position.' I figured she knew what she was talking about."

Teachers, students, and parents felt blindsided by the news. I had walked into the school auditorium on that humid August day excited about seeing friends and registering for ninth grade. Instead, I encountered confusion and uncertainty about the school's future. No public discussion, no warning. That was it. Game over. No appeal, final decision. I felt stunned; the grown-ups looked worried.

"It was a shock," said Heber Rogers, who had been on the PDS faculty since 1959. "And after we went back downstairs to help with registration, it was a moment of disbelief."

Ben Doochin '78, a student who arrived at the auditorium to pick up his textbooks, recalls "panic."

For some reason, the crisis reminded me of a moment I had learned about in seventh grade American History class from Ann Teaff: the surprise Japanese bombing of Pearl Harbor on December 7, 1941. Even though America had no clue of the impending attack, the United States didn't sit still in its aftermath. Instead, the nation mobilized, entered World War II, fought back, and prevailed. Just like America, PDS was a special place, a school beloved by students, parents, and teachers because of the way it blended academic and personal growth with individual freedom. Maybe, just maybe, I hoped, we could follow America's example and fight back to save our school. There was too much at stake not to try.

Outside the school building, the news media had started to gather. Oprah Winfrey, a young TV reporter and co-anchor at Channel 5, the local CBS affiliate, stood waiting to get reactions to the news that Peabody Demonstration School, whose history was intertwined with that of Nashville, was closing. Winfrey interviewed Thompson about the bombshell. "Being interviewed by Oprah is something we claim to this day," Thompson said.

THERE HAD BEEN A WARNING

In a confidential memo two years earlier, Peabody College President John M. Claunch had foreshadowed the possibility of closing PDS. In most years, Claunch observed, the school had lost money, putting financial pressure on the college's already strained budget. Furthermore, Claunch questioned whether the college would be better served having its student teachers get all of their experience in Nashville's public schools, rather than spending time teaching at PDS, which he viewed as a college preparatory school.

"From time to time, when the Demonstration School tuition has not produced enough income to meet all of its expenses, we have had the suggestions from different sources that the Demonstration School should be permanently dissolved or discontinued," Claunch wrote in the memo dated October 6, 1971. "This year the Demonstration School has the largest enrollment in many years and, speaking financially, is one of the bright spots in our total operation."

PDS, according to financial records, generated $135,272 for the college in 1971-72. The reason was a dramatic surge in PDS enrollment stemming from a federal court decree mandating cross-town busing to integrate Nashville's public schools. After the court ruled in mid-summer of 1971, PDS was immediately flooded with applications and phone calls from

Dr. Ed Pratt leaving his office in the Annex and entering the main building.

anxious parents; enrollment increased so much that the school had to lease five classrooms on the Peabody College campus to make room for all the new students.

Parents who contacted PDS, Heber Rogers said, did not want their kids spending hours each day on a school bus to attend unfamiliar public schools comprised of a 50/50 racial mix. "It was white flight," recalled Rogers, who estimated that PDS enrollment increased by more than 20 percent in one month, to roughly 800 students.

As PDS became more of a prominent private school, there had been periodic conversations about its value to the college for educational innovation. But just three months before Peabody College dropped the ax, its president, John Dunworth, had reaffirmed his commitment to keeping it open.

"Peabody should have a fine Demonstration School as an integral part of its teacher education programs," Dunworth wrote in a May 16, 1974 letter to a concerned parent. "One measure of a great school is that it helps a child to be as well as to know. As long as the Peabody Demonstration School accomplishes this objective, and in addition helps prospective teachers gain the insight and skills necessary for them to be truly great educators, be assured it will have my full support."

On August 29, 1974, a committee charting Peabody College's future delivered a report to President Dunworth and the college's board of trustees calling for PDS to be closed, describing it as a money-losing luxury the college could no longer afford. "It serves primarily as a private school for its paying clientele, contributing little to the realization of the central mission of the college," the report said. Its formal recommendation was made with added emphasis, using all capital letters: "THE PEABODY DEMONSTRATION SCHOOL SHOULD BE CLOSED."

That same day, former PDS teacher and Peabody College graduate Kathryn Edge made the case for keeping the school open in a letter to Peabody College President Dunworth. "No other school in Nashville offers the type of liberal atmosphere which I think is so important to the growth of a child's rational questioning nature. I want my son to be challenged at a school which places ideas above the mundane rules about dress and hair length. If the Dem School folds, my only hope is that the parents of its students start another school in the tradition of PDS."

There was also something fun-loving and relaxed that made the school unusual. "I would sometimes come out to my car at the end of the day and my Triumph

Spitfire would have been picked up and turned around," Teaff recalled. "The radio would be turned to blaring, and the windshield wipers turned on to high speed. I loved the zaniness."

THE RESCUE BEGINS

As soon as he heard the news about the PDS crisis, Bernard Werthan, Jr. spearheaded an effort by parents to save the school. With deep Nashville roots and a history of community leadership, Werthan and his family had long ties to PDS, Peabody College, and Vanderbilt University. While his father Bernard Werthan, Sr. served on the Peabody College Board which had voted to close the school, the elder Werthan had alerted his family to the news and floated the possibility that the school operate independently. Earnest and understated, Bernard Werthan, Jr. had the calm, friendly demeanor, coupled with the clout, connections and vision, to chart the best path forward for PDS. Wasting no time, Werthan met swiftly with Peabody College leaders to ask for their cooperation.

Werthan sought to stabilize the situation by asking the college for three things:

- the right to set up a new corporation that would continue using the "Peabody Demonstration School" name (the answer was "no," but a newly named school could use the phrase "Successor to Peabody Demonstration School" on its letterhead);

- the ability to lease the PDS building and grounds for one additional school year (the answer was "yes," for about $80,000 plus expenses);

- the opportunity to buy the PDS building and grounds, or enter into a long-term lease, in the future (willing to discuss, but highly unlikely).

Peabody College trustees described their discussions with Werthan as "friendly" and agreed to let PDS parents, the PTA, and students begin fundraising for creation of a new school immediately.

All of this was accomplished within weeks of the college's decision to close Peabody Demonstration School, laying the foundation for creation of a new school and stabilizing the situation quickly in order to retain faculty and students. But Werthan wasn't a one man band. A Transition Committee comprised of parents, students, and faculty members began meeting almost immediately on Saturday mornings, working to quarterback the herculean effort it would take to build a bridge from PDS to a new school that, at least in the beginning, did not even have a name.

In turning a crisis into a cause the school community could easily rally around, the Transition Committee launched an immediate contest for students to come up with a new name for the school. Ideas were encouraged, replacing fear of the school closing with the creativity, fun, and optimism that had long been part of the school's culture. Giving students a sense of ownership, the Transition Committee decided to allow students to vote on the new name, with the Transition Committee making the final decision. Nominations included Nashville Community School, University Center School, and the winner, University School of Nashville.

It wasn't merely the location adjacent to Peabody College and Vanderbilt University that made the name a natural. A stunning 187 parents, or one out of every four school families, were associated with local colleges and universities: Vanderbilt employed 113 parents of students; Meharry Medical College employed 24; Peabody College employed 20; Tennessee State University employed 15; and Fisk University and five other Nashville colleges employed 15 more. No other independent school in Nashville could match the diversity of the students.

The Transition Committee also formed a new entity, PDS Patrons Inc., to tackle the mission of raising the money needed to fund the new school's operations. Suzy Morris took a hands-on role, along with Werthan, as leader of the fundraising effort. The name of the organization was chosen thoughtfully; calling it PDS Patrons would play on 60 years of goodwill built up among PDS parents, faculty, and alumni, who had a vested interest in seeing their school survive. Morris and others organized the outreach to parents.

The pace was breathtaking. Within months, the school had a new name and more than $300,000 in contributions from 86 families, and teachers had been offered contracts for the following school year. Meanwhile, the PDS colors, maroon and blue, appeared on bumper stickers proclaiming, "University School of Nashville, Successor to Peabody Demonstration School."

"I forever will be grateful for that experience on the Transition Committee," said Ann Teaff, then a fourth-year middle school teacher, who would go on to become head of Harpeth Hall School. "I had the opportunity to observe the leadership of Bernard and Betty Werthan and other committed parents. Much of my philosophy of education emerged during that exciting time."

After some back and forth, Peabody College eventually agreed in June 1976 to sell the building, grounds, and adjacent properties for $800,000, enabling the newly-named University School to remain in its historic home. Suzy Morris, who co-chaired fundraising, described it as the fulfillment of a dream and a bargain too: "7.15 of the choicest acres in all Nashville, and at a reasonable price." Though there had been scary moments, the experience of saving the school reflected bold action, giving students a profound life lesson that dire situations could be turned into promising opportunities if they acted confidently, decisively, and swiftly.

THE "HIT LIST"

After the successful rescue effort, the early years of University School of Nashville were not without problems. Most notably, the first head of school recruited from outside, Harold Snedcof, had a short, stormy tenure. Looking to shake things up, he stoked fear among long-serving faculty that their contracts would not be renewed; rumor spread he even kept a "hit list" of those older teachers who would be the first to go.

But before Snedcof could pull the trigger, he was ousted in his first year when serious questions arose about the accuracy of his resume. The board immediately named the likeable Heber Rogers, who had been at PDS and University School for nearly two decades in a variety of roles, as interim head of school. His mandate was clear: restore morale, right the ship, and stabilize the situation.

Rogers knew just what he wanted to do first. Early the next morning, he went straight into his new office and began opening drawers and looking at files. He then discovered something he would never forget.

"I went through every scrap of paper in Snedcof's office," Rogers said. "I found the list of older faculty. And my name was on the list."

A Conversation with the Werthans

Betty and Bernard Werthan, Jr. played a leading role as parents in saving Peabody Demonstration School and creating University School of Nashville. In 1974, with the future of the school uncertain, Bernard chaired the Transition Committee and co-headed fundraising with Suzy Morris. Ironically, his father served on the Peabody College board that had voted to close PDS. The following is an edited conversation between David Vise and Bernard Werthan, Jr.

Q: How did you first learn about Peabody College's decision to close PDS?

A: The Peabody College Board met on August 29, 1974 and voted to close the school. When the board took a break, my father called Betty to let her know what had happened. With four children at the Dem School, she was totally devastated. She immediately called me and her dear friend Suzy Morris. All agreed that something had to be done to preserve the school. We quickly assembled several people we knew shared our love of the Dem School to develop a plan.

Q: Given his role on the Peabody College board, had your father tried to save the school?

A: He had inserted a provision for the possibility of an independent school totally separate from the college and in no way financially dependent.

Q: Why didn't you ask Peabody College to reverse its decision?

A: Although the college diligently applied development strategies, there was not enough money to keep the school going as it was presently constituted. Peabody Demonstration School was not self-sufficient, and it no longer served to demonstrate what teachers needed to learn for addressing the issues faced by inner-city schools, or by any public schools, for that matter.

Q: What happened next?

A: An elaborate plan developed in less than three weeks showed the urgency with which the Transition Committee addressed the many issues it confronted. There was a consensus that everything possible should be done to operate the school as it had been in the past, with as few changes as possible.

Q: Why was PDS worth saving?

A: It was different from any other independent school in Nashville. Life at Peabody Demonstration School was relaxed and informal. The Dem School was welcoming to all. It went beyond tolerance. Diversity was applauded and celebrated. The community that made up the Dem School family was an extraordinarily cosmopolitan one. University families were a large part of the population. Learning was valued, and great teachers were valued.

Q: How did you raise the money to support the new school?

A: Suzy Morris and I headed a development effort directed to parents and a few grandparents. Amazingly, the commitments were forthcoming primarily in the form of an immediate gift with monthly commitments for three years. As we look back at the list of those who contributed, it's amazing how many participated. It added up. By the time USN purchased its building in September of 1976, it had raised $900,000 and was able to negotiate a bank loan for the purchase.

Q: How do you feel about the way USN has evolved over the years?

A: Parents were in control and wanted a rigorous program that challenged students. Test scores soared, and today, year after year, USN has the most National Merit Finalists in Tennessee. But other virtues remain. USN is warm and welcoming and cosmopolitan and learning is still highly valued. Every year, Betty and I marvel that so many families choose USN. It is still evidently treasured by its constituency.

DAVID VISE

David A. Vise spent more than 20 years as a reporter for *The Washington Post*, and during that period won a Pulitzer Prize, received the PDS/USN Distinguished Alumnus award, received an Honorary Doctorate of Literary Letters, and was named to The Wharton School's list of its most influential graduates. He is the author of four books including *The Google Story*. David is a Senior Advisor at New Mountain Capital. He and his wife Lori have two daughters, Allison and Jennifer, and live in Bethesda, Maryland.

ACKNOWLEDGMENTS

"Saving PDS," the chapter on the 1970s, is the product of generous help and assistance from many current and former PDS/USN students, teachers, parents, administrators, archivists, and others. They brought the historic 1974 turning point in PDS/USN to life by sharing vivid recollections, documents from the era, and more. Many thanks to: Claire Ackerman, Andrea Barach, Connie Culpepper, Ben Doochin, Vince Durnan, Annette Abernathy Langsdon, Babs Freeman Loftis, Brittany McCauley, Mary Ann Pangle, Julie Reichman, Heber Rogers, Janet Carney Schneider, Jennifer Mathews Smith, Dana Morris Strupp, Ann Teaff, Claudia Thompson Hazelwood, Betty and Bernard Werthan, Jr., the USN Class of '78, and anyone I have inadvertently left off the list. This chapter belongs to all of you.

ANN MEADOR SHAYNE
Class of 1981

Weird or Not Weird?

I never took a class in unconventionality during my years at 2000 Edgehill, but that was the education I received: the importance of questioning, the tolerance of difference. It's a worldview, really. It's the sort of education that comes only after many, many small moments where something unfamiliar happens, and you ask the question: Weird? Or not weird? Good thing or bad thing? Embrace or reject?

PDS/USN in the 1970s provided a spectacular laboratory for testing my definition of conventionality—it was unlike any other environment I have ever experienced. Weird or not weird? The answer, of course, is yes.

THEN

My education in unconventionality began the first day I arrived at 2000 Edgehill. It was 1973, and our family had just moved to Nashville from Birmingham, Alabama. My dad had landed a job at Vanderbilt School of Medicine, so it was obvious and easy that the four of us would go to the school across the street. I started fifth grade at Peabody Demonstration School on crutches, recovering from two weeks at the hospital with a bone infection in my ankle. The lone elevator at PDS was used only to haul frozen pizza up to the cafeteria on the top floor, so I trundled myself up and down the stairs in a Tiny Tim, pathetic way.

People who were not blonde like me wandered the halls. My previous school in Birmingham had been founded in 1958, in the hot aftermath of *Brown v. Board of Education*. That school contained exactly zero African-American students, so it was astonishing to me, this integration at PDS. Impossible, not simply unlikely. One of these unblonde students was my locker mate, and she played the viola, that plump cousin of the conventional violin. She kept her viola in our locker, meaning 92 percent of our locker was inhabited by her viola. I dealt with this by carrying all my books with me, all day long, in my brown vinyl book bag slung over my shoulder where it whacked into my crutch hard enough to throw me off track. I was never, ever going to say a word to my locker mate about her viola. We rarely spoke at all.

I didn't know what to think of this place. This one building contained kindergarteners as well as high schoolers, a clear violation of the absolute truth that there were schools for little kids and schools for big ones. People were piled everywhere: on the floor, on the steps, on the ground. The high school students draped along the wall across Edgehill looked like the hippies on *Dragnet*, and there was nothing scarier than that.

My ankle mended, and I got the hang of PDS. We had one class called Variety Hour, and for one semester, Variety Hour was devoted entirely to assembling jigsaw puzzles. I loved it. I thought about the *Saturday Evening Post* a lot as I worked that Norman Rockwell cover, 500 pieces, over and over.

Occasionally, I would hear about other private schools in Nashville, and they sounded so orderly, rigid, and humorless. The boys at one school had to tuck in their shirts and wear a belt. The girls at another school wore a uniform.

By sixth grade, very little was predictable. Even the name of the school changed, just like that. When I arrived at 2000 Edgehill Avenue in the fall of 1973, the place was called Peabody Demonstration School. Within a year, it was announced that PDS would close, yet stay open under a new name. This didn't have much meaning to me, though I had never liked having the word *demonstration* in the name, because it sounded like people were supposed to protest things. (It was the early seventies. People on TV had been demonstrating most of my life, and demonstration seemed to involve limp bodies, yelling, and unpleasant interaction with The Fuzz.) The students at one point voted for a new name, which I loved doing, even though my choice, Winthrop School, lost out to the cumbersome

University School of Nashville. It should have sounded more classy, I thought. Winthrop was clearly the better choice.

Three sixth-grade classes linger in memory: Mrs. Edwards's typing class, where we pounded out QWERTYs on manual typewriters. Equally delightful was Mr. Ralph's mechanical drawing class, held in the attic of the house in the front yard of the school, the Annex. I never questioned why there was a rambling Victorian house left intact on the corner of the school property. (I spent many days admiring a drawing pinned behind Mr. Ralph's desk that my oldest brother Clif, bound for art school, had done: a cantilevered teapot so beautiful that I pointed it out to my classmates too many times.) The third class was so unusual that it wasn't even called Social Studies. It was called "Man: A Course of Study." MACOS.

John Garland was the teacher. For one thing, he was a man, unlike every other teacher I'd ever had. Even more exotically, he had a beard, and I had never in my life spoken to anybody with a beard, even Santa Claus at the mall. Mr. Garland was unfailingly gentle and good-hearted, and he led us through a class that I recall to this day in vivid detail. MACOS was my favorite class, ever. We watched movies of salmon laying eggs and swimming like hell up a stream. We learned how herring gulls fed their young by regurgitating food into the mouths of their babies. We saw baboons acting quite a lot like people we knew. Most spectacular, we spent a lot of time with the Netsilik tribe in the Arctic living a life that seemed ancient, timeless, and really smelly and grim. So much blubber! Ice fishing! Grubby fingernails! I was riveted, watching these people fight it out with cruel Nature, admiring the way every part of a seal was used for the survival of the family. I was delighted that my own mother was not one to scoop out a fish eyeball and offer it to me as a snack.

Amid all this distinctly un-Southern learning, my mother managed to get my sister and me through our Episcopal confirmation in seventh grade. Even we could tell that she had no heart in the matter, that she was fulfilling some contract she'd had in her head. By that point, Buffy and I were mostly bitter that we couldn't have bat mitzvahs like our friends did.

The first time I realized that this school with its significant Jewish population was unlike other schools in the area was when someone outside the school—a neighbor, I think—called USN "JewSN." I was shocked, hearing something like that. Coming fresh off a summer where I had read Anne Frank's *Diary of a Young Girl* maybe three times in a row, I was deep into an empathy with Jews that had arisen because of

Ann Meador Shayne, second from left, in her high school days.

my close friendships at USN. Would I have the courage to hide my friends in the attic, if it ever came to that? I fantasized that I would be a hero (our house had a staircase to the attic), though my fear was that I wouldn't. But hearing somebody call our school such a name lit a fire in me, an indignation that I carry to this day.

My family situation took a sour turn after eighth grade. I mention this because my memory of school becomes murky at this point, in terms of academics anyway. Within four years of our arrival in Nashville, my parents had separated, then divorced, in a neutron bomb of family destruction that came with no warning. It was such a seventies divorce. Our parents sat us down for family therapy that none of us could stay awake for, and all of a sudden, life altered. My father moved away to the Gulf Coast with his new wife. My sister and I would take odysseys through rural Alabama on a Greyhound bus to go visit him. My mother went back to school, then got a job teaching graphic arts and soon become head of the department at a local community college. My parents weren't on the scene; we just showed up at school most days, driving ourselves, embracing in particular the first part of the school's unofficial motto of "Freedom and Learning."

I had a bunch of classes in the Annex. Four years of English. Journalism. American History. French. In fact, the courses divided into two buildings as neatly as they divided in my interest level. If it was in the Annex, I was going to like it. If it was in the big building, well. Math and science I associated with counting ceiling tiles and trying to sleep with my eyes open and grabbing a seat in front of the fan. Delirium is the sensation I most associate with classes in the big building.

In the fall of 1980, my college advisor read to me the recommendation she had written for my college application. I don't remember the exact words, but the gist of it was that I had not performed to my academic potential because of the aftereffects of my parents' divorce. I thought: *That's not right! The divorce didn't have any effect on me; I just sucked at math, that's all.* But I never said anything to her about that recommendation—it suited my college-admissions purposes to be considered a survivor of a Broken Home. It made a better story than admitting that I had done my homework in front of the television, pretty much every single night.

Only now do I see that we children were the collateral damage in our parents' divorce, that a lot of nurturing can get lost in the shuffle when parents are busy despising each other. Those teachers who convened special conferences with me were aware of something out of whack in a way that I never was. I credit USN with keeping me on course during a time when I didn't even know I was off course. It was a steady place, feeding me Beowulf and Flannery O'Connor and Jane Austen to the point that I knew I wanted to be an editor when I graduated. It's only today, as I have teenagers of my own, that I see how life back then had gone wobbly, how I had bent my thinking in an attempt to make a lousy turn of events seem OK. It wasn't weird then, but it certainly seems weird now.

NOW

Years later, I married a USN guy who had graduated the year before I did. Our two boys attend USN now. Like many enduring institutions, the school seems polished, evolved. I have actually had the thought that things are too tidy now, too orderly. In 1996, news of the demolition of the Annex in particular hit me hard. Anybody can have class in an ordinary classroom—it's only a superspecial school that will teach you Melville in a small, Victorian parlor.

The world is different now. I look at the website for the white-flight school I attended in Birmingham, and there are students of many colors to be seen. I search the Internet for information about that MACOS course, and discover that there is a recent documentary about the controversy that killed the program. Unknown to me at the time, MACOS was considered a wild, America-busting, values-rejecting brainwasher of a curriculum. While I wandered in and out of Mr. Garland's classroom, an Arizona congressman was leading an effort to shut down the course's National Science Foundation funding. MACOS taught impressionable middle schoolers many, many awful ideas: murder of old people, gory butchering of animals in full and vivid color, divorce and trial marriage, religion treated as myth, evolution taught as fact. In 1975, MACOS ceased to be taught anywhere—but not before I got a full dose of this memorable, delicious class.

I drive by The Wall often these days, and there are no students who look like the hippies from *Dragnet*. The old building has been transformed with air conditioning (a miracle!) and fast elevators. They even renumbered the floors, which means the basement is now the first floor. The cafeteria is a modern marvel, no longer serving that spongy frozen pizza. Smart boards, not chalkboards.

Amid this lush environment, kids continue to hang out in the halls, on the steps, on the ground. University School continues to teach that basic lesson of unconventionality, of skepticism—I hear it from my boys just about every day. They tend to be wary of narrow minds. The impulse to do good is stronger than ever, as students stand up for causes that are complex, and hard. The USN of today rhymes well with the PDS/USN of the past.

Most important, middle schoolers now have their own lockers—but they still have to share a second locker for their backpacks. If ever there is a crossroads for cultural understanding, it is a shared locker that's a little too small.

THE FUTURE

As I write, my elder son David and his friends are in the next room, rehearsing the piece they are going to play in a few days at Senior Convocation. Flute, double bass, cello, violin, guitar. It's a James Taylor song, slow and sweet. Their conversation, in contrast, is hilarious: college gossip, teacher dishing, and a rash of jokes and sharp talk. These students are about to head out to every corner of the country for college, and they are ready. I wonder what lessons they will take from USN, but I have an inkling that they will soon discover, once they're away, how unusual their school is. How weird. How rare.

ANN MEADOR SHAYNE

Ann Meador Shayne '81 lives and writes in Nashville. She and her husband Jonathan Shayne '80 have two sons at PDS/USN: Clifton Shayne '18 and David Shayne '14. A graduate of Davidson College, she is the author of *Bowling Avenue: A Novel* and co-author of two books with Kay Gardiner, *Mason-Dixon Knitting* and *Mason-Dixon Knitting Outside the Lines.*

HARVEY SPERLING
Director, 1979-1990
University School of Nashville

> *The aim [of education] must be the training of independently acting*
> *and thinking individuals, who, however, see in the service of the*
> *community their highest life problem.*
>
> — ALBERT EINSTEIN, FROM AN ADDRESS AT
> ALBANY, NEW YORK, 1936, *IDEAS AND OPINIONS*, 1954,
> A BOOK THAT WAS GIVEN TO ME BY JON SHAYNE '80

Roots, Structure, and Vision

This chapter is dedicated to the people who were determined to save and sustain the newly formed University School of Nashville. The names of the board of trustees during my tenure should be indelibly etched upon the history and legends of the school, for they stepped forth during the most critical moments and provided the determination, resources, and wisdom necessary for institutional survival. My admiration and gratitude also extend to the countless and herein unnamed individuals who were willing to entrust their children to a school that often perched precariously between its continued existence and imminent demise. The words that follow convey a small part of the tale of the fall and rise of a great school. (Now thirty-five years after my first encounter with USN, I hope that I have not taken too many liberties in recalling the events of those days. If so, I apologize and gladly welcome greater clarity.)

Before departing St. Louis for Nashville in the summer of 1979, I had lengthy conversations with two remarkable individuals: Bev Asbury, the Vanderbilt University chaplain, and Bernard Werthan, Jr., the gentle pillar of reason and commitment at University School. Bev assured me that USN was a great school with the "right" values. He had recently established the Holocaust Lecture Series at Vanderbilt (now the longest-running such program at any American university) and appeared to be a very thoughtful and engaging community leader. I was most pleased that he would be a friend across the street. Bernard Werthan struck me as embodying the qualities that I hoped to see at USN. Bright, humble, and seeking no acclaim, Bernard knew that the school was essential to Nashville's educational landscape, for it provided a strong liberal arts education and a welcoming academic home to all individuals regardless of race, religion, or belief. The co-educational school was a bastion of diversity, unlike any other independent school in the area.

My wife, Cathie, and I had some reservations about moving to Nashville. Was the legacy of Southern racial segregation still pervasive? How "open" were the private schools to integration? Was the teaching of evolution an essential part of K-12 science? (Hopefully, the *Scopes* case was no longer being fought in Tennessee.) Was it true that Vanderbilt University coeds had to dress rather formally for the football games? (That issue deterred several of my St. Louis students from applying to Vanderbilt.) Did USN function as a demonstration, hybrid, or independent school? Was Vanderbilt, the school's close neighbor, committed to racial integration and religious diversity, women's rights, or even the survival of USN?

THE "UNCERTAINTY PERIOD"

During the late 1970s and early '80s, USN was perceived by many in the Nashville community to be an anomaly: an independent school with a laissez-faire philosophy and a ragtag group of students. In actuality, USN was quite different from other independent schools. It enrolled a wide array of conformists and non-conformists, believers and nonbelievers; those who looked different and alike; players of music, drama, Frisbee, basketball, ping pong, and chess; dancers, photographers, athletes, ponderers, young scientists and mathematicians, as well as thoughtful, outspoken, and timid souls—and all sorts of combinations thereof. There were also students who openly spoke of community or societal injustices, students with gentle natures, those who thrived in the arts and those who sought the life of the mind. Most of all, it was a community of young men and women, boys and girls, who genuinely believed that diversity, in every form, was not only acceptable, it was essential to schooling and the larger society. They all came together in common cause to value one another and to add additional luster and promise to the school community.

USN was indeed a haven for those whose values, backgrounds, and outlooks were in harmony with the soul of the school. The vintage building (a glorious McKim,

Mead and White structure but with antiquated and inadequate space), concrete and dusty campus, and very modest sports facilities were of concern but not enough to deter those who wanted their children to be immersed in the USN culture. The outward appearances did not define the school. The essence was, and remains, in the values and actions of its students and faculty. The school's diversity was a core value, long before other local or regional independent schools recognized the necessity of that critical component for any educational endeavor. Within USN, tolerance was not a signpost but a way of life, and there were no symbols of exclusivity. It was a family school, but the family was unlike any other in Nashville, and Cathie and I were delighted and enormously proud to be part of that family.

In 1979, the school was four years old, young enough to transition to a strong independent school model. It also had a sixty-year history as a demonstration school and, as such, was old enough in its ways to resist change. For many, moving toward an independent school model meant giving up perceived power and freedom. Others were concerned that retention of too much of the demonstration school model would dramatically weaken USN. The concept that was being batted about but often not articulated was "governance." Who should govern and how? What should be embraced or forsaken in that governance?

I was deeply committed to a "progressive" independent school model, an anomaly among the vast majority of conservative independent schools in the South. I was socially liberal, fiscally conservative, and adamant about a strong academic curriculum taught by highly competent teachers. Following rounds of meetings with board members, parents, teachers, students, and members of the larger community, I thought I understood many of the concerns and aspirations of the school's constituencies. I believed that we could achieve a consensus on governance that included a highly effective, appointed (as opposed to then current elected) board of trustees responsible for school policy, finances, facilities, and long-range planning, and a school director charged by the board to lead and administer all USN operations. My assumption was that the board and director would work collaboratively on all matters, and that the remnants of the decentralized demonstration school model would be transformed into a centralized model of independent school governance. It was evident that unless these fundamental changes took place, the school would remain unwieldy and unsustainable.

I soon realized that I had miscalculated the scale of difficulty in achieving those outcomes, and that it was quite probable that I would collide with failure at the next major bend of my school journey. We didn't have the luxury of a long transition period. Institutional change had to occur rapidly, very rapidly.

The most volatile and proverbial "buzz saw" issue was creating an appointed, self-perpetuating board of trustees rather than an elected board. The school needed the expertise of a diverse array of individuals with business acumen, financial savvy, Vanderbilt, Meharry, and Fisk connections, facilities expertise, legal insights, community affiliations, and the experience and understanding of how an effective board should function. We needed those who were philanthropic as well as those who were effective in raising money. We needed trustees who recognized their fiduciary responsibilities while also understanding the difference between policy and operations. We needed a board model that had been tried and successful at other independent schools. The new USN needed to remain socially liberal but conduct its operations in a fiscally conservative manner. Survival and growth would depend on increased school funds, essential institutional changes, and the wise stewardship of an appointed board of trustees. The idea of accumulating endowment or capital funds was, at that time, beyond our grasp, beyond reality. We were in a survival mode.

No one wants to contribute to a school woefully in debt, and that was the situation in 1979. We needed to establish financial sustainability while demonstrating, within and outside USN, the governing acumen and fundraising ability of the board of trustees. The degree to which the school would survive was directly correlated to the composition of the board and the manner in which it governed. I still have a bit of a visceral reaction when I think of the anger, emotion, and perhaps near mayhem that occurred at the open meetings of the patrons to discuss the appointed board option. It was a battle of control, of ownership, of power, of decentralized versus centralized decision-making. It was a struggle between keeping USN as an anomaly or transitioning once again, but now into an identifiable independent school. Endlessly, I explained the reasons for an appointed board, believing that the alternative would be a progressive balkanization of the school into factions that would preclude any semblance of effective governance. I had no desire to lead a school under those conditions, for leadership would merely be some form of consensus management at best.

After many gatherings, both calm and shrill, the appointed board concept was approved, thanks to the determination of a strong core of board members and parents. It was unequivocally the most important decision/action of my tenure, and it ensured the continuation and welfare of USN.

It was now time to institute necessary internal changes and, not unexpectedly, there was more than a modicum of resistance. USN was at a critical juncture of transformation, and all our change efforts would have been for naught but for the determined and dedicated trustees who were willing to endure chaotic times, difficult personalities, and long, tedious, and emotion-laden meetings. Board members did not become inappropriately involved in the operations of the school and continued to delegate those matters to me. I was most fortunate to have a succession of highly capable and skilled board presidents (Jayne Ann Woods, Gertrude Caldwell, Bill Tyne, Will Johnston, Bob Brandt, and Jane [formerly Krizelman] Lubow) who stood firm and were determined to support reforms while exercising their stewardship of the school. They were the institutional heroes and visionaries during my tenure and deserve our enduring gratitude.

During the rather tumultuous years of 1979-1985, the trustees did not allow the school to slide backwards into a decentralized pattern of governance and unfailingly supported me as critical decisions were made and operational changes were instituted. I recall the many late night coffee conversations with Gertrude Caldwell (then president) and husband Ben after long and tough board meetings. Change was a very difficult process, evoking passion and anger in some and appreciation among others. I recognized that in partnership with the board we could transform the school relatively quickly, but it would take its toll on many of us. I was convinced that unless governance, finances, leadership, and internal operations were stabilized, the school would, at best, languish. However, if we could structure the institution properly within a short period of time, we had the potential to emerge as a very solid, enduring, and top academic institution.

I would suggest that the decade between the birth of USN in 1975 and the emergence of an operational independent school by 1985 could well be dubbed the "uncertainty period." Regardless of the logic or calculus during those years, the only constant was uncertainty. There was no apparent equation that could ensure desired institutional outcomes, and thus uncertainty was an integral part of leadership during that ten-year period. (Perhaps uncertainty is a positive component of governance, for it is a variable that forces us to seek solutions beyond the conventional and reminds us that within the academic community "certainty" is elusive.)

The most essential part of my stewardship as director was the welfare of the student body, and that implied that they were served by the best possible teachers, had a culture of strong academics and humane values, and were able to think independently but coalesce as a vital and concerned community. For the school to function successfully, it was absolutely critical that it had the financial resources to support the mission, educational plan, and necessary facilities.

Unfortunately, I discovered upon my arrival that the school was literally bankrupt, owing $1.5 million (at an interest rate of 1.5% above prime—and prime was at 15%) for the purchase of the facility from Peabody College. The school had no reserve funds, no endowment, modest contributions, and an insufficient operating budget. Fundraising was not integral to the old demonstration school model and remained as such after the transition to USN. (Within a few months of my arrival, one faculty member advised me that such matters were not a major concern at USN, as money always seemed to appear magically at critical moments. I couldn't imagine operating on that premise and had an uncomfortable feeling that there was a belief among some in divine financial intervention, an interesting concept.)

BUILDING THE SCHOOL WE NEEDED

The main facility (the McKim, Mead and White building) was old and tired, with a cafeteria on the third floor (not too practical); an archaic sub-basement swimming pool that resembled an antiquated Roman bath; a gymnasium below the sewer system that flooded regularly, which resulted in elevated parquet floor sections resembling Egyptian pyramids; and inadequate classrooms at every level. The elementary school was desperate for spacious and age-appropriate facilities. We also needed a bright and engaging after-school space for the many families that could not retrieve their children at the end of the school day. We had terribly inadequate science laboratories, libraries, and spaces for the arts. The adjacent small buildings needed to be demolished. We had a dearth of outside play and sports fields. A rented space in Vanderbilt's Wesley Hall was used for P.E., although it lacked any semblance of level flooring. Our multipurpose auditorium was somehow still functioning but certainly tattered and frail with age. To my utter dismay, USN had a very old but vitally important underground steam pipe that was connected across the street to the Vanderbilt power plant, and the university was threatening to close the pipeline—a potentially catastrophic event as the school had no other source of heat during the winter months. (Obviously, we did

Construction of the West Wing, the new home to the lower school.

not have air conditioning, and perhaps our saving grace was the informality of the dress code.)

Although the staff and I were versed on the problems, I did not have the luxury of fixing them, as the school had an inadequate operating budget and no experience in raising capital funds. I was enormously grateful to the maintenance staff for holding the once-noble facility together. Also, the thoughtful spirit of students, faculty, and parents enabled us to exist as best we could without too many groans or facility comparisons to other schools. I felt both proud and thankful when one parent expressed, "We would send our children to USN even if it existed within a tent."

And herein lies the reason and rationale for the appointed board. The myriad of highly complex and seemingly insurmountable school challenges were "mostly" resolved because of the diverse talent pool of experts who were appointed to the board. Trustees with financial expertise arranged that terms of the school debt were modified, and shortly thereafter the debt was paid off, gone! Deferred maintenance was inventoried and addressed by board members with construction and engineering skills. Faculty salaries and benefits and student scholarships were increased, thanks to the generosity of board members, parents, and grandparents. The facility problems lingered but were finally addressed by a group of skilled board members. The main building was renovated and new additions (the West Wing/Lower School in 1986; Sperling facility in 1989), in harmony with the classic McKim, Mead and White architectural design, were built. These were the first new structures since 1925. Now teaching and learning could take place in more appropriate and comfortable spaces.

The capital campaigns necessary to construct the facilities were led and supported by board members, grandparents, parents, and friends of the school. Even the vexing issue of retaining the steam line between Vanderbilt and USN was resolved to our benefit. Board members who were associated with Vanderbilt in various capacities ensured a close cooperation between the two educational institutions. I knew that our future was inexorably linked to Vanderbilt, as a significant number of our parents were employed there, and our academic prowess would be tied to our association with that venerable university. Our connections to Vanderbilt, Meharry, and Fisk were greatly enhanced, as the dean of the Vanderbilt Medical School, two department chairs at Meharry, and the dean at Fisk were USN trustees. Our push for academic leadership was supported by university scholars on the board, and our need to increase the quality of our athletic programs received vital aid from a generous board member who was well-versed in sports. Those early years witnessed an unprecedented level of board accomplishments, the result of their talents, incredible diligence, and task/goal-oriented behavior. In a relatively short time, the school was stabilized, vital, and able to provide all the necessary educational essentials, and a few extras, for the welfare of students and teachers. We now had a well-functioning and sustainable independent school.

THE KITCHEN CABINET AND OTHER MENTORS

Wisely, I regularly called upon members of my "kitchen cabinet," school volunteers, and a group of trusted friends for advice, wisdom, and some necessary mirth. These individuals, and many others, ensured the well-being of the school through their dedication, involvement, and generosity. They were the organic bridge, the human elements that collectively formed the invisible undergirding that held the young USN together and allowed it to survive and prosper.

The "core group" included Joel and Bernice Gordon, May and Herb Shayne, Bernard and Betty Werthan, Suzie Morris, Raymond Zimmerman, Cecil Woods, Hank Foster, Howard and Betty Lee Rosen, Shelly Krizelman, Kathy Woods Van

Devender, Bill and Sandy Spitz, Sam Richmond, Kay and Keith Simmons, Sam Howard, John Harwell, John Chapman, Jim Kilroy, Bob Zelle, Harold Jordan, Gertrude and Ben Caldwell, Honey and Lamar Alexander, Mike and Ellen Ebert, Iris and Mike Buhl, Bill and Susie Tyne, Will and Lillias Johnston, Jayne Ann and Frank Woods, Bob and Betty Brody, Bob Brandt, Phil Bredesen, Jane (formerly Krizelman) Lubow, Clint and Gina Davidson, Jerry Williams, Jeannie Nelson, Harris and Diane Gilbert, Alan and Nancy Saturn, Judy and Noah Liff, Annette Eskind, Nelson Andrews, Charlie Wallis, Farzin Ferdowsi, Margaret Howell, Larry Fuldauer, Barbara Moss, David Rabin, Bill Stockard, Hal Maier, Hal Bigham, Cauley and John Lukens, Libby and Bob Corney, Flo Kidd, Karl Van Devender, Bob Gottlieb, Marty Rosenberg, Meredith and John Oates, Teri and Alan Cohen, John and Allis Dale Gillmor, Joan Bahner, Jimmy Schulman, Jack and Natalie May, Stan and Betsy Cherneau, Norihiro Takeuchi, Ann Wells, John Noel, Rick Blackburn, Ruth Johnson, Ronnie Steine, Weaver and Lucy Barksdale, Donna Hilley, Randy Falk, Jerry Gardner, Steve Fuchs, Bill Barnes, Emiko Ishii, Ricardo Tarantini, Larry Kown, Barbara and Marvin Friedman, and the list goes on and on. And I consistently sought the insights of members of the board of trustees, and they never disappointed me. My wife, Cathie, endured too many of my monologues about the school's woes and aspirations during our dinners and walks. Her thoughtful insights, suggestions, and customary calm were of enormous help.

From 1979-83, colleagues at other schools would often relate their disbelief at the many quandaries that seemed to emerge with great frequency at USN. For them, our school appeared ungovernable; for me, it was changing and hopeful. At that time, I did not meet any head of school who wanted to switch positions with me! Actually, I would not have traded, for I knew that USN had the talent and potential to be the envy of many of those institutions. However, I looked forward to dialogues with heads of other independent schools, for their vision and experiences could be of great benefit to USN. I sought ongoing discussions on complex issues that were common to our institutions. A few school heads and I formed a small seminar-like group, reading and discussing a wide array of literature that did and did not have direct applications to our schools (although *Antigone* provoked some fabulous discussions on leadership). We met in Cashiers at the home of headmaster Ned Fox of Charlotte Latin School. He and Bob Shirley of Heathwood Hall became my trusted colleagues and close friends. Our group leader and facilitator was most often the distinguished scholar and physicist Andrew DeRocco, who was always intellectually stimulating and refreshing. Ned, Bob, and Andrew contributed richly to my thinking and to the pathways I saw as essential for USN.

As a newcomer to Nashville, I had only a very sketchy grasp of the city's history, achievements, and woes. That changed in 1982 when I was invited to participate in Leadership Nashville, a yearlong program that focused on key segments of our community. Nashville was small, a mere one or two degrees of separation in many situations. However, the city also had wide chasms that seemed to defy closure. There were plenty of scars and remaining racial, educational, health, and economic disparities. I emerged from the program enormously proud of the leaders of Nashville's civil rights movement, recognizing their incredible courage in the struggle to integrate our city. From religious leaders and friends Rabbi Randy Falk and Rev. Bill Barnes and from USN parents, I learned more about Nashville's civil rights and social justice movements. I remain most grateful for, and humbled by, the actions of those individuals who risked their lives and futures for what was right, just, and moral.

Leadership Nashville provided the forums for discussions on critical urban issues, but it was with classmates and LN alumni that I had in-depth dialogues. I met with some of our city's leaders, dreamers, planners, builders, and skeptics from across the political spectrum. I was convinced that Nashville had the talent and potential to emerge as a remarkable city. I also recognized the need for USN to open its doors or at least bridge to many constituencies that were not associated with the school. I wanted far more outward vectors emanating from the school as opposed to its more traditional inward focus. Being a vital part of the larger Nashville community would better serve USN's interests and provide it with opportunities to contribute more directly to the welfare of the city. USN needed Nashville, and I wanted Nashville to need and support USN.

It seemed to work, as new families enrolled and community leaders extended themselves to the school. It was Nelson Andrews and some of my LN classmates who assisted me in building bridges outward from USN so that the school could be enriched by those who were unfamiliar, or even formerly critical, of its environment and practices. Borrowing from a Carl Sagan metaphor, USN was but a small blue dot, essential but part of something much larger.

From Leadership Nashville I gained some wonderful friends, advisors, and mentors. Nelson Andrews was top of that list, and I sought his input until he died in 2009. I often reflect on the insights I received from thoughtful and wise individuals, as well as from mentors who have been so important in my journey as an educator and human being. Mentoring is at the heart of a great school and should be sought throughout a lifetime. To be mentored and to mentor others is critical for the evolution of ideas, the extension of life experiences, and the transmission of values among generations. It is the great channel of learning between individuals and at the core of exemplary formal and informal educational systems.

LEADERSHIP

At the heart of University School's educational program was the curriculum, and it needed to be updated and refined. Technology had to be purchased and incorporated; academic disciplines had to be critiqued and changed as necessary; teaching needed an evaluative process; professional development funds were inadequate; highly talented faculty had to be recruited; and athletics and extracurricular activities needed to be expanded and supported. Faculty and staff salaries and benefits needed to be elevated to honor and reward those who were at the core of our success, and, indeed, USN had some excellent teachers and support staff. A very competent administrative team evolved, and it provided the essential curricular leadership to elevate our academic programs and outcomes. The administrators modeled what USN stood for, and their presence provided great confidence to school parents.

The division heads and I spent enormous amounts of time supporting, evaluating, and providing guidance to teachers; finding and hiring highly competent new teachers; handling a wide array of parent, student, and faculty issues; spreading "the good word" about the school; dealing with emergencies and crises that, fortunately, dwindled in number as the years passed; and meeting regularly with one another to ensure that we were building an exemplary, sequential, K-12 curriculum within a humane, tolerant, collaborative, and highly supportive school culture. I recruited Kathy Woods from the board of trustees to join Mary Emily Taylor as the leaders in the Lower School, and they became a legendary combination. Betty Pearson became an outstanding middle school head and then departed to Japan to teach and cement our relationship with our first overseas partnership school. Linda Wallis moved from being an exemplary biology teacher to being an equally stellar high school head. (I regret that I only had the pleasure of serving for one year with Rick O'Hara, who succeeded Linda as Head of the High School. I had recruited Rick and was quite sure that he would be a superb leader. He was.) The administrative team also included the enormously talented duo of Kay Simmons as Development Director and Jeanne McCutchan as Admissions Director. Those individuals provided the leadership necessary for the successful evolution of USN. We recognized that if we properly structured the educational environment, great outcomes were possible.

Thoughtfully and quietly witnessing all that was occurring was the very competent Bobbie Grubb who served as my secretary and administrative assistant. Her calm outward composure and confidential advice carried the day on many an occasion. Bobby Crutcher and Jimmy Mash ensured that the physical plant was upright and functioning, and Raymond Nowlin, James Fosten, Fred Minns, and others made sure that the school was properly prepared for the daily arrival of students.

Although USN used the designation of director rather than headmaster, the latter denotes an important concept. As head of the school, I was merely one master (teacher) among many great masters or teachers. As the head-master, I had the privilege to lead, but I was also a colleague, a fellow teacher. And teaching was a great

Harvey Sperling

joy for me, constantly reminding me of our most essential function: to teach, mentor, and support all the students who were entrusted to us.

I taught a course on Asian history/studies until a short-term illness precluded that activity. How fortunate I was to entice Mike Buhl to become my permanent substitute. He quickly surpassed me and elevated the course significantly. By extension, our role as educators is to have students (and faculty) surpass us, or little is accomplished and the status quo remains intact, a terrible condition for a great school. With pride and delight, I can attest that our students do surpass us (faculty and parents alike), and that is the promise and hope of our school community and larger society.

I also conducted a senior seminar at my home, where students conversed with the likes of Rev. Kelly Miller Smith, who was an integral force in the civil rights movement. I wanted our students to understand his values, courage, and vision at a critical moment in the history of Nashville, the South, and our nation. During these seminars, our students were always very engaging and thoughtful, struggling to discern truth and the human condition. They shared their insights and questioned assumptions in order to arrive at measured judgments. It reflected well upon their years at USN and the impact that teachers, peers, and families had on their thinking and values.

CONNECTIONS

From the time of my arrival to the day of my departure, I listened to and shared thoughts and experiences with USN students. During my first summer and early fall at USN, I met with a wide range of students who were simply terrific, reinforcing my initial belief in the very special nature of the school. Many of our former students are now our teachers and leaders in an array of fields, and I certainly relish learning from them. I often and easily visualize their youthful looks and hear their spoken words that echoed then and cling quietly now to the school's hallowed halls. I can see their smiles and occasional tears, their academic accomplishments and athletic triumphs and defeats, their inquisitive minds and gentle natures, and their unbridled laughter and forceful commentaries.

Recently, I read the names of those who graduated during my tenure, and with some exceptions I could visualize their faces, remember many of their parents, and even grandparents. I know little of their accomplishments since graduation and look forward to learning more about them. Of course, I am somewhat taken aback when I meet a former student and his or her face is not too similar to the one in my mind's eye. However, I look directly at their eyes and often find the recognition I seek. That is how I photographed many of them during their earlier years at USN. I focused on their eyes, knowing that would remain a constant. Now when I occasionally wander about USN, I notice the children of my former students, look for familiarity in the eyes and often find it in their gait! It's remarkable how children walk in a fashion similar to their parents and certainly display many of the same mannerisms. What I find most satisfying, but expected, is that the next generation of students admire and love USN with the same intensity as their parents or previous classes. The values of USN continue to have a dramatic impact on its students, and that is how a great school continues to function. It is the minds and hearts of children, not the brick and mortar, that constitute the quality of a school.

Ensuring that PDS graduates felt a kinship to USN (and vice-versa) was not an easy matter. Many believed that it was a far different type of school, not merely a name change. The PDS/USN Distinguished Alumna/Alumnus Award provided a strong bridge between the past and present. It was also a vehicle for me to develop ongoing dialogues and friendships with these remarkable graduates of years past. I hope that the stories of these distinguished alumni are catalogued and often shared, lest we forget their humor, wonderful tales, and life experiences.

I'll share a few insights on Stanford Moore, the 1972 Nobel Prize winner in chemistry (with William Stein) and the first recipient of the PDS/USN Distinguished Alumna/Alumnus Award. I believe that Dr. Moore is the only graduate of a Nashville high school (private or public) to receive a Nobel Prize, quite a coup for our school. I visited Stanford at Rockefeller University on several occasions. He was very gracious and shared many wonderful and relatively unknown tales about himself. Being modest, he did not want to frame his Nobel Prize and place it on the wall of his apartment in New York City and certainly did not want to store it in a safety deposit box where it would remain unseen. So how could he view it? Well, with his fine problem-solving ability, he decided to place the medal in an empty ice tray in the freezer compartment of his refrigerator so he could gaze upon it when he needed ice for an evening drink! Stanford also related to me that he was inspired by Charles Lindbergh's remarkable airplane flight from New York to Paris in 1927 and desired to pursue aeronautical engineering when he entered Vanderbilt University as an undergraduate student. However, he was told by a Vandy professor at the end of his freshman year that "there would be no future in airplanes," so he switched to chemistry. Such is the unexpected encounter that changes one's destiny.

I recall a dinner we arranged for Stanford Moore during one of his visits to our school. He talked about his distinguished career and related that he had been taught and mentored by some remarkable scholars and instructors, but "not one of them" compared to his high school teacher at PDS, Dr. Beauchamp, for "Dr. Beauchamp was the finest of all those teachers and mentors." The elderly and frail

Dr. Beauchamp sat tearfully at a table near the podium and slowly and carefully stood. "You, Stanford, you were the finest student I have ever encountered," he responded. Both men were crying as they embraced one another. No additional words were needed then or now to describe the special and lifetime bond that is often forged between a teacher and student.

In the 1980s, I met and befriended the shy and incredibly talented Dillard Jacobs, a PDS alumnus and retired Vanderbilt professor of mechanical engineering. Dillard was a superb photographer and a stellar filmmaker. In 1927, he brilliantly filmed *Masque*, the remarkable production of the PDS Cinema Club. I watched it with fascination and saw the teenaged Stanford Moore and Louis Rosenfeld and many of their classmates and friends. It was truly a window to our past. The film was in terrible condition, and it took considerable time and outside expertise to restore it. I officially declared it to be the PDS/USN Academy Award winner.

This chapter would be deficient in content if I did not list the PDS/USN Distinguished Alumna/Alumnus Award recipients during my tenure, for they helped me to gain glimpses of the legions of wonderful and talented people from years past, known and unknown students who remain part of the fabric of the school. These award winners also ensure our sense of humility, for they demonstrate what excellence is all about. They took diverse paths and contributed richly, providing enduring examples for all of us.

- Stanford Moore (who received the award the year prior to my arrival) – the scientist and Nobelist, a man for all seasons.

- Ethel Walker – the esteemed pediatrician of generations of PDS/USN children who dedicated herself to her patients, Siamese cats and Vandy basketball; the physician who assisted her patients at home whenever necessary.

- Merrimon Cuninggim – the leader, scholar, and doer; from Danforth Foundation to Salem College president; a Wimbledon tennis player; always making a difference.

- Louis Rosenfeld – the surgeon with a gentle soul and thoughtful presence; a Nashville exemplar.

- Robert Massie – the highly articulate scholar whose writings brilliantly illuminate history; a boy who pinpointed a war on his map; a great teacher who consistently inspires students and all who read his books or listen to his reflections.

- Lucius Burch – who lived the values we preach; a prominent attorney and civil rights leader.

- Bruce Henderson – the wise business consultant and founder of the renowned Boston Consulting Group; a business icon.

- J. Andrew Brown – the Admiral; he served to preserve essential freedoms.

- Mary Phillips Edmunds Gray – distinguished scientist and the academic rival of her classmate Stanford Moore; a legendary Vanderbilt scientist, mentor, and teacher.

- Willis Weatherford – President of Berea College, where the lives of Appalachian students are forever changed and enriched.

- Peggy Weil Steine – who fostered the arts and enhanced the city; a grande dame of the Nashville community.

- Vernon Sharp – the gentle, thoughtful businessman and naturalist who added richly to our city; a man to be admired.

REFLECTION

Serving as director of USN was the most challenging and meaningful leadership role in my career. In 1979, as a relatively young schoolmaster, I departed St. Louis for a school and community quite unfamiliar to me. I had to learn rather quickly about the cultural nuances; the school families; the business, educational, and community leaders; and the strengths, weaknesses, and taboos of USN. It was an essential but often daunting task. People expect you to know what is commonplace and taken for granted. Fortunately, board members and others willingly assisted me, although I certainly made missteps and thought and re-thought decisions during what should have been restful hours of late evening sleep.

From the time I met the USN search committee to the day of my departure as director of the school, my family and I had the great fortune of being embraced and supported by a myriad of fabulous individuals from the school and beyond. We received wise counsel and great assistance during our eleven-year stay, and many of the school families became our dear and trusted friends. We had no doubt that we would return to this community following my retirement in Wisconsin, for Nashville was indeed our home. As for USN in 2014, I am enormously pleased that Vince Durnan is at the helm. He has taken the school to plateaus beyond my vision, and he has ensured the continued ascent of this remarkable and necessary educational institution.

HARVEY SPERLING
Harvey Sperling served as Director of University School of Nashville (1979-1990) and Headmaster of University School of Milwaukee (1990-2000). Subsequently, he was the education program officer at The Frist Foundation and currently is a consultant to the Vanderbilt University Center for Science Outreach. During his forty-six years of marriage to Cathie (a reading specialist), Harvey has learned a great deal about early childhood education, art, music, literature, dance, gardening, and a myriad of other wonderful pursuits. Daughter Sarah is a member of the USN Alumni Board.

GREG DOWNS
Class of 1989

Stepping into the Same River

In May 1993, days before I actually graduated from college, I stepped back into the University School of Nashville that I had entered as a seventh grader ten years earlier. It was a school that meant an enormous amount to me personally, but its significance to me went well beyond the personal. In my four years away, I had come to understand that the extraordinary teaching at University School could be matched at a few—if only a few—other schools that my college friends attended. What I did not see matched was something rarer and more fragile. A vision of an inclusive, if not always beloved, community. A place where outsiders or alienated or awkward teenagers learned that their differences—real as they were—did not outweigh what they shared.

As I walked back into University School after my four years away, I could not help but experience Heraclitus's ancient maxim, sometimes translated as "you cannot step into the same river twice." While we call a river by a name, it is always in the process of becoming something quite new. Between yesterday and today, everything about a river changed; every single drop of water would be new. This is always true, of course, but I think those of us who returned to University School in the 1990s had a heightened awareness that things about the school were changing.

Most concretely, I did not step into The Oven, the "old gym" near the swimming pool with its spiral staircases to the fire exits, its musty smell of chlorine, its tiny rows of bleachers, its overpowering heat that made every step plodding, momentous. I stepped into the "new gym," with its impeccable lighting, its high rows of bleachers, its brightly gleaming floor, its high roof, and its soft and—to me—unbearable silence. Instead of our old cafeteria, shouldered into the back of the third floor, there was now the new, glass-walled one. Rather than hiding ourselves away from the world, we were opening ourselves to it, almost displaying ourselves for its admiration. There was a weight room, and proper band and music spaces, and there was also a palpable excitement over the next buildings that would come that have since turned that moldy pile of bricks into a true campus.

Debbie Davies with students, 1980s.

All of these, I could admit, were good things. And yet I could not help but fear that in the building up of something better and new, something that actually worked, the school risked losing something more valuable than competence. It risked losing its spirit. That September, in new teacher orientation, then-director Ed Costello celebrated the wisdom of older teachers who carried the feel of the school into their classrooms year after year. Finishing his remarks, he asked me, as the only alumnus in the room, to name the people who carried the legends of University School. Torn by my own sense that the old school might have dissolved in my four years away, I froze. For a terrible minute, as Ed's face tightened, I could not think of any reason to believe the school's essence endured. I thought of teachers who had retired or moved on, places in the school that no longer existed. Then, finally, with enormous relief, I began naming the teachers who had shaped me—Debbie Davies, Mr. Rod (Bill Rodriguez), D.C. (Gil Chilton), Doc Ann (Wheeler), Pat Miletich, Alys Venable, and many others.

While I had no doubt about the virtues of those teachers, and many others, I was not all so confident that Ed Costello was correct. The buildings at University School had become shinier and quieter, and so too, I thought, had the students and so perhaps had its spirit.

THE OLD NASHVILLE

It is impossible for me to talk about University School in the 1980s without talking about race. That is because it is impossible to talk sensibly about the Nashville of the 1980s without talking about race. No matter how indomitable University School seemed, it did not live separate from the city around it, even if it often seems in retrospect to have lived in opposition to that city.

While I did not understand this at the time, the defining event of 1980s Nashville was the fight over federal court-mandated busing in Metro schools. Although the Supreme Court had invalidated legal segregation in the famous 1954 and 1955 *Brown* decisions, school districts—including those in Nashville—moved very slowly to implement any changes. By 1960, only one percent of black students in Nashville public schools sat in integrated classrooms. Despite increasing pressure from federal court judges, the city edged begrudgingly toward desegregation. By 1970, Nashville had created only 12 seriously integrated schools out of a total of more than 140. Legal segregation was dead, but the proof of it was hard to see in the city's classrooms.

In 1971, the Supreme Court empowered judges to take the bold step of busing students from racially segregated neighborhoods to distant, integrated schools. Forced by federal courts, Nashville in the 1970s bused about half its students, but integration remained elusive; about one-quarter of all schools were exempted from busing. Ominously, white enrollment dropped by about 20,000, as some families moved to outer counties, and others placed their children in the newly forming private schools termed "segregation academies" elsewhere in the South. Panicked city school board officials proposed dismantling busing altogether for elementary school students, a measure that would have re-segregated younger grades. After the federal circuit court blocked the implementation of a variant of that plan, schools opened three weeks late in 1981. Over the next years, the school board, civil rights lawyers Avon Williams, Jr. and Richard Dinkins, and federal courts arrived at a compromise that required the busing of all students except kindergarteners and the creation of new magnet schools. (In 1998, Nashville schools entered a consent decree that dramatically reduced busing.)

In this historic, fraught transition from legally buttressed white supremacy to an as-yet-undefined new Nashville, University School seemed at once a strange anomaly and a beacon of the future. In 1964 Peabody Dem had become, with Father Ryan, one of the first private schools in Nashville to integrate, and among the earliest schools in the South. While University School no doubt at times gained some white families who fled the busing orders, it gained a great deal more from an influx of black children from old-time Nashville families as well as from the offspring of Meharry, Tennessee State, and Fisk professors.

Combined with the school's longstanding, and also unusual, attachment to the city's liberal and secular Jewish communities, University School was a place of people who seemed not to fit the typical Nashville private school profile. It was becoming strange to the city in a way that outsiders moving in to Nashville recognized at once. By the time I reached high school, there was no center to hold in terms of demographics. As a white Protestant, I felt like a minority, though I admit I have not had the will to go back and count precisely. When I joined the varsity basketball team, I was one of only two (out of 12) WASPs in uniform.

Coming, as I had, from schools in Kauai, Hawaii, where whites were a small minority, the racial experiences I had at University School did not strike me then as strange as they do now. I would not want to let a veneer of nostalgia imply a utopia that did not exist. Yet my friends, both black and white, in our years after high school could not at times avoid that word utopia as we encountered a world in college and beyond where even racially integrated spaces were rarely sites of actual inter-racial communication or community-building. At University School, we sat together and ate together and dated together and sometimes fought together or against each other. It is true, in retrospect, that the silences around certain racial issues were more meaningful than I understood at the time. There were, no doubt, aspects of my friends' lives that I did not understand, and perhaps do not now. But that was not the entirety of the story. (The clearer silence in my memory was around sex. While we knew, at least intellectually and sometimes concretely, that there were gay students and teachers around us, and, in my memory, people were mostly—though not always—careful not to invoke this negatively, the idea of speaking openly about that issue seemed impossible to me at the time.)

While we lived inside a fragile shell at University School, the Nashville around us always threatened to intrude. There is no point in being silent about this. The Nashville we lived in during the 1980s was not just poorer and less hip than its current incarnation. It was a meaner place. In fact, it was in many ways a truly mean place. That meanness, I believe, had its beating heart in the fury over court-ordered busing and the enduring anger at the closing of the schools for the first weeks of the 1981-1982 school year. When my mother, newly arrived from

Kauai and with her own memories of 1960s Kentucky, decided to send me (against my will) to University School, a businessman told her sneeringly that only "fags and liberals"—words he said with equal disdain—sent their kids to that place. In Franklin, where we lived before moving in to Nashville, a group of whites drove into the town and began firing shots and yelling racial epithets. When black men fought back, in my memory killing one of the assailants, the town of Franklin was placed for a few days under martial law with enforced curfews. We drove back from University School to armed men in uniform standing at our intersection, inspecting cars. When I returned to University School in the early 1990s, one of our own students was assaulted at gunpoint at a classmate's house by a neighbor who believed he was stealing electronics. Disgracefully, that classmate's family asked the assaulted student to try to understand the neighbor's position. Even in polite society, the expectation was that we use our energy to understand the racists, not to understand the impact of racism upon African-Americans.

In sports, because of our small size, University School played against the segregation academies that had grown up in the 1960s, 1970s, and 1980s, white, largely religious schools established on the fringes of the city for people who wished to escape the integrated school system. In the face of the court orders, the percentage of white students who attended private schools had skyrocketed; about one-third of all white students in the city went to private schools, mostly at these just-created institutions. While those institutions presumably served many useful purposes, they became hotbeds of white racial resentment and anger. In the 1980s, some already seemed poised to outgrow their heritage. In others, however, the anger was palpable. I remember watching a grown man call one of my teammates a "sand nigger." Entire crowds, including adults, jeered us for not being Christians. "We got Christmas yes we do/We got Christmas how about Jew." There was always a buzz of racial tension. Some of their school administrators—the best one can call them is cowards—sat blandly and passively in the stands. It is impossible to say that they did not know. Most likely, they did not think there was anything remarkable or objectionable about it. Their Nashville—mean and small—was something whose contours and triumphs and limitations they took for granted. It was the shape of the world.

IMPROVISATIONS

Inside the walls of the old building, University School of the mid-1980s was a continual act of improvisation. Still struggling through its growing pains and still struggling to pay its bills, the school at times seemed held together by little other than faith. It was if the teachers—remarkable and dedicated—conjured it into being anew each morning, turning the sometimes-crumbling walls from a near-ruin into a school. There were few facilities; there was an enormous amount of creativity. Students flowed in and took ownership because there weren't enough people to do things for us. Want something? Start something. Clubs flowered and died, and projects rose and fell with the whimsical inclinations of teenagers.

I experienced this side of that University School in my admissions interview. Baffled by the school system, fresh from four years in Kauai, we understood nothing of the culture of private schools in the city. Blindly, I interviewed at almost all of them, from the old standards to the still-new segregation academies to the schools in the painful process of transitioning from the one status to the other. Without anyone telling me so, I understood that my job was to reinvent myself to fit their vision. I lied shamelessly. I sat across from thick-necked admissions officers and responded that yes, I very much looked forward to playing football and always imagined myself as an offensive tackle, though I had never touched a football in my life. To solemn men who asked me about my relationship to Jesus Christ, I promised to use my gift with words for preaching, though I had been inside a church fewer than 20 times. To skeptical, well-dressed interviewers at the older schools, I explained away my inappropriate attire and described—absurdly—the sports coats and ties I had left behind in Kauai in our hurried move.

At each school, I could see a palpable vision of what I was expected to pretend to be. What a relief. By this point in my life, I had lived in San Francisco and in a trailer in Kapaa, Kauai, and on the fringes of a Kauai commune, and (twice) in a house against the mountains in the jungly backwoods of Kauai, and in my grandmother's house (at least twice) in Elizabethtown, Kentucky, and in the high eastern valley of Hyden, Kentucky, and in my uncle's extra bedroom in Brentwood, and in an apartment in Franklin, and I understood that I could, if needed, be anything anyone wanted me to be. I had my own life, a private realm of multi-player historical board games, of books I rewrote in the margins, a dream life of a future in which I gave speeches that I rehearsed endlessly in my mind. (If I only knew how unglamorous it is to give public speeches!) But that was not something to be handed over lightly to people who might never give it back. Better to disappear.

When I walked up the dismayingly soft and creaky stairs in the old administration building at the corner of 19th and Edgehill, I was not prepared for what I saw.

As they led me through the school, I could see no order, no form. The school was exuberant and chaotic, as if the things a kid should keep inside his head were instead plastered on the walls. People sitting cross-legged on the floors of classrooms instead of in desks. Kids arguing with an obvious and serious sincerity in class, instead of just nodding along. The unimaginably aged seniors on the steps chattering boisterously at the end of the third-floor hallway. Didn't they have somewhere they were supposed to be? Wasn't there something they were supposed to be doing? There were, still, the remnants of punk in the air, including a boy with an illustrious mohawk. But mostly there was what seemed to me a frightening and kaleidoscopic confusion.

"What do you like to do?" That was the question I recall admissions director Jeanne McCutchan asking me in my interview. It seems absurd now, but in my memory it was the first time that anyone at any of the schools had asked me such a thing. Had spoken as if my wishes mattered. What an irritating question. Didn't she understand what we were supposed to do here? She was supposed to signal to me what I was supposed to be, and I was supposed to signal back to her that I would pretend to be exactly that. "Who are you?" she said. "What makes you you?"

I decided then and there that I would not attend University School. Any place that could not tell me what they wanted from me was a place I did not want to be. It was not so much that I wanted to fit in; it was that I wanted the promise that I could disappear back into my own private world, behind whatever screen they wanted to lower. Everyone else at every other school seemed to understand this distinction between act and actor, self-presentation and the self, except the people at University School, and I wanted nothing to do with them.

But it was not my choice to make. A different, much-more-sincerely friendly businessman told my mother that University School of Nashville was, despite its name, the only private school that was not fundamentally "of" Nashville. That touched, I suspect, some ambition she had for me, and so off I went. For weeks I lived in a state of constant mortification. These people had known each other since kindergarten! There was a language of west-side street names that I could not map, a litany of stores I could not find, rituals I had never heard of. Dutifully, people invited me to bar mitzvahs (I had just missed the bat mitzvahs of the previous year) and I lumbered around anxiously, asking absurd questions about Jewish rituals and the Hebrew language. Missing the point, as usual.

I lived also, I should say, paralyzed by shame. A more suave person could have spun my past into some kind of glamor, invented himself into a surfer. But I felt my past not as a succession of strange and wonderful places—of mountains and beaches—but as an unraveling. I went, for messy reasons, by a last name that was not my own name, a fraudulence I felt every morning when I answered attendance. I felt at that period orphaned not just from my father but from myself. Sometimes, when people called on me by that name, I forgot to answer. I wrote my new name on the cover of my notebooks, my old name on the interior pages.

And, we were truly, though it turned out temporarily, poor. When our refrigerator had died the previous winter, we could not replace it, so we went without milk; I remember looking forward to the winter so we could once again set milk on the windowsill and count on finding it cool and unspoiled in the morning. But there were other aspects to the winter I did not like. There was a sizable and rusted-out hole in the center of my mother's VW bus where cold air, and occasionally rocks, swelled up onto us. We walked to the car bundled in blankets like swamis. When we pulled off I-65 and neared University School, I lobbied my mother relentlessly, cruelly, to push her blanket down to her knees so no one could see us as we were. Then I made her promise not to pull the blanket back up over her lap until she was safely onto 21st Avenue. Every field trip and every expense at school was a little trauma those first few years, before the clouds lifted.

One day, driving in to Nashville, the back wheel of our VW bus shrugged itself free and bounded eagerly down the hill, as if it too were running away from us. Baffled, we stood by the car, swilling the sound and the exhaust of the passing traffic, paralyzed by bad luck. When my French teacher, Ms. Marcum, happening to pass by, pulled over and offered me a ride, I wanted desperately to run into the woods. Dutifully, I climbed in, abandoning my mother to the wreckage. That day, I shuffled into class, ready for Ms. Marcum to expose me, but, miraculously, she said nothing about it at all, neither then nor ever.

Over time, mysteriously, in the face of other silences and other kindnesses, I forgot to be ashamed. I forgot to keep myself a secret. I went back to my real last name, and, amazingly, no one asked me why I had another name or what had become of my last one. I shed that mis-named, mistrustful person like a skin. The person I actually was, Greg Downs, was not so wary. When Ms. Venable saw that I was bored writing bland sentences on our spelling tests, she told me to do something interesting. Instead of answering the quizzes normally, I began writing out

Greg Downs speaking at his Commencement.

page after page of detective stories and horror stories and historical fiction; proving I knew the words was immaterial. For years, I would persist in this, handing over long and formless stories to Ms. Venable and then Ms. Grimes and then Dr. Wheeler. In History, Dr. Clements and Dr. Chilton recognized that I had an unusual, maybe unnerving, interest in the past and told me to do something with it. Later, after I began bombarding Ms. Miletich with long discourses on the roots of segregation, on the formation of the system that was just being dismantled by federal judges and civil rights lawyers outside our classroom, she set up an independent study with one of her former Vanderbilt professors, Sam McSeveney, who graciously let me bore him with stories about Ben Tillman and James K. Vardaman and the other architects of the disfranchisement of African-Americans.

Only later, after I left University School, would it occur to me that there was anything unusual about this. My friends at USN were doing the same thing, inventing their educations almost on a whim, with the support but not necessarily the direct guidance of their teachers. The teachers trusted us, and also they needed us to take ownership. Friends worked on increasingly difficult math projects with the legendary Ms. Davies and Dr. Van Voorst. Dr. Bibring and Mr. Rod led other students through baffling science experiments. Kids took classes at Vanderbilt. Kids made up their own classes. In theater, an area I knew nothing about, students under Gus Gillette seemed to be designing and building impossible sets. The number of students who went on to work, successfully, in music and theater is a tribute to the program they built. In a version of *Pirates of Penzance*, Kenneth Burns added lines to one number that openly, if lovingly, chided our director, Mr. Sperling, for his love of the words "plurality" and "diversity."

Everyone was doing everything. There were so few of us that things like Quiz Bowl or band or the literary magazine could only stumble along if people participated in all of them. In my memory, though it seems unlikely to be true, those of us who played both band and basketball would go up to the narrow, assuredly illegal, platform above the gym and play the intro music for halftime of the girls' games, then go change in preparation for ours.

Of course I sentimentalize away divisions. But, still, in my memory, the divisions were not the important things. After I taught a section of Algebra II for Ms. Davies' class, an older kid—scruffier and cooler and savvy about bands I could not name, someone who had not spoken to me all year—leaned over and said, "You should be a teacher." I winced, waiting for the mockery, but it didn't come. "I'm serious," he said. When Ms. Davies heard him, she repeated it to the class, and no one snickered. When I won, embarrassingly, every trophy at a state history competition, a girl I barely knew, someone else cooler and savvier than I was or am, ran up to tell me the news, more sincerely excited than I was. Even people who did not care so much about grades honored learning; even the kids who frequently struggled saw that their teachers struggled with them.

We had nothing like the sports prominence of the '70s and early '80s, when legends like Fred Humphries and Randall Moody and Ronnie Lawson walked the hallways (and sometimes came back to school us), but our athletics teams battled. With the help of Mr. Rod, kids started a swimming team, and later baseball under Mr. O'Hara and then Coach Baynham. Soccer and tennis thrived. We boys played slow, smart-paced basketball under crusty, brilliant Coach Matthews, a second father to me. When Alex Ericson arrived, the girls' basketball and volleyball immediately became excellent, then dominant. And yet, still, the teams were full of people who were captains of both sports and Quiz Bowl teams.

In the midst of this, almost as an afterthought, students went on to staggeringly impressive colleges. It did not seem at the time a matter of importance; it seemed a matter of course. People who liked to learn would find places where learning mattered. With the gentle guidance of Ms. Schneider, kids went to an amazing range of places, Ivy League colleges, and top Southern schools, and liberal arts colleges, and state schools. Every year, in my memory, a kid went to Yale; the year before me, it was my friend Kent Chen, the year before him the talented Melvin Chen. I had my own family reasons for wanting to go there, and so I went.

A NEW CITY, A NEW SCHOOL

Four years later, when I walked back into University School as a teacher, things seemed different in ways both subtle and profound. Some of the differences were heartening. The shiny gym, the weight room, the cafeteria. Who wouldn't prefer to sit in the light? There was an influx of teachers, idealistic and ambitious women and men from all over the map who came to University School not because they sentimentalized what it was but because they saw what it was becoming. In my classes and on the practice court, I saw the undeniable passion and joy of the students. Their unbearable willingness to sacrifice.

Master teachers—Betty Pearson White, especially—taught me to coax from students something more than they thought they could give. A few years earlier, Ms. Pearson White, catching me kicking my locker to try to force it closed, had taught me how to arrange objects. Now, she taught me how to talk to students about their writing, how to turn assignments into extraordinary film projects, how to make education truly international. My students humbled me; they were prepared and organized in ways I had never been. They humbled me in other ways. They taught me that I did not know what I thought I knew. I did not always know more than they did. They ran the newspaper class that I advised; in English, they organized themselves into small groups; in basketball, the kids would be lined up for practice before I entered the gym. What I did not know, what I was too green at age 21 to know, was what to tell them. In meetings, I saw the astonishing dedication of the teachers—whom I now had to learn to call by their first names. When Mr. O'Hara led us through a reading of Maya Angelou's inaugural poem, "A Rock, a River, a Tree," with its invocations of the different roles that rocks, rivers, and trees play in the world, Ms. Melchiore said, "Okay, so we need to be rocks and rivers and trees for our students." When I asked why some of us couldn't be rocks, and some others rivers, and some others trees, she laughed. "Because we have to do everything, Greg!"

From my job in the admissions office, I had the extraordinary privilege to walk the halls, to peek into classrooms, to hear our teachers teach. I learned about the lower school, which I had never attended, and saw Mr. Hoover-Dempsey crack up a room of fourth graders, and Ms. Noel quiet a whole class with a bemused look, and Ms. Princehorn smile the children into the joy of music, and the legendary Ms. Dickinson nod gravely as six-year-old-boys recounted their adventures. I saw Ms. Knox and Ms. Hicks and dozens of other extraordinary teachers whom I had heard about but not ever experienced.

In the admissions office, I also saw something both heartening and also heartbreaking: the waves of parents who desperately wanted to send their children to University School. Over the late 1980s and early 1990s, University School shifted from a place apart to a place above. Instead of a school for the alienated and the strange, for families or children who in one way or another didn't fit in, it became a place where people went so they could fit in to some new order of things. It had become a place of aspiration. Schools which had once sent only a few students to University School now overwhelmed our admissions office.

No doubt, there was something wonderful about this, just as there was something wonderful about the school's concrete expansion. Just as there was something pleasant about seeing University School compared by teachers and faculty to other independent schools across the country. But there was also something disquieting. University School had seemed special because it was weird, even proudly weird. If the school now attracted people who seemed unnervingly normal, could it retain that weirdness? Was a University School that could be compared to other places still University School?

When we returned, I and my friends and classmates saw these differences immediately and as a threat. In truth, some of these changes had been taking place while we were still in school. Some of us had wondered this as the school finished the "new building" with its clean and air-conditioned classrooms. The kids seemed richer, shinier, kinder, less troubled. There was deep, abiding goodness in them, more I suspect than there had been in us. When I chaperoned the school community service trip to New Orleans, our biggest problem (other than my driving) was negotiating menus between vegetarians and carnivores. The school seemed quieter, more peaceful, less rebellious. There seemed, from a distance, less alienation, less creativity, more conformity, and it scared us. There were hundreds of schools across the country that were wonderful places to send one's children; there was in our minds only one University School.

In ways I could not understand, the school was in fact conforming to the world around it, but not so much because the school itself was changing. Nashville was changing. It was hardening its bones, adding muscle. It was becoming richer and less Southern. You could see it in the "Batman building," completed at the end of my first year back at University School. You could see it in Vanderbilt's campus. From the admissions office, I could see it in the parade of Northerners—attached to Vanderbilt or one of the healthcare companies—who entered our office. There had always been people, like me, who were not Nashvillians at University School, but they had always been aware that they stood out in a city that seemed insular. Now, the outsiders had no such self-consciousness. They had become the city, in a way, turned it inside out. Arriving in such sweeping numbers that they washed away many of the old habits and manners and prejudices of the old city, they expected Nashville to cater to them, and they saw in University School the Nashville they intended to live in. It was as if University School had conjured up not just a school but a city. As if its creativity had created a new place.

For years, I searched for a clue as to why University School seemed to have changed. Were people inside the school trying to discourage oddballs from entering? In fact, that was not the case. I was part of teams that accepted home-schooled students and kids who had grown up on The Farm in Summertown, kids whose experiences should have made them as self-conscious and alienated as I had been. But, miraculously, they were not alienated; they dissolved into the student body like sugar into water. The city was changing; the culture was changing. It was no longer clear what University School should be fighting against. It was sometimes clear that University School had in fact won whatever battle it had been fighting.

In retrospect, this, too, goes back to the meanness of the 1980s. The final defeat of government-sponsored segregation had unleashed an enormous amount of anger but also of creativity. While many of the city's manners and customs were charming, the city's conservatism had been rooted in something that was not charming at all, the conviction that the way of life grew from a racial order codified, sustained, and defended by the government. As the United States shifted over the early twentieth century, places like Nashville became increasingly strange to the country. In the 1980s, we at University School had been alienated not from the world itself but from a particular, dying strand of the world, a world of Southern segregation.

Nashville changed because civil rights activists and the federal government forced it to change. In the process, however, the city learned something. Segregation was not just an affront to the moral sense of human dignity and equality; it was an affront to common, business sense. With the end of legal segregation, Nashville returned to the United States. It was no coincidence that outside businesses flooded in. It became possible to tell workers in Detroit or New Jersey or California that they could relocate to Nashville. This human and financial wave washed over everything in the region—its universities, its neighborhoods, its restaurants, its manners. In making Nashville like the rest of the country, this wave did not, of course, fashion a utopia. Nashville recreated the problems of the 1990s and 2000s at home, the stark inequality, the informal segregation that thrived even as public and governmental racism faded.

It would have been strange, in retrospect, if University School had not changed, too. A school that was not "of" Nashville, as my mother's friend told us, now represented an aspiration for Nashville to many people. In those circumstances, with hundreds upon hundreds of people clamoring to enter University School, how could the school have remained alienated? As Nashville's culture changed, what precisely could the school have been alienated from? Soon, too, it became evident that this wave of outsiders washed over Nashville's old families. As the city re-entered the nation and left behind the fixed, limiting attachment to region and race, University School became one of the gateways from the city to the world. Its students moved in numbers not just to Atlanta but to New York and Washington D.C. and San Francisco; they entered a new, cosmopolitan class that ranged beyond the country's borders. People who never before would have considered University School sent their kids here because they feared being left behind.

THE PULL OF GRAVITY

After two years, I left University School for other worlds and other lives. Recently I returned to campus for my 25th reunion. The nephew and namesake of a classmate led my wife Diane and me in a hardhat tour through the construction project underway in the old locker rooms and hallways of the lower level of the old building, past the old raised platform where the band played, through the pool. It was now possible to get lost inside University School. Standing inside it, I felt the disconcerting, uncanny feeling of being in a place I had visited in a dream, inside rooms that were familiar and also utterly strange. Even though the rooms had been hollowed out, one of the other people on the tour could name the rooms by the flooring. It was possible to catch a detail like that and remember, yes this was the shower, this was the locker room, those were the Myles Maillie murals my classmates filled in with greens and reds. This was the coaches' office, where I used to come down with my lunch and sit in the extra chair and listen to Coach Matthews talk, as if I could ingest his certainty with my sandwiches. This is the poolside step where I cried openly after we lost by one point to Hume-Fogg, our rival and one of the magnet schools created by the federal consent decree. All of that lived in the air. Yet it was also impossible to resist the feeling that nothing, not even the green paint on the Maillie murals, was quite the same. The hanging lights and hollowed walls all showed the signs of purpose and professionalism, as if we had rudely walked in during the middle of a Broadway actor's preparation. The finished product wasn't complete, but it most certainly would be finished.

As Nashville became normal, it also became rich, as the city no longer starved itself from national commerce through self-destructive segregation. That wealth flowed through University School, too. Making it look to outsiders like myself almost entirely new, with its River Campus, its extraordinary arts center, its enviable kiln, its lovely student sculptures. A proper library, gorgeous and light. A senior class hangout with games and comfortable seats, instead of the old stairs. When the school completes its current renovations, the entrance itself will change, too. Instead of steering visitors past closed classroom doors and through narrow hallways, it will welcome them proudly. What we called the new building had become old; the old building, under renovation, was in the process of becoming new. An entire generation's skin has been shed; a new creature has been born inside the old one.

At the end of the reunion lunch, ticking off the names of the teachers who once inhabited each classroom, wondering at the names in place now, playing the boring but inevitable game of describing what once was where now something is, we drifted into the staggeringly gorgeous art building. Through the narrow windows, we could see strange, even disturbing sculptures snaking up the walls, and an off-putting, almost aggressive video installation. Paintings and pottery, and all the signs of the urge to create—the essential claim of I Am that is at the heart of who were are as people, and of what a school should aim to nurture. None of those things were in place when I walked the school as a teacher or a student, no sculpture room or video installations or kilns, and yet they also filled me with an unearned pride.

About rivers, it is possible that Heraclitus was wrong. Of course the molecules all change. But is a river simply a collection of molecules? A school nothing more than the accumulated attributes of its concrete forms? Is it possible that a school, like a river, is defined not by its particles but by its current, its force that moves you inevitably, even against your will, in a common direction? For 100 years, Peabody Dem and University School have drawn thousands of students forward, carving hard cliffs when they came up against granite, and swelling wide and soft when they reached the deltas. That gravitational tug, drawing in some mysterious way from the teachers in their classrooms and the students in the hallway and the administrators in their offices and from all of us, must be—more than the buildings or the precise composition of the student body—the thing that defines, and one hopes, will continue to define University School, a place I am still proud to call mine.

GREG DOWNS

Greg Downs graduated from University School in 1989. He is an Associate Professor at the City College and Graduate Center of the City University of New York. He has published one book of history, *Declarations of Dependence*, and one book of short stories, *Spit Baths*, and has another book of history forthcoming in spring 2015. He lives with his wife Diane and their two daughters in New York City, where he still plays basketball regularly, though not with the same intensity as he did when Coach Matthews was hollering at him.

PAT MILETICH
History Teacher, 1986-Present

The Happy Child Decade

Leaving behind the "squirrely school" of the 1970s (as a survey mid-decade reported) and the heavy lifting required to establish the successor to PDS in the 1980s, USN in the 1990s focused on becoming the kind of school that produced the "happy child." As both a parent and a teacher, I can attest that this goal, as hard as it was to define a happy child, motivated the loyalty and enthusiasm of the still young USN community to become truly exceptional. Kay Simmons, Interim Director for the 1990-1991 year after Harvey Sperling left and before Ed Costello arrived, summed up what would be the foundational principles of the 1990s: cooperation, community, and commitment to quality.

Many elements came together in the 1990s to make that elusive happy child. It was a collective effort that began with a strong board of trustees contributing financial and business expertise, administrative and staff leaders who worked effectively together, an increasingly stable and well-compensated faculty, and growing numbers of capable, diverse, and talented students. Supporting all these were parents who appreciated and loved the school, a place most felt "had an extraordinary commitment to nurturing children and helping them find the best in themselves" (from a 1992 parent survey). In order to make the vision a reality, the school's finances and physical space needed to grow.

The 1990s saw ambitious projects, both physical and in terms of teaching and learning, as well as the ability to support them. Instead of always doing more with less, the USN community committed itself to achieving the means to support the students in all areas: academic, athletic, and artistic, and in exploring the larger worlds of engagement and service.

As Director Ed Costello remarked, USN in the 1990s was blessed by the leadership of the board of trustees. Bob Brodie, Bill Spitz, Weaver Barksdale, and Larry Fuldauer served as board presidents and chairs of crucial committees, spearheading ambitious plans that required prioritizing needs and articulating a vision for the school. PDS/USN had always attracted the philanthropically inclined, but the decade was marked by a new emphasis on adding board members with financial and business expertise as well as the energy to push the school forward.

Such an aggressive attitude brought about the 1992 Strategic Plan and its comprehensive series of goals and timetables for achieving them in all areas from program and plant to faculty and diversity. Two areas receiving attention that would prove instrumental to success in future years were marketing/public relations and alumni. During the 90s, marketing/public relations expanded beyond enabling USN to attract the best students, faculty, and financial resources. It helped us all think about and define the identity of the school. USN's image and place in the larger community as one of the preeminent independent schools, a place where students came first and where achievements were acknowledged beyond its walls, did much to overcome lingering feelings of "inferiority," as Ed Costello remembered.

Establishing an alumni association with a Director of Alumni Affairs united the far-flung PDS/USN graduates, and beyond any support for promotion and development united the generations. Proclaiming honorary members of the board of trustees—first Joel Gordon, Raymond Zimmerman, and Bernard Werthan; later Suzy Morris, Betty Werthan, and Henry Foster—honored the founders of USN during its early struggles and gave more than a nod to its history as PDS. The marble plaques in the entry hall crafted from the stalls of the locker rooms during a renovation recognized equally the contributions of the board presidents and of staff who committed decades to the school. School governance continued developing on a business model with its strategic plan, feasibility studies, customer satisfaction surveys, and an ever-expanding school bureaucracy whose overriding goal was to support student learning and well-being.

The board, the director, and the development office set ambitious financial goals for the school. Spearheaded by an energetic and enthusiastic board composed of individuals set to "give, get, or get off," as one former chairman remarked, success followed success. At the opening of the decade, Capital Campaign II surpassed its initial multi-million dollar goal. Later the school met a fundraising goal of $5.5 million for another wing of the school and necessary remodeling as well as expanding the endowment. USN saw its first million dollar gift. The fundraising successes reflected a school deeply appreciated by all segments of the PDS/USN community. Annual giving expanded with nearly 100% faculty support, and planned giving was introduced. One of the most innovative fundraising efforts was the establishment of Evening Classes, which allowed the Nashville community to take short courses for very low fees on topics from literature to cooking to computers. The proceeds helped fund student scholarships.

Successful fundraising allowed for one of the most significant areas of change in the 1990s: the transformation of the physical footprint of the main campus on Edgehill and beyond. Following the 1980s construction of the West Wing and the Sperling Center, the 1990s began with the community building a playground and ended with the acquisition of the River Campus. In between, the East Wing reconfigured the daily existences of teachers, students, and staff. When the decade ended, the plans left undone—a new library, arts wing, and other aspects of the strategic plans— would fill out the footprint on Edgehill. The goal of these projects was to allow the physical space of the school, whether at the Edgehill or the River Campuses, to reflect the teaching and learning taking place every day. As Ed Costello said, USN was "trapped" in a physical space that needed to reflect and enhance the work of students and teachers. By the end of the decade, USN was not only filling in the footprint but moving well beyond it.

A CAMPUS TRANSFORMED

The 1991 USN playground project signaled the themes of "generosity, cooperation and hard work," according to Interim Director Kay Simmons. That year marked the fifteenth anniversary of USN as well as the completion of the capital campaign. Tucked in a corner of the field behind the school, the playground project brought the community together designing, planning, building, fundraising, and celebrating. The ribbon cutting, student performances, and a benefit concert by Crystal Gayle culminated a year of hard work to bring the playground to fruition—an effort spearheaded by Simmons and chairperson Louise McKenzie. As high school students recalled, the playground resulted from "a long weekend of hard work," with everyone "proud to have completed such a demanding project."

The most transformative projects occurred at the end of the decade: the construction of the East/Gordon Wing, the acquisition of eighty acres on the Cumberland River that would become the River Campus, and the renovations of the main building and the West Wing. The construction of what would become the Gordon Wing mesmerized the students during the 1996/1997 school year. As students watched the building rise from the ground up, the construction infiltrated the curriculum, with fifth graders making quadrants to measure the height of the building, other students throwing a party to wish the giant crane farewell once its work was done, and high school physics classes making their own building model.

As Jerry Gardner, head of the board's Building and Grounds Committee, said, the East or Gordon Wing was to be "functional with some pizzazz." It housed the middle school and provided needed high school science classrooms. Other renovations during the decade air-conditioned the main building—a near miraculous occurrence that eliminated window fans. In addition, all three divisions of the school now were housed in separate wings: the West Wing for the lower school, main building for the high school, and the Gordon Wing for the middle school. Each division had some autonomy, yet all were tied together through the use of the auditorium and the physical education, music, and art facilities.

The school badly needed athletic fields. Prior to the acquisition of eighty acres off Briley Parkway, students had to travel about town for athletic practices and games. The limitations and deficiencies of such a situation strangled the competitive sports programs. In addition, student safety concerns arose when a team at one crosstown practice encountered gunfire. Ed Costello, director and athletic booster, worked tirelessly to find a solution. Many possible solutions met severe setbacks, and even Costello was hesitant when the land along the Cumberland became available. Concerned about the financial risks, Costello remembers board member Mike Shmerling telling him, "Ed, don't be a jerk. We'll buy the land, and if it doesn't work out, we'll sell it."

Not only has the acquisition been spectacularly successful for the athletics program, giving us fields for soccer, lacrosse, softball, and baseball as well as a track and tennis courts, the River Campus Wetlands have become a focal point for outdoor education from kindergarten through high school. Costello notes that within the first year, a prospective buyer offered almost double the price USN had paid.

Costello's decade at USN was marked by a strong commitment to recruiting and retaining an excellent faculty and building a strong administrative team. When he came to USN in 1990, teachers considered themselves committed to a life of service and financial sacrifice. Working with the board, Ed steadily raised faculty compensation, closing the gap between salaries at USN and those in the Metropolitan Nashville public schools. First giving an across the board salary bump that benefitted the lowest paid faculty members, annual tuition increases largely went towards funding faculty compensation. In addition, such compensation was now tied to evaluation and integrated with an Improvement of

Ed Costello

Instruction Plan. The result was significant; the yearly faculty turnover slowed and students had the advantage of a stable teaching staff.

ENDING THE BATTLE

Costello remained at USN until 1999, when he became Head of School at Durham Academy in North Carolina. Looking back on his time here, Costello characterized USN as a "people place" where the faculty cared deeply both about the students and about their own fields of expertise. He rejected any attempts to see the school as one-dimensional. Although academic excellence and quality of education were extremely important to all within the USN community, Costello saw the educational experience of students as far wider. A great fan of athletics, he told the board, "I think I should also state that I view the seemingly inevitable battle between arts and athletics to be both unnecessary and unhealthy." When Costello left USN, athletic fields had been acquired, but plans for an arts facility remained a critical but unachieved goal of the strategic plan.

Athletics became more and more important during the nineties. The Sperling Center gave USN its first-rate gymnasium, and the women's basketball team won the district championship, with Jenny Boucek '92 on her way to becoming the only woman in the elite basketball 2,000 point club. Wil Howard-Downs '99 was named Tennessee's "Mr. Basketball" for two years and became USN's all-time leading scorer. Ed Costello donned the Tiger mascot suit for pep rallies, and support for athletics became more enthusiastic. Volleyball teams won state championships, and individual excellence in many sports focused attention on providing support for student athletes. In addition, new sports were added to the athletic repertoire: girls' soccer, boys' lacrosse, and Ultimate Frisbee/"Brutal Grassburn," or as one student remarked, "USN's answer to football."

One sport not included was football. A survey found parents placing football as the lowest priority sport and some threatening withdrawal of their children if USN added football. As the survey takers concluded, "The issue is obviously divisive and has apparently been brought up more than once." Parents and students both valued athletics as a key to lifetime fitness and "character development learned through team sports."

NEW WAYS OF LEARNING

Academically, the nineties saw innovation at every level. In the high school Advanced Placement courses expanded and attracted more students. As students in 1990 remarked, "A.P. Means Added Pressure," but the rigorous workload "no longer scares away" students who do not consider themselves elite. Teaching innovation addressing a variety of learning styles became one reason students found advanced courses more accessible.

1990 was also the year Debbie Davies was awarded the Presidential Award for Excellence in Science and Mathematics Teaching. Davies, one of two high school teachers from Tennessee so honored, was characterized by her students: "She is crazy; she is fun … she is simply one of the best, especially in students' hearts."

Hands-on learning was the focus at every level, from lower school math solving real world problems to "real science" with experiments, labs, and the science fair. Whole language and Morning Meetings occupied lower school children, and technology became a high priority for the school, with computers increasingly integrated into the curriculum over the decade. High school students observed that the "Computer Highway Starts at USN." With emphasis on a wider and deeper curriculum, concern for varied learning styles prompted the hiring of a learning specialist in the lower school. The middle school experimented with several programs addressing learning styles in the middle school, and high school incorporated more varied teaching strategies.

Students and faculty were enthusiastic about the arts. The lobby and central hall of the main building hosted an art gallery of revolving student work. Lower school students had an additional gallery outside the lower school office. Musicals and plays continued to be performed by students in the middle and high school, while lower school students charmed all levels with the productions of music teacher Doni Princehorn. Band and chorus groups attracted huge numbers of students and required multiple bands and choir groupings culminating in pep band, jazz band, as well as advanced, select, and show choirs.

The track at the River Campus

Co-curricular activities reflected student interests in the serious as well as the silly. Everything from Amnesty International, Human Rights, and Gender Issues Clubs attracted students who might also attend Star Trek, Dining, or Trivial Pursuit Clubs. Political groups included Republican Clubs, belying the stereotype of a universally left-leaning student body. The PEAs (high school's peer educators and assistants) gave expression to students' desire to help each other cope with new concerns about stress. Parents' Networks formed in response to similar concerns, particularly about stress turning students to alcohol and drugs. High school students had a different response, calling such networks "vigilante societies," and one student complained that "[his] parents did not want him to have any fun during his prime teenage years."

The middle school held field days and activities such as Tennessee Jeopardy or Volunteer Day to emphasize Tennessee history and culture. For high school students, having a designated club period during the day encouraged a vast array of quirky clubs that addressed important issues of intellectual and personal growth. A member of the Tabula Rasa Club, Sameer Kirtane '94, concluded, "Our world of thought is a diamond mine ... we sift these diamonds from the flint in a nonarrogant sort of way." The Community Service and Environmental Clubs allowed students to "be selfless and fight apathy."

Student traditions continued in the nineties, and new ones were introduced. Retreats and special programs took students out of traditional classrooms. Seniors tried to have two senior skip days rather than the traditional one but succumbed to faculty disapproval and satisfied themselves with the senior prank. Hurling water balloons at freshmen got seniors into particularly hot water one year. Senior Superlatives became a standard in the yearbooks. Way Out Winter Wednesdays and internships were tried out in the high school, while the lower school looked forward to Fun Fridays. The Student Council adopted service as part of its agenda and embraced the Halloween UNICEF trick or treating project. The Community Service Club expanded its mission as mentors to children in the Nashville community, first at the YES program and also at the Friendship Outreach Center near the Andrew Jackson Apartments. In 1995, the tradition began of holding an annual Community Service Day for the entire high school.

Diversity became an important topic in the nineties. USN's enrollment went up dramatically—to nearly a thousand by the end of the decade. Yet with growing popularity came growing concerns about keeping a diverse student body, expanding diversity of the faculty, and making USN a truly nurturing atmosphere for all students. Affinity meetings focused on the issues of specific groups as one of the most deeply valued aspects of life at USN. People thought the diversity of the student body was worth fighting to maintain.

Costello sent high school English teacher Ann Wheeler to a SEED workshop. The goal of Seeking Educational Equity and Diversity was to nurture change in schools through groups of teachers reading, thinking, and meeting together to discuss issues of diversity. As one of the members of the SEED group, I remember reading a variety of fiction and nonfiction works by authors exploring issues of race, ethnicity, gender, and sexual orientation. Out of the discussions came both changes in personal perception of diversity issues and also changes in school policy, such as urging USN to publish statements of commitment to nondiscrimination. The board developed a sexual harassment policy for employees and students. USN helped sponsor a visit to Nashville by Dr. Peggy McIntosh, a founder of SEED. USN joined the Multicultural Alliance to help recruit faculty of color. USN's relationship with Kwansei Gakuin High School in Japan continued. The USN community grew to include a number of international students from Asia, the Middle East, and Europe. English as a second language classes helped make USN a place where a diverse population could be comfortable and successful.

What was it about USN's environment in the 1990s that made for a "happy child"? The students themselves characterized the qualities as: opportunities to "learn about themselves and about each other," gaining "self-confidence ... by interacting with other individuals," "more opportunity to express yourself," and the always popular "more freedom."

Reflecting on his tenure as Director through most of the decade, Ed Costello attributed the growth and development of the school to an effective and committed board of trustees, innovative faculty, his assistant Bobbie Grubb (who "never let me leave without having done what I needed to"), and an administrative team that worked together for the good of the students.

Let the last words be those of a 1990s lower school student: "I'm having a good time in school."

PAT MILETICH
Patricia Miletich came to USN in 1986 to teach in the high school history department. A native Californian, Pat traveled to Tennessee for graduate school at Vanderbilt University but stayed because of her love of University School and its students. She is the parent of USN alumni Dorothy Lee Miletich '01 and Mathew Stephan Miletich '07.

VINCENT W. DURNAN
Director, 2000-Present
University School of Nashville

We Lift Our Voices Upward

In 1970, twelve students in Leland Johnson's *American Problems* class wrote a remarkable little history book. One of its authors contributed a chapter to this Centennial volume, forty-four years later, and all of its authors provided inspiration for our current efforts to tell our school's story. Their choice of a title, *The Past Is Prologue*, is borrowed from Shakespeare, from *The Tempest* in fact, and from the inscription on the National Archives building on Pennsylvania Avenue, beneath the 1935 statue of *Future*. Those students hardly imagined the tempest ahead for their school later that decade, as their book's final words looked to the future, not the past.

This concluding chapter intends to frame our present circumstances, after the preceding pages explain what made today possible. My aim is to provide the 21st century segment of the hundred-year journey, a segment still in process. I write as someone who arrived as Director at the start of the new millennium, drawn to this campus by its singular place in the independent school world, fascinated that it could be completely autonomous of and directly contiguous to one of the nation's great research universities. One of the first gifts made available to me at USN was a copy of *The Past Is Prologue*, and I note with sadness the passing of Leland Johnson (who went on to author a series of books for the Army Corps of Engineers) just this year. My hope is that he would look favorably on this project—he was generous of spirit whenever we asked. And we, in turn, now look to the school's future appreciating the wisdom of our predecessors, approaching the crystal ball with equal measures of excitement and humility.

The contemporary story of University School, and very likely the continuing story on this and almost any campus, is the intersection of **accomplishments**, **challenges**, and **opportunities**. Managing the pace of change, setting the next targets, and understanding what is timeless at the center of our narrative as a school community has called for the best work of a broad range of constituents here. What follows is an earnest effort to place the past fourteen years in context, knowing that there is always more to tell.

A TIME OF GROWTH

We've been the beneficiaries of increased interest in the school on a number of levels. Perhaps most fundamental is the growth in enrollment, continuing a trend reaching back to the 1980s. We opened the doors last year to 1,053 students in grades K-12, up from 987 in the year 2000. The change has been incremental and steady, largely a function of an expanded high school, given the four-classrooms-per-grade scale of the lower school and the five-section team model in middle school. That has combined to mean 64 kindergartners, 72 first through fourth graders, 80 fifth through eighth graders, and high school classes of just under 100 students at present.

To reach and remain this size, we count on 500+ applications each year, combined with very low (by any comparative standard) attrition numbers. Fewer than 5% of our students leave USN for any reason each year, even with the family mobility that comes with contemporary Nashville and all the reasons there are to make such changes in the life of a child. The new group of students we welcome each August typically comes from more than 60 different prior schools, and they help us maintain a community that includes passports from more than 50 other countries and racial diversity of about 30% in our enrollment.

The space available to provide educational program for these students is both finite in terms of acreage and expanded in terms of square feet. The first facility addition of the new millennium was the Tibbott Center, named for legendary Demonstration School art teacher and *Hee Haw* motif creator Christine Slayden Tibbott at the insistence of her big fan, Nashville philanthropist Cal Turner. Architect Marion Fowlkes and department chair Liz Mask drove a process that gave us a building to be proud of. Modesty made Chris demur when I asked her permission to inscribe her name on the building in 2003, but her love of helping people make art ultimately let us move forward, replacing a decades old double-wide trailer in the 19th Avenue parking lot in the process. And best of all, Chris still visits the studios regularly, well into her 90s.

The Tibbott Center's companion project was a new library, ultimately named with the consent of its lead donors, Heidi and John Hassenfeld '75. Knowing the daily life of the school could accommodate only one project at a time, our board voted to do art first and library a year later, not one or the other but both, with the corresponding responsibility to raise the $10MM it would take to construct and endow the maintenance of both buildings.

The grand opening of the Hassenfeld Library in August, 2004.

The library, at 20,000 square feet, roughly the same size as the art building, met a mandate imposed by our accrediting association and filled a substantial need for a central gathering place, a town hall and office space of sorts for faculty and students. Librarians Jill Eisenstein and Martha Hooper worked to plan the program spaces, and alumnus architect David Plummer '86 designed a space that is regularly mentioned locally and nationally as a building to be seen—and it opened in 2004, a year after Tibbott. Both spaces benefit from a 110-well geothermal energy system that set a standard for in-town installations and preserved our big back field by putting seven miles of water lines under that green space.

Those seven miles approximate the distance to the River Campus, purchased in the late 1990s, when its 80 acres seemed a limitless resource. But starting with an eight-lane track in 2001, then on to an environmentally self-sufficient restroom facility, a set of wetlands boardwalks, eight tennis courts, a maintenance structure, field lighting, baseball dugouts, a perimeter walking trail, and most recently a 140-foot solar installation, we always seem to have another River Campus improvement project in the works. We now use virtually every bit of field space for all of our outdoor sports, and the original co-op arrangement struck with the turf farmer who worked space we never used has become a casualty of progress.

Growth in the student body and growth on our campus corresponded with growth in support. The cornerstone of that philanthropy continues to be our Annual Fund, which has more than tripled its target goal over the past fourteen years. To reach this year's goal of $1.3MM, from two thousand donors, we can count on more than four-fifths of our current parents and more than one-fifth of our 4,000+ alumni. While families of current students continue to drive this effort in both dollars and organizational leadership, giving from our graduates grows by the year, and we compare impressively nationwide in support from the parents of our alumni—perhaps not surprising given the modern history of the school.

The great philanthropic rallying point of recent years was The Campaign for Arts and Letters. The purpose of that effort was to fund those two new buildings and reserve twenty cents on each dollar contributed to be held in perpetuity, thereby more than doubling our endowment at the time. Three years and hundreds of volunteer hours later (we neither followed the feasibility study's modest prescription nor added staff to help us reach the $10MM announced goal), we faced a hard slog getting much past $8MM of that target. Then one spring day, our three largest gifts ever, for one million dollars each, changed our trajectory—after a remarkable conversation that joined the Garrison, Hassenfeld, and Shmerling families in making USN history.

What followed was a boost in giving from a range of sources, with a correspondingly elevated target set by an appreciative board, and we crested the $12.5MM mark. Then, another remarkable moment: the Malone Family Foundation, launched by communications entrepreneur John Malone and headquartered in Denver, called to announce that University School had been chosen for a $2MM scholarship endowment grant. Ours was the only such gift made in Tennessee by the foundation, dedicated to encouraging the most able young minds who also demonstrate financial need. With that grant, still the largest in our history so far, from a source with no prior link to USN, the campaign ended at nearly $15MM, an unprecedented figure and a powerful next step for us in coming of age as a school.

Recognition from the Malone Foundation came alongside other examples of wider national attention for the school. In 2001 the Morehead-Cain scholarship program at the University of North Carolina invited us to join their very limited group of nominating schools, and we've had four scholarships offered since. The Goizueta Foundation in Atlanta endowed a scholarship at USN. In the 2006 Leading Edge recognition, the National Association of Independent Schools named our fifth grade's civil rights unit as its Equity and Justice exemplar.

Just this year, the Edward E. Ford Foundation chose USN for one of four national leadership grants, funding curricular work uniting our high school faculty with Vanderbilt counterparts. We've seen four Presidential Scholars invited to the Rose Garden since 2000, including two named the same year. We've sent runners to the Olympic trials. Every year Scholastic Arts and Writing national gold medalists have earned invitations to be celebrated at Radio City Music Hall. This year we led all Tennessee high schools, regardless of size, in our National Merit Scholars total. And we engage more than ever in our home city, with a transportation fleet of a dozen USN buses of various sizes busy daily connecting people with program.

These varied and considerable initiatives and accomplishments flow in large measure from a set of 2001 strategic planning sessions, ably chaired by board veteran Thelma Kidd and led by a dynamic steering committee spanning decades of experience. That strategic exercise drew hundreds of participants and generated six priorities (along with miles of poster paper), areas of focus reaffirmed in 2007 and visible in our work together today:

- Academic Excellence

- A Multicultural School Climate

- Community Networks

- Arts and Athletics

- Creating Balance in Life

- Financial Resources

Through these six lenses we should see the host of facility improvements, outreach efforts, communication improvements, schedule changes, broader philanthropic ambitions, curricular innovations, and budgetary commitments. Each priority generated specific initiatives. And driven by our annual School Renewal self-review process, we've continued to build on prior successes, with faculty/staff committees making recommendations to help us grow in our capacity to provide a breadth of experiences here at 2000 Edgehill.

We've become a center for Responsive Classroom professional development to help lower school teachers, worked to improve literacy instruction, and developed a model program for young naturalists. Now we're exploring a groundbreaking word study curriculum for grades K-4. Our middle school recently launched a one-to-one laptop program with a wide range of new materials and methods, continues to develop its team-teaching model, and draws dozens of colleagues from other schools to see its mindfulness initiative up close. Our high school has added classes in every department, and its remarkable faculty continues to offer independent studies to more than 40% of our juniors and seniors. A new alignment in our athletics league has brought still greater success to our teams.

Constant through these changes has been leadership from key administrative colleagues. Each head of a division—lower, middle, and high school—has given the school more than a dozen years of service and guidance. Our other administrative team colleagues provide a constant source of perspective and expertise. This continuity in leadership opens doors and builds confidence in times of change.

A similar source of strength through these years is the stability of our faculty. Our average length of service now exceeds fifteen years, and the school is ever grateful to these dedicated teachers. Consider the amazing Gil Chilton, whose service now extends into a fifth decade. That same faculty, under direction of Robbie McKay and Beth Interlandi in successive years, completely overhauled our evaluation and compensation models. In each of the school's divisions (K-4, 5-8, 9-12), faculty leadership helps us strike the optimum balance between autonomy and coordination, between innovation and demonstrated best practice that strengthens a professional culture here that's generations old. Our teachers push where we need to be pushed, sharing a wonderful sense of the possible.

NOT WITHOUT OUR CHALLENGES

With growth and advances in critical areas, we nonetheless encounter vexing questions and difficult tradeoffs. We no longer face worries about whether a young, reinvented school can stand the test of time. Instead, our existential issues are those invoked by a consideration of what will happen if current trends continue far into the future, issues that come with longevity. We worry about decisions today that preclude options years from now. Interestingly, and perhaps predictably, many of our toughest knots to loosen flow directly from some success in that same area of school life—short term causes for celebration that carry longer term notes of caution if we make time to think as hard as we should.

Start with admissions. We've grown steadily and gradually, but not in each grade and not in sync with interest from families. There's no guarantee that we'll have space in each grade each year, or even that we'll have openings proportionate to the interest in each part of the K-12 sequence. Most painful at present is the situation in middle school, where a host of factors brings a host of families to look at our program in a segment of the sequence where we have little capacity to welcome new families. As a result, we see an uptick in kindergarten visits (not a bad thing at all) and some difficult conversations about possibly waiting around for ninth grade, where we add 20+ students to start high school.

Responding to this phenomenon by changing the shape of our enrollment carries risks of another sort—for example, what if we realign and then Metro Schools reorganize their grade groupings to leave us out of step? What would become of our middle school team-teaching model if we grew substantially in those grades? And what would we do with the correspondingly increased enrollment once those students reached high school? Fewer new ninth graders? Enrollment limit decisions have long tails. And saying no to great families, to our Nashville neighbors, takes a toll.

We wonder about the ultimate carrying capacity of our historic campus, now more than 50,000 square feet of interior space larger than it was in 2000. Moving through the arbitrary limit of 1,000 students, we've been able to make room for the school to work for everyone, but at some point the marginal cost of adding just one more young learner will be astronomical—we'd need to change the size of everything. At the risk of being proven wrong by our successors, it seems we have reached a ceiling in student numbers.

Adjacent to questions about enrollment are decisions about tuition. For many, many good and defensible reasons, what we charge to attend USN grows faster than the general price level and faster than average incomes nationally—we are not immune to this cross-sector educational phenomenon. It may be that USN families constitute a different sample and are earning faster than the rest, but assuming so feels presumptuous. The facts are these: since 2000, our tuition has basically doubled, even as our five-year average annual increase has been managed down from 7% to under 5%, all in a broader environment where consumer inflation measures have stayed under 3% by most estimates. The effects of compounding this growth are sobering—the ratchet only works upward.

In response, our need-based financial aid resources have tripled in that same time period, though the proportion of our enrollment receiving tuition assistance (21%) has not quite doubled, as the average award size increases. Financial aid budget discussions are among the most heart-wrenching moments on each board calendar—keeping a USN education accessible to students from a range of incomes is mission-critical for us. Generating the resources to help us keep that promise is just as critical.

To be worthy of that kind of support, whether in the form of tuition or philanthropy, we continue to enhance and improve program offerings. Those classes and activities, in academics and the arts and athletics and service learning, translate into some correspondingly very busy student lives. Different young people have different preferences and tolerances for packed schedules, but all students need time to reflect, and that time can be scarce. High-aspiring schools like ours tend to be additive and not subtractive with program, not wanting to miss a chance to provide chances for students to excel. Our students often share that tendency, adding to their cumulative set of commitments quite readily but loath to pare down, sensing that much is at stake.

Their teachers are busy people too. A central driver in our tuition increases has been a strong interest in raising faculty compensation—and in fact, since 2000 the average salary has grown by nearly 60%. Correspondingly, we ask faculty to communicate more than ever, to innovate more than ever, to be relevant more than ever in the life of the school and its students. The flow of information within and beyond the campus continues to grow in volume and frequency, as we strive to be leaders and not caretakers in our field. A glance at our daily school calendar or a link to our Twitter feed reveals a pace quickened by technology and by new opportunities to pursue and demonstrate excellence, whether at a math competition in Knoxville or a Big Brothers-Big Sisters event in the Edgehill neighborhood or a lacrosse game at the River Campus. One sign of the times is that we staff the building seven days a week, sixteen hours a day now.

Our packed and interconnected days stand in contrast to what can be the norm in many public schools, and finding a way to build bridges to those environments remains a challenge. The difference between what a child will experience at USN and what might be the case elsewhere in Nashville makes for difficult transitions, placing a corresponding burden on students and teachers on arrival here. The importance of and focus on state-mandated test results makes education more a product and less a process, making it harder for us to find common ground with our public school colleagues, even if we could find or make the time. My strong sense is that the disparity between the best and the worst education available in our city continues to grow, despite determined efforts by good people. And we, given our school's DNA and our own commitments to our community, want very much to be part of the solution, not part of the problem.

THE OPPORTUNITY OF THE CENTENNIAL MOMENT

Combining the raft of encouraging developments in recent years with the challenges that come with that success puts our 100th birthday in proper perspective. Our planning for this milestone draws on themes mentioned throughout this chapter, starting with an appreciation for the resolve and resilience of our predecessors— we aim to work as hard as they did in their turn at the wheel. While the specific circumstances of our day might have been hard to predict decades ago, the need to balance a range of worthy priorities is probably a constant. So too is the need for leadership, a quality that has been evident in abundance of late.

Consider the Centennial building project. For the past seven years, we've been working on a way to restore our historic McKim, Mead and White building's last untouched spaces, now nine decades old. We began with a goal of returning the pool to optimum function and recasting the old locker spaces that had become our bookstore and changing area for swimmers. That goal soon morphed into something more ambitious. We determined to address a range of needs, most visibly the need to enter the school in a single, consistent, coherent way from the north side. What resulted is a five-story concept that ties the school together at the ground floor and

The new 19th Avenue entrance to the school as it appeared in mid-July, 2014, a few weeks before the project's completion.

meets emerging needs from basement to roof level, at the heart of the building, combining the best of old and new.

To complete this project took the commitment of hundreds of students and teachers (primarily in high school) who bore the disruption through months of classes, of hundreds of extracurricular participants who persevered through altered venue routines, of a hardworking Building and Grounds committee who met almost weekly to review plans, and of our imaginative architect Manuel Zeitlin '72, who cares so much about a legacy for his alma mater (after his design transformed our Sperling Center dining area in 2012 with the first glass and steel modernism on the campus and signaled the Centennial's approach). And it took the support of a donor community willing to contribute once our board authorized a start date that would permit us to cut the ribbon before the first day of our Centennial school year.

In addition to caring for the educational space, we've been able to make important strides providing for people on this campus as we reach the 100th birthday milestone. We've endowed a second faculty chair, following on our last campaign's Shmerling Chair for Excellence in Teaching, by creating a Bovender Family Chair to recognize leaders in their fifth to fifteenth years of experience. The honor rotates every few years, and announcing those recipients, starting with Dee Holder Bradshaw Hicks '58 ten years ago, is a highlight for me at Convocation. Another watershed moment was the establishment of a new set of endowed scholarships, thanks to a gift from the Bredesen-Conte family. The opportunities to secure component pieces of our future trace directly to the challenges of our evolving financial algorithm.

Past these essential considerations, our responsibilities today extend to seeking ways to make the most of our autonomy in an age of national educational reform. In that spirit, we've helped launch the first synchronous distance learning consortium (letting students see and hear each other in real time via high-definition video link), in the company of other Malone Scholar schools across the country. Closer to home, we've accepted an invitation from Horizons National to become one of thirty sites connecting an independent school host with a nearby economically challenged elementary school—for an eight-year looping program of summer academic enrichment. And our recent E.E. Ford leadership grant to support curricular development work with Vanderbilt, linking high schools and colleges, provides another great opportunity to lead, to set a precedent.

The question of our optimum relationship with our university neighbor, while different from the Demonstration School's with the original Peabody College, remains a potentially defining issue—especially so with Peabody's prominence as a national leader in its field. In fact, Peabody classes, primarily in teaching methods, have returned to our campus under Vanderbilt auspices. Connections in other areas may never have been stronger, with Vanderbilt adjunct lecturer PhDs joining our faculty (five in the past decade), graduate students continuing to serve as lower school teaching assistants, and USN board leaders who are Vanderbilt deans and program directors.

It could be accurately stated that University School's origin story, fiscal and governance independence, and location at the heart of what the Carnegie Foundation called a Research I university puts us in our own category of one. My own doctoral work, completed just this year, thanks to many colleagues, confirmed that supposition. The resulting "Vanderbilt Question" looms large without imposing any particular imperative for action. So too the question of our connection with Belmont or TSU or Fisk, each of which has been important for USN past and present, here in this Athens of the South.

How we choose to intersect with the nascent charter school movement, such a flashpoint in our city at present, and how we respond to the Common Core national standards initiative, so political and contentious, and whether we will find ways to be part of the larger conversation about great education in Nashville across all school types remains to be seen. In light of the intensity of these issues, this Centennial moment could not be better timed, inviting us to think big, to dream big, and to reflect on the reasons we've stood the test of time.

THE NEW PRAGMATISM

At the end of *Past Is Prologue*, Leland Johnson and his students offered an assessment of their school and its prospects for the future. They lamented the position of the school within the college as a deficit-prone budget burden, and they highlighted the need for long-deferred maintenance of their classroom building—though they saw no viable means of funding. But their optimism never flagged, having identified a "heritage of achievement," great loyalty from constituents, and a willingness to embrace new measures to honestly address familiar challenges.

Vince Durnan at the 2011 Commencement.

They went on to acknowledge that the school's history revealed no obligation to any specific educational school of thought or philosophical orthodoxy. Instead, they found "something tough about the school," in the words of the venerable Peabody administrator J.E. Windrow, and that something was the Peabody spirit. It strikes me that the great and continuous resource connecting generations on this campus, through changes and challenges that might have proven insurmountable without our adaptability, is that spirit. In that spirit we found the courage to invent and reinvent the school that began as PDS and became USN, willing to do the hard work and expecting to build a school students would love.

Those are the constants in our story of change. Those are the cornerstones in our school culture, at the heart of our narrative. To understand the USN story, we are well served to look to the Peabody spirit. It's visible in the words written in 1980 (her first year at USN) by lower school music legend Doni Princehorn, creator of Grandparents' Day, who reminds us in our school song to "lift our voices upward," in the company of our elders and our young ones.

What might be the next steps inspired by that spirit? Ours is the chance to imagine and pursue a future worthy of our past, of the uncommon dedication that created the Demonstration School, made it thrive, saw the Transition through against all odds, and brought it to prominence as an independent school. Finding the way forward will likely include another experience in pragmatism, addressing at least three central and interconnected questions.

First, what financial model will best serve our aspirations? What blend of tuition, fees, and philanthropy will combine to ask the right amount of material support from the right people? What blend of salaries, need-based tuition assistance, program funding, and campus maintenance will combine to produce the best education any school could offer within reason? What assumptions should we make about the inalterability of current trends in educational finance? To what extent should we see higher education as a road map and to what extent a cautionary tale?

At every turn in those budget algorithm conversations, we should seek the educational model best suited for our times, our resources, and our future. The configuration of eighteen students (or so) in a room with a smart, caring, committed adult has proven remarkably impervious to change for the past century—and many would argue for good reason. The radio, the television, and so far even the personal computer have not wrought structural change in our student/teacher foundation.

Maybe those changes are just around the corner, and maybe USN will help define a blend of educational experiences that becomes the norm in schools that might learn from our example. Again in the closing reflections of *The Past Is Prologue*, its authors stated with conviction, "The history of the school reveals a perpetual dialectic between educational theories, for even the name 'Demonstration' school appears to have been a synthesis . . . . The name had enough flexibility to harmonize opposing theories about the nature of such a school."

It may be that the ideal educational experience of the next generation is revealed to be a synthesis of individual and group work, of time on campus and time in the wider community, of learning face-to-face and learning via video link, of research and internships, of mastering the basics and shaping personal areas of study. Maintaining flexibility and seeking harmony will move us further, faster, and complacency is to be avoided if we intend to be relevant.

Essential to the longer range conversations about USN's future, conversations we were formally encouraged to engineer by our reaccreditation team just this spring, is determining the size and shape of our school at its best. The question of how many students in what grade configuration would best suit the financial and educational models we choose, and vice-versa, gets to the heart of the matter. We've grown incrementally in scale and scope for at least a generation, living in the present as a means to live to see the future.

We've earned, by dint of hard effort by a great many people for a very long time, the right to think as our founders did, when it was all new. The Centennial reminds us to think of our place within this university campus, in this dynamic Edgehill neighborhood, in this high-flying city of extremes, in a nation struggling with educational reform, in an ever more globally connected world. Should we grow enrollment to be larger, scale down to be smaller, reach out more substantially to our Metro School colleagues, help sponsor a charter school, find a way to provide an international experience for more students and faculty? Picture USN at its very best for this next century—what do you see? Those big planning conversations will benefit from keeping our feet on solid ground and our eyes on the horizon— and they represent the most exciting prospect in our uncommon story.

VINCE DURNAN

Vince Durnan serves as Director at University School of Nashville, where he arrived in 2000 after stints in California, Hawai'i, and Connecticut. He recently completed an Ed D at Vanderbilt's Peabody College, writing on the governance connections between major research universities and their K-12 independent school neighbors--inspired by experience at USN. Earlier degrees came decades ago at Williams College and Harvard Graduate School of Education. His three daughters, Avery, Nani, and Julia, are USN alumnae. This Centennial book is the fulfillment of a long-time aspiration for him.

ACKNOWLEDGMENTS

Before closing, I'm compelled to offer a heartfelt word of thanks to the remarkable board presidents whose care and wisdom have meant so much to me personally and professionally. To Ann Fundis for her patience in teaching me the ropes, to Mike Shmerling for teaching me to combine detail with the big picture, to Frank Garrison for teaching me the power of active thinking, to Mike Schoenfeld for teaching me the value of our story told well, to Bert Mathews for teaching me persistent optimism, to Gail Williams for teaching me to listen to every voice, and to Dave Kloeppel for teaching me to work the plan. The importance of their leadership cannot be overstated. And through it all, the institutional good sense of Bobbie Grubb running my office has been the pearl of great price.

My special gratitude extends to the writers who helped, through this book project, to tell our school's story. We are, after all, the sum of all our stories, and maybe some days a little more than that—as a school community. What has happened here at 2000 Edgehill Avenue, and what happens today, is an adventure in demonstrating school at its best. The enduring question remains— what is a great education and how can it be generated here? Like so many of us, and to quote Bob Massie '46, "I can't wait to see how it all turns out."

— VINCE DURNAN

STUDENTS OF THE
AMERICAN PROBLEMS CLASS
1969-1970

Remembering *The Past*

In the school year 1969-70, high school students in Leland Johnson's class wrote *The Past is Prologue, Peabody Demonstration School 1915-1970*. Following are excerpts, including Mr. Johnson's Preface and a list of the students, all class of 1970, who contributed. We made no changes in the passages we selected.

From the THE PAST IS PROLOGUE

Preface

An elective was added to the curriculum of the Peabody Demonstration School in 1969 to provide senior high students with an opportunity for independent study and research. The course was named "American Problems" to avoid limiting the topics for study to any one area, although it was expected that the class would orient itself toward political problems and local government. As the class investigated the various topics it had selected, it discovered that many American problems are related to the American system of education; it also concluded that many of the nation's problems could be solved only by improving the quality of the educational system. Hence, this study of the efforts of the Peabody Demonstration School to improve American education was undertaken in the belief that a knowledge of what has been attempted in the past might be a prologue to increased efforts in the future.

During the progress of the study, the history of the Demonstration School began to assume meaning in relation to the history of the nation and the history of developments in American education during the past half century. It is the sincere desire of the class that their study will be of interest not only to the thousands who have taken part as administrators, faculty, and students in creating the distinguished record of the school, but also to those who are not members of the "Peabody family," because the history of the school, in the wider perspective, reflects vigorous conflicts in educational theory and several problems common to the nation—American problems.

The class discovered that a strictly chronological narrative of the history of the school was ineffectual, hence the topical organization of the history. Two departures were made from this organization, however, by developing the history of the Winthrop School, 1889-1913, and the early history of the Demonstration School, 1915-1925, as separate topics for study. Apologies must be extended to the preschool and elementary divisions of the Demonstration School. Although diligent search was made, few records were discovered of the activities in the school below the senior high level. School publications are generally written by senior high students, and most of the surviving records which deal with the activities in the lower grades are merely curriculum outlines. The authors suggest steps to remedy this problem in the concluding chapter.

The area of study chosen by each student was as follows:

Phillip Mintz	History of Winthrop School, 1890-1913
Janet Clodfelter	Early Years at P.D.S., 1915-1925
Bruce Davis	Environment and Physical Plant
Barbara Pearl	Financial Affairs
Jim Coddington	Athletics
Anne Schoggen	Student Government
Charles Lutin	Special Events and School Traditions
Hilda Wilsdorf	School Organizations and Administrators
Theresa Bell	Members of the Faculty
Kyle Ellis	Curriculum
Randy Hurt	Student Body
Julie Reichman	Alumni

The study was a cooperative enterprise with each student contributing to the work of the others and offering constructive criticism. The instructor attempted to coordinate the study and to synthesize the collective thoughts of the students in a concluding essay.

The class must express its deep appreciation to the hundreds of alumni, administrators, and faculty members who kindly contributed to this study by sharing their reminiscences with the class. Many were so kind as to grant interviews and to undertake an extensive correspondence with the class—so many that it is impossible to mention each of them by name; personal mention must, however, be made of Dr. J.E. Windrow, a past administrator, who shared his personal papers with the class. Thanks must also be expressed to the staff of George Peabody College Library for their patience and aid and to the present administrators of Peabody Demonstration School, Dr. L. Edward Pratt and Mr. Robert Smotherman, without whose aid the completion and publication of this study would have been impossible.

Leland R. Johnson
Instructor, 1969-70 American Problems Class

EXCERPTS

Chapter 1
Garnet and Blue: The Heritage of the Demonstration School

The Peabody College for Teachers suspended its operations on the old University of Nashville campus with the end of the school session of 1910-1911. With the suspension of the college, the Robert Winthrop School was left without the aid of the college and the college authorities. Dr. Albert Barrett, however, who had served as director of the Robert Winthrop School since its reorganization in 1908, decided to continue the school as a private preparatory school. The school was moved by Dr. Barrett from the Winthrop Model School building to another building located on the corner of First Avenue and Carroll Street near the old University of Nashville campus.

Two senior classes graduated from the high school before Peabody changed campuses, and two more classes graduated from it after it became a preparatory school under the personal control of Dr. Barrett. The school's first graduating class, in 1910, consisted of ten members, while the graduating class of 1911 contained forty-nine seniors; the class of 1912 numbered thirty-five, and the class of 1913, the last before the end of the school's existence, contained twenty-eight.

The controversy in the last decade of the nineteenth century over the advantages of the "model" school versus the "laboratory" school represented the clashing of two different educational philosophies on the part of Dr. Payne and Governor Porter. Payne abhorred the concept of allowing unqualified student teachers to practice their newly acquired classroom knowledge on young children. He was a traditionalist in educational techniques; wary of new ideas in teaching. When President Payne retired from the college and President Porter became the chief administrator, the Model School's purposes altered. Porter, who was receptive to the newer trends in educational techniques, discontinued the elementary department of the Model School while widening the scope of the secondary school. He initiated the program of allowing college students to supplement their classroom training with practice teaching in the Winthrop Preparatory School.

When Peabody Demonstration School was founded on the new George Peabody College for Teachers campus in 1915, a mixture of both the observational and the practice or experimental methods of teacher training was instituted. Hence, the Winthrop School and the controversy over its purposes established the character of its successor, the Peabody Demonstration School. One indication of the continuity of history between the Winthrop Model School and Peabody Demonstration School is that the latter still carries the colors of the former and of the University of Nashville—garnet (maroon) and Columbia Blue.

Chapter 2
Early Years at the Demonstration School, 1915-1925

The Demonstration School began with a small summer school for children, used for observational purposes, in the basement of Jesup Psychological Laboratory. This marked the beginning of an educational project which was to become one of the leaders in the reorganization of education in the Southland. Fifty-nine such schools have been erected in the South since 1935.

The Peabody Demonstration School was organized to provide laboratory facilities for students in the process of becoming teachers and administrators. The administrators and faculty members were and are concerned with the development of a democratic way of life, the nature of learning, the changing social and economic order, and the growth of the individual in "intelligent self-direction and in richness of personality."

From 1915 to 1919, the Demonstration School was located in the Jesup Psychological Building on Peabody College campus. In 1919, a building was built especially for the Demonstration School, "The Stucco Building." It was built to house the kindergarten and the first six elementary grades (this building is now a college maintenance building), while upper grades remained in the Psychology Building. In 1925, with a benevolent gift from the Rockefeller Foundation, the school was able to move into its present building on Edgehill Avenue. This fund also financed the building of Vanderbilt Hospital and Medical School.

The first teacher at the Demonstration School was Professor Harvey Guy Swanson. For a salary of $800 a year, he served as principal and also taught history and civics. Several people thought the idea of a laboratory school an excellent one, but only Mr. Swanson was willing to undertake the financial risk. According to Dr. Thomas Alexander, it was this man who put the school on its feet within a short three-year period. The Demonstration School had an enrollment of over three hundred and a long waiting list when he left in 1918.

Dr. Joseph Roemer was assistant principal during these first years. Part of his duties were to keep the children off the grass, act as head janitor, and make sure the children did not enter a door used by adults. It has been said that Dr. Roemer was the "chief disciple of joy." He and Professor Swanson completed the combined administrative and janitorial staff for the first year.

According to Dr. Alexander, there are three prominent women to be considered among the builders of the school and in the program for the education of the girls during the early years—Miss Anna Cooper, Mrs. E.L. Parsons, and Miss Nell Crain. Each of these women was employed to teach a particular subject—home economics, Latin, and physical education, respectively. They left great impressions on the minds of the girls by reflecting their love for them and upholding the ideals of womanhood. "The girls in this school seem to me to excel any other similar group physically, mentally, and morally—all of which is due to the work of Miss Crain, Mrs. Parsons, and Miss Cooper," said Dr. Alexander.

Two other important men worked behind the scenes during the early years. These men were Dr. Charles A. McMurry and Mr. E.W. Connell. Neither of them took active parts in the administration of the school, but both contributed greatly to its support. Dr. McMurry attended faculty meetings and offered much advice on school operations. Mr. Connell worked on the financial end of things and guided the faculty in many ways.

Dr. Thomas Alexander left his position as a faculty member of Columbia University in 1914 to begin the planning of the Demonstration School, and occupied the position of chief administrator until 1924. Dr. Alexander, sometimes called the "Father of Peabody Demonstration School," is still living today, retired in North Carolina.

....

From 1915 to 1925, the Peabody Demonstration School struggled for existence in the basement of the Psychology Building and the Stucco Building, but by the time it began operation in its present location, the labors of its founders and early administrators had endowed it with a distinctive and enduring character and spirit.

On February 19, 1925, the new and permanent home of the Demonstration School was dedicated. Seated in the beautiful new auditorium on that day were hundreds of parents and friends of the school, and on the stage were the students and alumni. Familiar faces were everywhere as former faculty members and students gathered to join in the dedication of the new building. Dr. Bruce Payne presided in his amiable manner, and the program of music and speeches proceeded in fine fashion until the climax of the program was reached. Dr. Alexander, the "Father of Peabody Demonstration School," rose to speak, but was unable to do so because of the prolonged outburst of applause. When the roar subsided, he spoke to the audience just as he had done in the classroom, with snappy, frank, ironic and humorous comments.

Dr. "Alex" began with the birth of the Demonstration School, telling of the first year—of the financial difficulties, of the people who had aided—how the first students were recruited (recruited is correct), and how the school expenses during the first year, 1915, with nine teachers had reached the astronomical sum of three thousand dollars! He told of the dark days when classes were held in a basement, when College people complained of that "noisy Demonstration School bunch," and "Keep off the Grass" signs prevented the children's play. He concluded by thanking all who had made the school possible—Dr. Bruce Payne, college faculty, Demonstration School staff, and the parents who had been brave enough to send their children to P.D.S. during the formulative years. He explained how their criticisms and cooperation had combined to produce the Demonstration School.

Is it necessary to describe the applause which overwhelmed Dr. "Alex" when he finished his dedicatory speech?

Thus was the new building entered with enthusiasm and dedicated with impressive ceremony. The early struggles for a permanent home were successfully concluded, and a new era was beginning in the history of the school. Although thousands of people have passed through the halls of the school since the day of dedication, the building still stands and still serves the Peabody and Nashville community. It is the story of this service which is to be pursued in the following chapters.

Chapter 3
School Environment and Financial Affairs

Although many changes have been made in the Demonstration School Building, there were many more suggestions which have been postponed or canceled altogether. One such postponed proposal concerned the seating in the gym. Until 1940 Peabody was using either folding chairs, or bleachers which resembled folding chairs, as seats for the spectators during athletic events. Dr. T. Ross Fink, director at that time, asked for new bleachers and the question was brought before the Peabody Demonstration School Committee. The answer came back in the form of a bulletin from the Director of Business and Finance. Because the cost of the bleachers amounted to $3,000, it was decided that they were too costly and the matter was dropped. Bleachers were finally installed a decade later at a cost of $4,000.

During the mid-fifties the use of the open-air balconies came to a close. These balconies, located at either end of the third floor, were once used as roof gardens. Meetings and social affairs, such as the Easter Breakfast, were held on them in the fresh air. As a result of the slow deterioration of the roof garden, Dr. McCharen ended the use of the balconies.

Another part of the school building which has been closed is the health room in the sub-basement. The health room was once used sporadically as a dressing room for the opposing football team, according to whether or not Peabody played football that year. In 1951 it finally met its end as a football locker room as did football. Seven years later, in 1958, Coach Howard Stubblefield refurnished the room as a locker room for the opposing basketball team. After three years, this too was discontinued and the room was converted into a health classroom. It now serves only as a bomb shelter, with Civil Defense survival supplies available for emergencies.

The most radical and complete changes which have come to the building were those made necessary by the 1954 fire. Dr. McCharen, then director, lived near the school. One June 5, 1954, Dr. McCharen was eating breakfast when he heard fire engines. He leaned over to his wife and said, "Someone's having a hot one." Twenty minutes later the Nashville fire chief called to tell him that the Demonstration School was on fire. Ironically, only a short time earlier, Dr. McCharen had told the fire chief that he didn't believe the school could be burned with a blow torch, a belief unfortunately still too common among the students.

There were many opinions as to how the fire began. The opinion of Dr. McCharen centered around a large fan used in the auditorium. He believes the fan caught in the draperies, became overheated until it shorted out, and a spark jumped to the draperies which caught fire. The auditorium then proceeded to burn. The fire spread onto the second floor through the French doors at the back of the balcony (now the faculty lounge). The windows in the auditorium burst under the heat and the wind swept flames down the second floor halls and up to the third floor.

The opinion of the fire chief was that the rheostat dimmers used for stage lighting were left on overnight, overheated and broke. The gas from these dimmers seeped into the auditorium and, when a spark jumped from a short-circuited dimmer, the gas exploded, blowing out all the windows, including the windows in back of the auditorium. The wind then blew the fire into the second floor where the paint on the walls caught fire, spreading the fire down the hall and on to the third floor.

The fire gutted most of the rooms on the second floor and many on the third; those which were not destroyed by the fire were badly damaged by water; many valuable books were damaged in the library. The total cost of the fire amounted to $250,000, but because the fire started at six on a summer morning, there were no injuries.

There were many changes to the school after the fire. They gym floor was again replaced, most of the classrooms were treated with sound-absorbing ceiling tile, and the lobby was enlarged to include the offices now occupied by the principal and the director. The balcony in the auditorium was converted into room space and now serves as a teachers' lounge, and the windows behind the stage were walled up.

....

Tuition will be raised to $900 in 1970-71. This additional income will go primarily to increase the salaries of the teachers. In this coming year, there are no plans for building, nor any radical financial changes in the operation of the school.

Thus, we see that the operating expenses of the school have been met in the past by tuition charges and grants from Peabody College. The recent increase in tuition rates, necessitated by the recurrent inflation of the past two decades and the rapidly rising costs of modern quality education, has practically ended the need for aid from the college, at least currently. It should be pointed out, however, that inflation lowers the real value of the tuition a great deal; it is believed that the current tuition rate may, in actuality, be little more of a burden to parents and students than $150 was in 1940 or $300 in 1960.

Major improvements in the physical plant have been financed, in the past, largely by grants from foundations of a benevolent character and by patrons and alumni of the school. The school will continue to rely on this source in the future for the renovation and expansion of the physical plant to meet the needs of space age education.

Chapter 4
PDS Sports: Olympian Efforts and . . .

The 1925-26 school year was marked by the move into the present building, which of course, included the Joel Cheek gym, named after the donor of the funds to build the gym. Described at the time as one of the most "spacious" gyms in the South, it remains today virtually unchanged. This new gym, after a 2-2-4 record by footballers and a 5-9 mark by the boy cagers, saw the girls capture the "Little Tenn" Championship with a 10-1-1 record. With this first "Little Tenn" Championship, a new era dawned in Peabody sports, for in the next decade the Demonstration School would be a vital part in this conference of Mid-State schools, which was established to promote amateur athletic and academic activities.

The following fall, the formation of the Tennessee Secondary Schools Athletic Association was another significant event for PDS. W.H. Yarbrough, PDS principal, was an important figure in the establishment of this organization which even today governs the athletic contests of the state. Ironically, Yarbrough and Peabody College, also instrumental in putting the TSSAA together, would be investigated by the

TSSAA Board of Control in 1936, just ten years after Yarbrough had become one of the first members of the Board of Control.

With these developments off the field, the 1926 fall edition of the football Tigers marched on to the Little Tennessee Championship with a 5-1-2 record, by beating the teams of Carthage and Columbia. Overshadowing this, however, was the girls successful run at the state title. After a perfect 13-0 mark in regular season play, the girls entered the state tournament, which was held in the PDS gym. With Peabody College housing and entertaining the teams, the tourney got under way and PDS clobbered cross-city rival Hume-Fogg 36-15. Two wins later the girls were once again in the finals, this time faced by Hampshire. This game was tight all the way until it seemed PDS had won it at 24-22. However, a last second bucket gave the Hampshire girls another chance. But Peabody was not to be denied, and with Misses Caldwell and Harris stopping the opposition cold, reserve Kay Early dumped in the winning tally in overtime at 26-24. The fine play of the girls in this tourney not only won them the championship, but also the sportsmanship award.

....

The 1932-33 and 1933-34 seasons were not noteworthy, although they were the prelude to the full blooming of the "Golden Age" in Demonstration School sports. With the arrival of Coach Bill Schwartz on the scene, hired by President Payne to dispel the "sissy" image which people attributed to the Demonstration School, the football team would rise from a dismal 0-6-1 record in 1933 to a brilliant 23-1-2 record for the next three years. These years would also see a rise in basketball fortunes as gridiron stars Roy Huggins, Mickey Flanigan and Herb Dunkerley dribbled the ball around Cheek Gymnasium along with the great Jack Irby. Baseball would also find the Tigers one of the best in the city as Coaches Schwartz and Nance Jordan put the material together. But all of these great feats would be forever tarnished as the TSSAA and Peabody ran afoul of each other, eventually causing PDS to be expelled, temporarily, from the TSSAA.

The fall of 1934 found Peabody with a record-setting football team. Not only did the team go 9-0 for the season, but they were unscored upon in all nine games, amassing a total of 190 points to their opponents' 0! After crushing all nine opponents, the team was awarded the Little Tenn championship by the league heads, making it the Tigers' third championship. This team placed Dunkerley and Flanigan on the All-Little Tenn team and Dunkerley and Huggins on the All-City team. Flanigan and Huggins were only sophomores while Dunkerley was a junior, boding well for Demonstration School athletics the next few years.

Baseball saw Peabody field another winner, the team finishing with a 7-3 record in Nashville league play. With Coach Nance Jordan leading the team, the crown was not lost until the final games of the year. The season climaxed with the selection of Mickey Flanigan, centerfield, boasting a batting average of .376; Roy Huggins, third base, an average of .417; and Dick Polk, shortstop, .500, to the All-City team. Polk, a senior, was the leader of this team, perhaps the best diamond nine PDS ever fielded. The successes of 1934-35 did not stop with the major sports as Peabody also laid claim to a tennis championship. Moreau Estes marched over all his opposition in the city tourney to take the crown by beating Bill Travis 6-0, 6-4, 6-4.

With veterans Dunkerley, Huggins and Flanigan returning, the '35-36 campaigns looked promising. After crushing Ashland City 63-0 first game, the 10 game streak came to an end with a scoreless duel against Donelson. The unscored upon streak would remain intact until the last game of the season against East. By the time the East game rolled around, PDS had a 5-0-2 record, having had another scoreless tie with Murfreesboro. East, however, intercepted an early pass for a touchdown against the Tigers, ending the streak at 16 straight games unscored upon: final score—East 6, PDS 65!! PDS's 65 points was an NIL record at the time, as was the 30 points Flanigan compiled during the game. Those 30 points pushed the Peabodian ahead of teammate Huggins in the NIL scoring race, as they finished 1-2. Once again Huggins and Dunkerley made All-Nashville, this time joined by Flanigan. Senior Dunkerley was described as capable of "doing everything," junior Roy Huggins as "a savage tackler," and Mickey Flanigan as "a hip-loose ball carrier." The entire team under Coach Schwartz, himself an All-Southern end at Vanderbilt, was called the best in years in Nashville.

This tremendous string of successes was exploded on November 30 with the announcement by the TSSAA Board of Control that Peabody had been expelled from the association, and thus would be unable to play any of its teams. The reasons for the expulsion, as stated in a letter to Dr. Roemer were: "The Board believes that your coach has too much authority in your athletic program . . . It is reported that your coach has been heard to say that he was going out and get [sic] him some athletes . . . . The Board also believes that friends of the school are paying the tuition of some of your boys." Peabody replied that it was innocent, for all of its actions had been entirely open for the Board to see. Included with this reply was a statement asserting that PDS had presented the names of all its candidates for scholarships, six for athletics, to the Board of Control. The Board refused these scholarships on the grounds that all six were freshmen between the ages of 17 and 19, and thus were offered scholarships for strictly athletic purposes.

The issue was further clouded when the Mid-South Association of Private Schools tabled Peabody's application to participate in its conference. So now it became apparent that unless the TSSAA was satisfied, PDS would have no interscholastic athletics.

Several Peabody athletes announced they would attend other schools. Harry Dailey, star quarterback, left at the end of the first semester, while Flanigan and others were making plans to leave the next fall. Schwartz, whom the TSAA had said would have to be removed before PDS would be readmitted, had organized a full intramural program at the start of the new year, because only games with BGA, TIS, the Vandy freshmen, and Terre Haute, Indiana, could be scheduled.

On January 3, the Demonstration School Committee met and called for the abandonment of all interscholastic competition until some later date. Finally, on January 11, the whole issue was resolved as Peabody was reinstated to the TSSAA, on the condition that Yarbrough would be in complete charge of athletics thereafter. The decision came after a member of the Demonstration School Committee had met privately with the TSSAA Board of Control, and agreed to its conditions, which included the requirement that no one receiving a scholarship could play athletics. The same day the PDS faculty met and decided to accept reinstatement, while also deciding to limit the basketball and baseball games to one a week and to commit the Demonstration School to full development of an intramural program.

With the issue settled, and all except one of the players back, apparently paying their own way, the Tigers took to the hardwood. The team finished 3-5, with Coach Schwartz still at the reins despite the TSSAA objections.

The fiasco with the TSSAA apparently did not hurt the Tigers of the 1936-37 campaigns. The football squad boasted an 8-1 record, and scored a record 329 points, as Mickey Flanigan closed out his career with Peabody. The lone loss of the season came at the hands of the mighty juggernaut of Riverside Military Academy, 36 to 13, and was the first defeat the Maroon and Blue had tasted in 21 games. Outside of this loss, the Tigers ran roughshod over all their opposition on the strength of Mickey Flanigan's scoring. With Huggins hurt for three games, Flanigan, along with Ed Hiestand at end, carried the burden well, as he eventually totaled a tremendous 121 points, a school record for points in a season. Another school record set during the campaign was most points in a single game, as the '36 Tigers clawed Hohenwald 67-0; also set was a record team-scoring average of 33.2 points per game. The team won all four of its city games to ramble the city championship, the last ever for a PDS football team. The team's potent offense was led by All-City selections Roy Huggins at fullback, Ed Hiestand at right end, and Lee McKinney at left tackle. Flanigan's brilliant year earned him All-City honors and All-State choice at right half. It was certainly a great way to end a great era of Peabody sports, for the next year PDS would sponsor only intramural athletics.

During those years, 1924-1937, four Huggins brothers appeared for PDS: Louis, Harold (Skinny), Jim and Roy (Red). All were great performers, as both Harold and Jim became stars on both the gridiron and hardwood at Vanderbilt. But Roy was best of all, as he became a Vanderbilt great on the football field and continued in the professional league; he is, so far as the author was able to discover, the only PDS athlete to become a pro athlete. Always remembered for their efforts will be Flanigan, the Hugginses, the Askews, Jay Armistead, and other great gridiron stars.

Success in those years did not end at the hundred-yard line, as Jack Irby led the hoopsters to the city championship in 1936. Undefeated in city play and suffering only one upset loss to Linden, the team climaxed this season, the only one in which a Maroon and Blue quintet captured a city title, with a trip to Terre Haute. Here PDS demolished the pride of that city, in the heart of basketball mania, 35-7. Jack Irby became an All-City selection at guard; he would be the last Peabodian to gain such an honor for almost two decades.

In the winter of 1954 a new face appeared on campus as basketball coach and with it came a new look to the basketball teams; Coach Dan Finch took over a team which had won three games in five years of NIL competition, and with some willing players put together the best team Peabody had seen in years. This team finished at 6-6 in NIL play and 8-10 overall behind the play of Ben Rowan.

Coach Finch molded this crew into a team between courses at the Vanderbilt Law School, where he was working towards his degree. The previous three years, he had been

THE SAME RIVER TWICE

a standout for the Commodores' basketball team, being selected All-SEC his last two years. One of only ten VU players ever to score over 1000 career points, Finch began to re-establish a winning tradition at PDS. The 1954-55 team posted the best mark for a Tiger team in 10 years, but was certainly not the best under Finch.

Finch was called to Korea after this first campaign, and Elmer Cooke inherited the team with all five starters back. Their 1955-56 season was the year of Ben Rowan, one of the Demonstration School's greatest athletes, as he set several school records during the course of the season. While leading the Tigers to a 14-7 record (best since the City Championship days of 1937), the 6'5" center scored 570 points for an NIL record of 26.43 points per game. This great performance led to his being named NIL's most valuable player and also to his being the first Peabody representative ever on the All-State basketball team. Recruited heavily, Rowan cast his lot with Vanderbilt as most great PDS athletes had before him. There, he was a three-year starter, being named to the All-SEC sophomore team his first year. Rowan had fired the first stage in Peabody's rocketing basketball fortunes.

Rowan, however, did not stop at basketball, for in the spring he took to track and tennis. In track, Rowan won both the broad jump and high jump in the *Banner* Relays, scoring more points than any other individual at the meet. In tennis he was part of a squad led by Steve Riven and MacNeil Stokes, which challenged MBA for the city crown. The team lost a tight 3-2 match, finishing second to the perennial Big Red champions.

With the loss of Rowan, whose 1,235 career points would be a school record for only a few years, and the other four starters, the cagers of '56-57 could manage only a 5-13 record. In tennis, however, Dave Nicholls and Bruce Stratvert laid claim to the city doubles crown, as the Tigers were again fielding a strong tennis team.

Dan Finch returned in 1957 as PDS coach and again forged a winning team, 13-8. This team was paced by juniors Gene Ericksen and Edwin Anderson, establishing a firm nucleus for the team the next year. The team finished out its season by copping the district sportsmanship trophy.

The edition of the PDS Tigers which appeared in 1958-59 was an awesome offensive machine which crunched the opposition and school and NIL records left and right. Louis Finkelstein and Bill Stratvert at guards, Bill Darby and Edwin

Anderson at forwards, and the virtually unstoppable Gene Ericksen at center, combined into a well-trained juggernaut which eventually piled up a 23-4 regular season record.

The season started well and by mid-December the Tigers seemed to have a bid to the annual March of Dimes games in the bag. A stunning upset loss to Howard killed this opportunity, so the Tigers went to Franklin for the first annual Middle Tennessee Invitational Tournament. Here, with Gene Ericksen destroying everyone and Edwin Anderson cleaning up, the Tigers defeated West, BGA, and East in that order to claim PDS's first major trophy in 21 years.

With this great performance behind them, the cagers settled to the task of also capturing the NIL crown. With Ericksen, continually the big point man, and Edwin Anderson, cleaning the rebounds off the backboards, PDS raced to 16 straight triumphs, including a 67-48 thrashing of previously unbeaten Goodlettsville. During this stretch the team began to build its point totals until by the end of the season they had reached record proportions. Gene Ericksen and Edwin Anderson continued their 1-2 punch; Ericksen as the NIL's top scorer, and Anderson as one of its top five.

PDS then took revenge on rival West by a 73-64 tally to finish third in NIL play, marking the Demonstration School as a spoiler in the tournaments; however, here it stopped as the Tigers, winners of 19 of their last 20 games, ran afoul of hot West in the second game. West, according to the *Tennessean*, "stunned mighty Peabody 60-58 with a fourth quarter rally that has never and may never be equaled in District 18 tournament play." Coming from 10 points behind with less than four minutes to play, the Blue Jays won on two lay-ups in the last 16 seconds, to snuff out Peabody's tourney aspirations.

The best way to measure this team's success is in the numerous records it set. Gene Ericksen's 705 points were most ever by a Peabody cager in a single season and second most ever, at the time, by a NIL performer. The team scoring average of 66.9 was a school and NIL record, as was the 1,942 point total overall. Ericksen, NIL scoring king, and Anderson, fifth in NIL scoring, both placed on the five man All-Nashville squad, while Ericksen became one of only two Peabodians ever to be honored on the All-State team. But greatest of all were the team wins which included PDS's first basketball trophy in 21 years and culminated in its best record ever, 24-5.

Graduating Ericksen, Anderson, and guard Louis Finkelstein, Peabody rebuilt on Bill Darby and Bill Stratvert in '59-60. Darby led the NIL scoring, while leading the Maroon and Blue to a 13-12 mark. The team highlighted its season with a rousing 48-46 upset of West on Darby's last second basket. Coming in fifth in the 18th District tournament, Peabody saw Bill Darby become the third cager in two years to make All-Nashville, this time for Darby's performance throughout the season at center. This season was an interlude, however and the *Nashville Banner* marked this, on February 13 after the West game, by saying "Harry Ward and Jack Gayden . . . promise to develop into crackerjack guards before they graduate . . . ." Certainly these sophomores lived up to that billing the next two years.

Juniors Harry Ward and Jack Gayden found themselves guiding the Tiger fortunes from the guard position in 1960-61. The team started slowly, losing five in a row to post a 2-5 mark after seven games. Then the team caught fire, especially after finishing the holidays with another victory in the M.T.I.T. Here the team finally got together, downing Murfreesboro, West, and BGA, all in the state tournament the year before, on successive nights to take the title for the second time in three years. To Coach Finch, this tournament was " . . . the best three night tour in Peabody history." It propelled the Tigers into the season as they rambled on to win 18 of their last 20 games, ending regular season play at a tremendous 20-7. Led by Ward, who led the NIL in scoring much of the year and ended with 501 markers, the team also featured Gayden, Jim Darby, and Tom Nixon at forwards and Robbie Lagemann at center.

The Tigers did not stop winning when the District 18 tournament came up as they took a state rating, which at times was as high as fourth, into the tourney. The Maroon and Blue defeated Mt. Juliet, West (avenging a final game of the season loss to the Jays), and Hume-Fogg to advance to the district finals. Here Ryan pressed the Tigers into submission 52-39, holding stars Ward and Gayden to a combined ten point total. However, this team became the first PDS team to advance to the Region 5 tournament.

Taking on Hume-Fogg in their first outing, PDS ousted them by 46-40, as Lagemann dumped in 13. Then going on to play Gallatin, the Demonstration School avenged an early season loss, by a count of 51-41. Again Lagemann was a key with 19 rebounds, while Gayden tickled the twine for 17 tallies. Now PDS was in the regional semi-finals, just one win away from a berth in the state tournament. In the semis, the Tigers ran into the Cinderella team from Donelson, which sported a terrible record but a lot of key wins. And once again the Dons took the game they needed as Peabody succumbed 50-37.

The year was a tremendous success though, as the Tigers advanced further in tournament play than any other PDS boys' basketball team, and also brought home the M.T.I.T trophy again. Ward's second place finish in the scoring race earned him a spot on the All-City team, while the team's second place finish in the district was also the best ever for a Peabody team.

With the mainstays Jack Gayden and Harry Ward returning for the 1961-62 campaigns, the outlook was strong for PDS. Playing along with these two seniors were Jack Smith at center and Ned Davis and Knox McCharen at forward, while Harvey Wilker played guard when Ward was positioned in the front line. Ward, chosen for *Dell Magazine's* All-America honor roll at the beginning of the season, proved his versatility as he played three positions during the year.

The season opened against rival West, whom the Tigers dumped 51-36, starting a long trek up in the state rankings. Ripping off eight wins in its first eleven games, the Maroon and Blue then collided with powerful Kittrell in what was, to say the least, a memorable game.

Kittrell, rated in the state's top ten all season, and at the time, No. 1 by Litkenhous, came to the MBA gym (where the game was moved from Peabody so the crowd could be accommodated) with "Monk" Montgomery averaging 30 points a game, and the team hitting a 70 point clip. Coach Finch attempted to counter this by moving Ward to a new position, center, and sent his light-weight crew into the tussle ready to play its usual aggressive defense. The Tigers started out hot and never let up, as Ward and Ned Davis blew PDS to a 36-29 half-time bulge. The third quarter opened with the visiting Devils getting the hot hand, eventually narrowing the PDS lead to 50-49. It was here that Ward made the difference, as he bucketed 10 of Peabody's 23 fourth quarter points to complete the stunning upset, 73-63. With teammate Gayden chipping in 18, Ward had led PDS to perhaps its greatest victory ever. The Demonstration School's fantastic performance was reflected in the torrid 52.3 field goal percentage with which they blistered the nets.

Rocketing off this victory to a state spot which reached as high as fourth, PDS eventually finished second in the 18th district play to Cohn.

Carrying a 17-7 record into the tournaments, PDS barely nudged Hume-Fogg from the competition, 42-40, as Harvey Wilker dumped in a spectacular last second lay-up. Encountering Lipscomb's Mustangs, Peabody suffered a 60-51 defeat at the hands of one Clyde Lee, who dumped in 28 points to knock the Tigers into the crucial consolation game against Cohn. Here, with a bid to the Region V tourney on the line, Peabody rose again, handing the Black Knights a solid defeat.

For the second year in a row, PDS was appearing in the region tournament. Clobbering Greenbrier 54-29, the Tigers prepared to meet the East Eagles for the third time in the year, having beaten the Eagles just two weeks prior to the tourney clash. However, the Demonstration School's lack of height caught up with it, and the season ended with a 50-36 count against Peabody.

The end of this season was the end of another era in Peabody sports. Not only were veterans Harry Ward and Jack Gayden graduating, but Coach Dan Finch was closing his coaching duties after six years at PDS.

Ward and Gayden, who played on Peabody teams that won a total of 85 games, closed their magnificent careers; Ward being honored for the second year on the All-Nashville team and also being named second team All-State. Ward, the most prolific scorer in the annals of Peabody cage history, at a total of 1,446 points, had led the 1961-62 team to a final record of 20-9. Gayden, for his part, had played in Ward's shadow for much of the three years, but in his own right was a great player, as he combined both strong defense and strong offense, netting 1,112 points in his career. With their graduation came the loss of Peabody's last winning basketball team to date.

Coach Finch also closed out his career at the end of the 1961-62 campaign; former PDS star, Ben Rowan, was his successor. Finch, with a six-year record of 107-57, had taken over a team in 1954-55 which lost as a way of life, and molded it into a winning outfit. Returning several years later, and coaching continuously from 1957-62, Finch established a winning tradition at PDS, which overflowed the little gymnasium. With great players like Gayden, Ward, Bill Darby, Gene Ericksen, and Ed Anderson, Finch forged a powerful machine which instilled fear in the opponents and tremendous spirit in the students, who, according to Coach Finch, made the difference in more than one or two winning efforts. These great teams were culled from a collection of possibly 110 eligible boys, certainly the smallest in Nashville; yet, Coach Finch was able to garner state rankings and region tournament victories. He summed up these years best when he said, "Well, at least they aren't playing the subs against Peabody any more."

Chapter 5
Student Government at Peabody Demonstration School

The S.A.C. [Student Activities Committee] seems to have been the most active council of the school's history, as far as initiating social events is concerned, and the disciplinary function seen in early councils has practically disappeared. Some of the projects of the S.A.C. since 1955 have been: a Book Week Assembly, the painting of a classroom, the donation of a television to the library, and a Career Day. In 1958 the S.A.C. organized a pep band and a citizenship committee. In 1965-66 Peabody began an exchange program with students from another school. This program was carried out for three years and involved public high schools in Vicksburg, Michigan, Ames, Iowa, and a private school, Francis W. Parker School in Chicago, Illinois.

Until recent years, the S.A.C. has retained basically the same type of organization with only a few significant changes since its organization in 1950. In 1964, the constitution was amended to provide for the election of S.A.C. representatives biannually instead of annually. The Junior High (grades 7 and 8) declared its independence in 1967 from the Senior High and set up its own student government. This revolutionary council lasted only three years, however; as it was eliminated when the Middle School (grades 6-8) was formed in 1969. The discontinuation of student government in those grades is, according to the administration, an attempt to avoid the creation of "super-stars" so that every student has an equal role.

The S.A.C. expanded its interests in 1968 to include curriculum with the establishment of the Student Curriculum Committee. The main project of this group was the engineering of "Student Education Day," when students decided what they wanted to learn and, using lectures, seminars, and workshops, planned their curriculum for a day. Student Education Day was expanded to two days in 1969. The day was held on "Earth Day" in 1970, but participation was small.

The fourth phase of student government is more difficult to identify because the school and the nation appears to be in the midst of a transition in student government philosophy. In recent years the theory of the three areas of authority in a school has been questioned, particularly in colleges and universities; students have been asking for more voice in the area formerly reserved for the administration. This idea is now filtering down to the high school level and at Peabody is apparent in recent Student Activities Committee projects, such as the revision of the dress code and especially Student Education Day.

In 1970, Dr. L.E. Pratt recognized a need for more cooperation among students, teachers, administration and parents, with the establishment of the Advisory Committee. This committee, which acts in a strictly advisory capacity, has representatives from faculty, parents and students. Its purpose is to provide a forum for airing a variety of opinions on issues vital to the successful operation of the school.

In summary, it appears that there have been at least three phases in the history of student government at Peabody Demonstration School, and at the time of this writing a fourth phase seems to be commencing. The first phase, represented by the Cooperative Student Council, had a largely disciplinary function. The Student-Faculty Planning Committee, the second phase of student government, provided for serious cooperation between students and teachers and emphasized learning citizenship through experience in government. The first years of the Student Activities Committee marked a third phase. The S.A.C. was an exclusively student organization which concentrated its activities on social events, rather than discipline, the formulation of school policies, or the curriculum. The fourth phase has commenced in the last few years. The S.A.C. is currently revising its constitution, and included in this revision is a re-evaluation of the goals of the S.A.C. At this point, the trend appears to be toward making student government a means to represent the interests of the students in all matters pertinent to their education at the school, including matters of curriculum as well as extra curricular activities.

Chapter 6
Dramatic Productions and Special Events

The first dramatic activity at the Demonstration School came in its first year of existence! Near the end of the school year 1915-1916, the eighth grade put on a short play entitled "The Steadfast Princess" under the auspices of its English teacher, Miss Ruth MacMurry. It should be mentioned here that many such plays have probably been produced by the lower grades, and, as nothing was written down about them at the time, they have been completely forgotten except by the participants.

The first of many operas directed by Mr. D.R. Gebhart, the very popular Glee Club instructor, was "Pinafore." This Gilbert and Sullivan production was given in the old Orpheum Theatre in May, 1917. The following year, Mr. Gebhart continued in the Gilbert and Sullivan tradition by producing "The Mikado" in the same theater. All productions between 1916 and 1925, the year the present school building was opened, were given either in the Orpheum or on the Peabody College Campus. These operas were very elaborate, involving a cast, chorus, and group for musical accompaniment, and, as might be expected, each opera was the climax of an entire spring of rehearsals and hard work.

Mr. Gebhart began work on "Chimes of Normandy" in 1918, but abandoned the project for one year in favor of Balfe's "Sleeping Queen." This four-character opera was given outdoors on the Peabody College campus on a May evening. Mr. Gebhart also directed the fourth, fifth, and sixth grades in a cantata, "The Three Springs." The following year found Mr. Gebhart producing, in addition to "Chimes of Normandy," an operetta called "The Feast of the Red Corn" with the fifth grade.

The opera of 1921 was a huge production and a great success. The cast, chorus, and group of dancers totaled 71 people, all directed by Mr. Gebhart and Miss Ruth MacMurry. Mr. Gebhart described the event in the Annual:

> *Artistically, the opera was a success; financially, it was a success; as an*
> *illustration of what high schools should do in the line of entertainment, it*
> *was a success. There was not a real hitch or bobble in the performance . . . .*
> *Will Carter was a heroic 'Thaeus,' and played his part much better than is*
> *usually done in professional companies.*

In 1923, Mr. Gebhart directed his sixth full-scale opera at the Demonstration School—Gilbert and Sullivan's "The Two Vagabonds." The productive association of the Demonstration School and Mr. Gebhart ended in 1925 after the productions of Gilbert and Sullivan's "The Pirate of Penzance" and a second elementary school version of "The Feast of the Red Corn."

These first years of the School saw the inception of several traditions and the presentation of many fine programs. The first Dramatic Society was founded in 1918 under the sponsorship of the high school English teacher, Miss Flemma Snidow. Will Carter, later known professionally as Jacques Cartier, was the president of this club in its first two years and vice president in 1921, the year he graduated. Other activities included two skits by the Girl Reserve Corps, one about a débutante and the other a black-face comedy; the French Club, *Les Bonnes Amies*, gave a play entitled "Every Girl," the proceeds of which went toward the support of French World War I orphans, and the Annual was partially financed by a Stunt Night program that filled the auditorium of the Social Religious Building beyond capacity and produced $150 profit. The Dramatic Society of 1919-1920 gave a Christmas program and two short plays in March, "Making Good" and "Just Women." The second Stunt Night included one act in particular that reflected the social consciousness of the Demonstration School students, a skit entitled "A Suffrage Meeting, As Men Imagine It;" women had just been given the right to vote.

A fundamental Demonstration School tradition was established on Easter morning, 1919. The eleventh grade (the first graduating class) had held a class picnic earlier in the spring with such success that they decided to repeat the adventure. The junior class met before dawn at the Social Religious Building, and drove until they found a suitable spot on the banks of a small creek. By cooking their breakfast, they set a precedent for a tradition that has endured for 31 years, the Easter Breakfast. (The first Junior-Senior Banquet was not held until May, 1922.)

....

E.J. Gatwood, a musician and choral director from the Peabody College Music Department, took over direction of the Demonstration School's musical program and Glee Club in the fall of 1926. He began work on the sonata "Pan" during this school year, but had to suspend the project for one year. Gatwood, sometimes assisted by Peabody College drama majors, continued to produce musicals at the Demonstration School until the school year 1938-1939. His second production, aided by Miss Bantam, was a repetition of the 1923 opera, Gilbert and Sullivan's "The Pirates of Penzance." Two more Gilbert and Sullivan operas were given in 1932 and 1933, "Pinafore" and "Chimes of Normandy," both of which had been done before at the Demonstration School by D.R. Gebhart. Gatwood directed two operas in 1935: "Jerry of Jericho Road" and "Maid in Japan." In 1936, a shortened version of the opera "Bon Voyage" was presented on the school's second radio broadcast on "Teacher's College of the Air." This program also featured short speeches on the purposes of the broadcast by Dr. W.H. Yarbrough, Dr. A.L. Crabb of Peabody College, and Dr. Joseph Roemer.

Gatwood's Glee club formed the core of the production of Gilbert and Sullivan's "The Two Vagabonds" in 1937. In addition to this undertaking, he directed the sixth and seventh grades in the operetta "The Feast of the Little Lanterns." The opera of 1938 was Mr. Gatwoods's second production of "The Pirates of Penzance," and the influence of the movies was reflected when "Hollywood Bound" was presented in 1939. The last Demonstration School production directed by Gatwood was Gilbert and Sullivan's "Chimes of Normandy" in 1940.

Other activities flourished during Gatwood's stay at the Demonstration School. The seventh grade undertook an ambitious project in Shakespeare's "A Midsummer Night's Dream" for the May Festival of 1927. The newly formed Cinema Club made a mystery movie called "Masque," which was praised in passing by both *Movie Makers* and *Photoplay*. The Cinema Club of 1928-1929 produced two films and a one-act play. One of the films was another mystery movie, named "Retribution," and the other was an unnamed three-character comedy; the play was "Spring." This club bought much lighting equipment for these filmings, and this proved very useful in later dramatic productions.

....

After 1949, the various school functions were shifted and juggled constantly in an attempt to find a schedule that would not have an unacceptable number of special nights to prepare for, but would stir interest among the students. The Senior Tea, given by the faculty in early spring for the seniors and their parents, was substituted for the Easter Breakfast for a few years, but died from lack of interest in 1954. The Easter Breakfast itself was revived in 1954 and 1955, but then disappeared until 1970. The last homecoming celebration was in the fall of 1950, as the football team was disbanded in the middle of the following season. There was for a time a big party called the Junior Hoop-Dee-Doo, and Christmas Carol Services were sometimes given. The Valentine Dance was first held in 1953, and has continued more or less regularly until the present time. Senior Proms became annual affairs around 1960. In addition to these, there have been assorted S.A.C. sponsored parties, picnics, spaghetti suppers, PTA dinners, a 1953 *Volunteer* Stunt Night, and a 1960 Senior Play entitled "Chicken on the Roof."

The Dramatic Club was not actively revived until 1966-1967, when Paul George formed a group in the second semester of this year. The club produced "Pierrot, Poltroon" under the direction of Chris Schoggen, a senior member of the club.

James Stelling, an English teacher from the Nashville public schools, took over the club sponsorship in 1967-1968; and produced three one-act plays: "the Blind," "Ana De Capo," and "Zoo Story." "The Crucible," a five-act play produced later in the spring, featured some brilliant ad lib when one of the characters forgot to bring on a prop and threw off an important entrance. The dialogue became hopelessly fouled up for about 10 minutes of the play. Stelling also taught a summer drama workshop that culminated in productions of "A Midsummer Night's Dream" and "Antigone" in August. The Drama Club of 1968-1969 gave three April performances of the French comedy, "Madwoman of Chaillot." In Jim Stellling's summer of 1969 workshop, productions of "Electra," "The Bald Soprano" and "Thieves' Carnival" were presented.

John Offutt, another teacher from Nashville public high schools, took charge of a Drama Class in 1970 that has so far produced four one-act plays: "Twelve Angry Men," The Brick and the Rose," "Egad What a Cad," and "Endgame." Plans are being made at this time for a May production of a longer play, "The Ghost Sonata." The last two of these reflect the current Demonstration School trend toward the Theater of the Absurd playwrights which began with the production of Ionesco's "The Bald Soprano."

Chapter 7
Administrators and Faculty

Dr. Robert Owens Beauchamp, who taught in the science department at Peabody Demonstration School beginning in 1923, became associate director in 1947, and held an administrative position longer than any other person in the school's history. Beauchamp majored in physical science at Peabody and received his B.S. degree in 1924. Still pursuing his interest in science, he went on to earn his M.S. and Ph.D degrees at Peabody, while also doing graduate work in physical and industrial chemistry at Vanderbilt. As associate director, Dr. Beauchamp advised all high school students, planned their schedules, communicated with colleges on behalf of students, and handled all records. His belief in high standards of education has been a distinct and lasting contribution to the spirit of Peabody Demonstration School.

....

Dr. William Knox McCharen came to Peabody in 1951. McCharen was raised on an eighty-acre farm in Toccopola, Mississippi, where his parents taught him that hard work was no disgrace and that responsibility builds character. These teachings left a lasting impression upon him.

As an undergraduate at the University of Mississippi, McCharen majored in education. To pay for his expenses at college, he and one of his three brothers managed a farm. He taught high school mathematics at McCool, Mississippi, in 1922-24. By 1926, he had received his Bachelor of Arts degree from the University of Mississippi and had accepted a position as principal and coach in Winona, Mississippi. From 1927-1932, McCharen acted as superintendent of schools in McCool, Mississippi. He came to Nashville for the first time in 1932 when he entered George Peabody College where he received a B.A. degree in school administration and a degree in library science. While working toward his degrees, McCharen served as librarian at Tennessee Polytechnic Institute, and also taught courses in library science. His students say that he was practical and thorough in his teaching and that he employed simple but meaningful methods.

McCharen was appointed a member of the training division of Tennessee Valley Authority in 1935, where he was in charge of the whole educational program. McCharen left his position with T.V.A in 1940 to become head librarian at Middle Tennessee State University; later becoming chairman of the department of education. McCharen developed an interest in small community schools which led him to often load his car with students to drive to rural schools to observe and study their problems; he did his doctoral dissertation on the subject of community schools in the South. In 1947, McCharen received his doctorate degree from Peabody College and became associate director of the Division of Surveys and Field Services in 1949. McCharen worked with other leading educators to make a survey of school systems throughout the country.

McCharen became director of Peabody Demonstration School in 1951. He often taught classes in order to continue his understanding of the classroom problems of the teacher. To better understand the problems of the students, he sponsored the Student Activities Committee, taking great interest in the organization.

McCharen's devotion to his work, his sense of humor, and understanding of other people's problems made him very popular at the Demonstration School. His emphasis on a warm and informal atmosphere will never be forgotten by the students who attended during his years as director: 1951-1968. He still works with young people today as state director of the High School Student Ambassador Program.

Chapter 8
Curriculum Development and Extracurricular Activities

The students of the school, in general, do not recognize what educational theory is behind the learning situation in which they are placed, and memories of graduates over the years remain pretty much the same. The oldest graduates have memories of the classrooms in the basement of the Psychology Building or the Stucco Building—the "Keep Off the Grass" signs on the lawns, the flowers and plants in the classrooms, the scratched and initialed desks, and the smell of chalk dust. Those who have attended since the present building was constructed have similar memories and others, such as working in Miss Pitts' garden, feeding the animals, and watching fish in the aquarium float magically by in the little sea. All can remember tiptoeing "like little mice" to the restroom, and the pranks they played when there were a bit older and "wiser." But these priceless memories do little to explain how and why learning took place. Perhaps one of the reasons for this lapse of memory is because the teachers at the Demonstration School have always labored heroically to make the learning process fun rather than work.

The team-teaching method adopted recently is new to the Demonstration School, but most teachers in even the earliest years were not alone in the classroom. The school has had throughout its history a large staff of resource teachers and specialists who contributed greatly to the educational environment—specialists in music, physical education, art, guidance, and so forth. Students at the Demonstration School have also been blessed with many fine student teachers, adding greatly to the amount of individual attention which may be given to each child in the classroom. Thus, teaching has always been a team effort at the Demonstration School.

....

In 1949, Hazel Lundberg started a Math Club at Peabody and continued as sponsor for a decade. She recalls the first Math Club as being busy decorating their room. The members drew designs on the walls, made drapes and geometric designs in them, and used their art work for pictures to hang on the walls. The club took many field trips to banks, insurance companies, and businesses with new computers. Professors often spoke to the club on topics related to mathematics. The club's meeting varied from collecting for the needy to solving tedious puzzle problems. Several members of the club participated in the Tennessee Teachers Mathematics Association contest, which was and still is the main contest each year. While Mrs. Lundberg sponsored the club, Peabody won the Middle Tennessee division each year. In all the years that the state scores were figured, Peabody came in first. Many individuals from the Math Club won the highest honors in the State of Tennessee. In 1968, Mrs. Lundberg left Peabody and with the loss of a dedicated teacher came also the loss of the Math Club.

Although there is no club, the math teachers at Peabody continue to prepare the excelling students for the math contests. In 1969, Peabody ranked second in the state of Tennessee, and students won regional and other honors. In 1970, Peabody still retains their outstanding mathematicians, for representatives are still being sent to Birmingham, Alabama, for the contests.

Records concerning the Science Club date back to 1937. Its purpose was to further the interest of its members in the field of science. The club even published a magazine composed of articles condensed from current periodicals. The activities of the Science Club after 1951 are vague until 1960 when Mr. Lawrence Bradley reorganized the club to supplement classroom activities.

Until 1969, the club met twice a month, but because of a new computer project, the club now finds it necessary to meet every week. Gregg Williams, a senior at Peabody, is currently conducting a class in computer programming. This project seems to be very interesting to Science Club members, especially since the students have access to the computer on the Peabody College campus. The National Science Club of America has definite goals to which Peabody Science Club members adhere. The club has been honored by many guest speakers over the years, and has made several trips to Vanderbilt University and the Bill Wilkerson Hearing and Speech Center, all to increase their knowledge of science.

A Nature Club was organized in the spring of 1936 with membership limited to sixteen students. The purpose of the club was to develop powers of accurate observation and to foster an appreciation of the dignity and beauty of the out-of-doors. In 1938, a Bird Club was organized at Peabody. The members learned to recognize the different bird families and also learned more about the bird's nesting and migrating habits. The Bird Club's meetings consisted of lectures, discussions, slides, and movies. Evidently, this club was still active in 1942, for in that year the club was engrossed in making feeding stations for the birds in the winter months. This interest in our natural environment still exists at Peabody today; however, recent interest has been in the preservation of the natural environment, rather than its study. The threat of pollution is of major concern to the student body, and the Youths for Environmental Stability (Y.E.S.) has been organized.

Chapter 9
Student Body and Alumni

Another graduate working in the field of history is Robert K. Massie, who has combined history and literature with a happy result. Massie, co-editor of the *Volunteer* and quarterback of one of Peabody's great football teams, graduated in 1945. While a student at the Demonstration School, Bob Massie excelled, above all, in history and writing; several of his stories and essays appeared in school publications. Since graduation, he attended Yale on a scholarship (Class of 1950) and Oxford for three years on a Rhodes Scholarship. He served for three and a half years in the Naval Air Intelligence, stationed in Korea and the Mediterranean, then turned to a career as a journalist, writing for such magazines as *Collier's*, *Newsweek*, and the *Saturday Evening Post*.

More recently, he has written a book *Nicholas and Alexandra*, concerning the last Russian Czar. The book, which was on the best seller list for weeks, is to be made into a movie. At present, this Peabody graduate is in Paris, working on a book on Peter the Great.

Many graduates of the Demonstration School have entered the medical profession, perhaps influenced in their decision by science teachers such as R.O. Beauchamp. One of the best known of the Demonstration School graduates currently in the field of medicine is Dr. George Mayfield, a certified Anatomic and Clinical Pathologist. Dr. Mayfield is a graduate in the class of 1944. He attended Vanderbilt University for his college and medical studies (Phi Beta Kappa and A.O.A.). Today, Dr. Mayfield is a practicing pathologist, serving many hospitals in the State of Tennessee. He resides in Columbia, Tennessee, but his practice takes him all over the State. He still finds time, however, to pursue his interest in nature study and music which teachers at the Demonstration School fostered twenty-five years ago.

Many Demonstration School graduates have remained in Nashville and are now outstanding members of the community. At least three of them have returned to Peabody Demonstration School as faculty. Teaching in Nursery School is Miss Gean Morgan, a 1931 graduate. She has been teaching at Peabody Demonstration School for 24 years. Marvin Wilker, a Middle School math teacher, was graduated from the Demonstration School in 1964. Before returning to this school, he spent four years at Emory University in Atlanta, Georgia, and taught in a Nashville City School. Charles E.L. McCary, a French teacher in the Middle School and the High School was a 1952 graduate. After Peabody Demonstration School, he attended the University of Lausanne and Vanderbilt University. Not only has he spent many years at Peabody, but his parents, Joe T. McCary and Caroline Little McCary, were 1923 Peabody grads.

Chapter 10
The Past is Prologue

When Dr. Fink again donned his uniform, the third of the Demonstration School's great administrators took the helm. Knox McCharen, that genial little man with the wry sense of humor, took charge and remained in charge until his retirement in 1968. Dr. McCharen was a traditionalist in educational theory, but he fervently believed that the teacher was in command in the classroom and should be free to experiment with methods and techniques, which promised better learning situations for the students. He cultivated that friendly, informal atmosphere which has become a mark of the Demonstration School, and accomplished wonders in harmonizing the conflicting educational theories which were so divisive among educators and teachers. Dr. McCharen's students remember him for his unusual knowledge of human nature; his special knack of dispensing an encouraging, or on the other hand, discouraging word at the proper moment. His special interest in student government took the S.A.C. to new heights.

One must also mention Dr. McCharen's associate director, Dr. R.O. Beauchamp, who stood with him like a rock in defending quality education at the Demonstration School and fostering the "spirit of Peabody." Dr. Beauchamp is a distinguished science teacher who had taught at the Demonstration School since 1923 before becoming associate director in 1947. It is believed that Dr. Beauchamp holds the record of longest service to the school, having been associated with it for forty-three years before his retirement in 1966.

In carrying out our theme of the dialectical quality of the history of the school, we find that the McCharen administration represented a synthesis, a harmonizing, of conflicting forces. The early history of the school, to the end of Yarbrough's administration, was characterized by a traditional and academic approach to education. This is not to say there was no opposition to such a program; there was a healthy opposition which supported the progressive theories. During the Thirties and Forties, under Joseph Roemer and especially J.E. Windrow, progressive theories were implemented in the school curriculum; courses were added which emphasized skills and preparation for life, rather than academic preparation for college. Of course, the traditional program was not abandoned; it still had many vociferous adherents, and besides, academic courses are preparation for life for those who plan to attend college and enter business and the professions, which most graduates of the school have and still do. But, there was a definite movement toward progressivism during the Windrow years.

The synthesis of these conflicting theories of education was accomplished during the McCharen years, because of McCharen's belief in the autonomy of the teacher in the classroom. Each teacher was allowed to carry out his own methods, whether traditional or progressive, by which he achieved the best results in the classroom. Rather than supporting a specific theory, Dr. McCharen did his utmost to foster a spirit of freedom and a friendly atmosphere conducive to learning at the Demonstration School.

One of the problems of the analysis of any history in dialectical terms is that the dialectic progression is perpetual—stability is never achieved; there are always new conflicts, new controversies, new challenges. The synthesis achieved during the McCharen years gave the school a certain stability, but it could not endure forever—the result could be stagnation. Arnold Toynbee developed a thesis in his study of world history which might be appropriate to mention at this point. He concluded that the challenges with which a people were faced created their civilization. When challenge no longer existed, stagnation occurred with consequent decay and an eventual end to civilization. There is little doubt that the same concept is applicable to the history of the Peabody Demonstration School. The end to conflict and controversy—the end to challenge—would mean the decay and eventual termination of the existence of the Demonstration School.

Today the Demonstration School is again meeting its challenges in the spirit of adventure bequeathed to it by its predecessors, renewing its quest for excellence in education. The "Peabody family" greatly regretted Dr. McCharen's retirement, but the new administration has taken up the challenges facing the school with vigor. The winds of change are blowing through the hallowed halls of Peabody Demonstration School.

....

What should one call this new approach—this effort to continue the heritage of achievement of Peabody Demonstration School on the basis of a realistic assessment of the situation? The authors would like to suggest the "New Pragmatism," or, as one wag in the group punned, the "New Prattmatism." Names, of course, are unimportant; what is important is that new efforts are being made to meet the challenges which have faced Peabody Demonstration School since its very inception.

The authors have found that Peabody Demonstration School possesses a remarkably loyal student body, and it retains that loyalty after the students have left to make their own places in the world. It is perhaps this intense loyalty and feeling of belonging which is the school's greatest asset and its hope for the future.

The authors also believe that the school's greatest present handicap is the outdated physical plant which is in need of major renovation and the construction of additional space. The building when it was constructed in 1925 was probably the finest in the Southland and it is still a basically sound structure which could serve the Nashville and Peabody community for another half century. But the wear and tear of fifty years, during which perhaps ten thousand students have attended, is beginning to be seen. The building is in need of extensive modernization to meet the demands of space-age education.

Of course, the renovations cannot be commenced until the necessary financial support is forthcoming. The school operated on a deficit for years and was a heavy burden on the budget of Peabody College. Recent increases in the tuition rate have made the school practically self-supporting in its day-to-day operations, but there are no funds available for large scale improvements in the physical plant. The authors have observed that the renovations which have occurred since the school was originally constructed have been financed largely by the alumni and friends of the school in the "Peabody family." The support of its patrons is vital to the continuing efforts of the school to provide quality education in the Southland.

In writing the history of the Demonstration School, the authors found that the keeping of many records which would enlighten the history of the school has been neglected. Complete files of the school newspaper have not been collected and secured; as a result, much information which would have been invaluable in the creation of the history of the school has been lost. Over the past half century of the school's history, hundreds, perhaps thousands of experiments, tests, and studies have been made by college students, college professors, and Demonstration School staff which have utilized the resources of the school. The students of the school are the subjects of what seems a continuous cavalcade of programs designed to test this teaching method, support that doctoral dissertation, and so forth. Yet, records of these investigations appear to have generally disappeared. The authors were able to locate a few such studies collected in the Peabody College Library, but they strongly believe that some record of each of these investigations should be retained in the Demonstration School itself, perhaps bound and collected in the faculty or administrative libraries.

The authors deplore the loss of contact with alumni which has occurred (the last important effort to locate and communicate with *all* alumni took place in 1946), and it lauds the revival of the custom of the Easter Breakfast reunion during 1970. They strongly believe that the support of the thousands of distinguished alumni of the school is paramount to continued service by the school.

Peabody Demonstration School has completed its first half century of service. It faces the next half century with the same spirit of adventure which brought the pioneers to Middle Tennessee two hundred years ago. Rumors to the effect that the existence of the school was about to terminate have circulated sporadically through the Nashville community for more than thirty years, but, as Mark Twain was reputed to have said when an account of his death was circulated: "The reports of my death are greatly exaggerated." J.E. Windrow was told by certain friends when he accepted the directorship of the Demonstration School in 1937 that he was making a mistake; the job was a dead end. Dr. Windrow remembers this with considerable amusement today. "There is something tough about the school," he says. The authors are convinced that the "something tough" is the "Peabody spirit"—the warm feeling of association in the quest for excellence in education.

A Sampling of Work by the Historical Methods Class

From 2000 until 2006, his first years as Director of University School of Nashville, Vince Durnan taught a seminar class for seniors called "Historical Method," in part as a way to learn about the school's story and in part to connect with the student experience here. The class aimed to research and write the history of the school since the transition time of the 1970s, following a precedent set by *The Past Is Prologue*, created by the PDS American Problems class in 1970. Students conducted scores of interviews, visited archives, and read primary source documents, searching for a definitive version of events that had already become the stuff of legend. The dream in those years was to publish another book, but the research always overwhelmed the editing in a race to a finished product. Selected passages directly from some of their papers follow, as examples of what was a great educational adventure. We present them without further editing; this is the work submitted by the students.

From a January, 2002 paper
JACKSON MURLEY
Class of 2002

The class leaped at the chance to interview Dr. Ida Long Rogers, a longtime Peabody faculty member and administrator, on her role as co-author of the 1974 report which recommended closing PDS. John Dunworth, upon assuming the presidency of Peabody in early 1974, commissioned a report on the future role of the College, "Design for the Future," from a select committee of three highly respected faculty members, including Dr. Rogers, Jack Allen, and Raymond C. Norris, with the mandate to "dream big." Dunworth's background had all been focused on public education, and he preferred mainstreaming teachers in public schools.

According to Dr. Rogers, he was not very popular with the faculty and with certain members on the select committee. The report recommended that the College be broadly restructured, cutting or trimming many departments. Often referring to the Field Services Report of the year before, the Committee recommended on the subject of PDS that:

> *Inasmuch as the Peabody Demonstration School cannot assume a*
> *major laboratory school role for the college and cannot become a fiscally*
> *independent, high quality private school under a comprehensive program of*
> *cost accounting, the Peabody Demonstration School should be closed.*

On the morning of August 29, 1974, the Board approved the recommendations of the report, deciding to cease operating PDS after May 1975, to a standing ovation. Later that day, Registration Day 1974, the closure was announced.

Dr. Ida Long Rogers asserts that the Demonstration School "should have seen it coming."

Yet faculty, staff, faculty and parents universally proclaimed shock upon hearing news of Peabody's decision. Even the much-beloved Heber Rogers, at the time Associate Director, said he reacted "like a bombshell had been dropped." Peabody conducted evaluations and issued reports every few years, but the reports became increasingly urgent with the worsening financial situation of the College as a whole and the recession in the U.S. economy. Dr. Pratt's reports seem to become ever more defensive, especially the December 1973 report in which he argued in revealing language that the school was not useless to the College and that he should have more influence over what the school's financial responsibilities are and how they should be evaluated.

However, PDS had been showing a willingness to strengthen cooperation with the College. The Demonstration School Faculty in early 1974 recommended expanding student and Peabody faculty teaching program and increasing interaction. Dr. Pratt reported in May 1974 that "We are convinced that the School can contribute heavily to the central purpose of the College. To do so, however, there must be communication and planning between the two faculties, and the School needs to share in the program of the College." Dunworth wrote PDS patroness Peggy Hays a few days after this report, assuring her that "I agree that Peabody should have a fine Demonstration School as an integral part of its teacher education programs."

The Select Committee Report describes the laboratory school theory as "vestigial remains of an earlier era in teacher education in America" and the conversion of PDS to a laboratory school as educationally and economically unfeasible. The only other option in the eyes of the Select Committee was the transformation of PDS to "strictly a private school serving only the needs of its clientele." University School today, though independent, provides demonstration and student teaching for Belmont and Peabody, proving the fallacy of the "all-or-nothing" options presented by the Committee. The Committee concluded that PDS "cannot become a fiscally independent, high quality private school," arguing that "the income level of the Demonstration School would have to be increased very substantially (probably by as much as 50%) if it were to become an economically viable institution." The tuition would have to be raised $550 or more per student to $1500, a tuition $200 dollars more than that of Harpeth Hall and Montgomery Bell Academy. Some of the new income (approximately $400,000 per year) that would need to be raised would, according to the Committee, go towards raising faculty salaries by a total of about $132,000 per year in order for the school to retain and hire teachers at "an acceptable professional standard" (however, the school had consistently attracted excellent teachers at salaries below public school levels), but most would go towards a one time cost for physical plant renovations estimated at $325,000. The new costs do not add up to balance such a high tuition raise. The financial justifications in this section appear weakly supported and greatly exaggerated.

In spite of the decision of Peabody to close the school, PDS was far from defeated. The last sentence of *The Past Is Prologue* reflects on former Director Dr. J. E. Windrow's assessment that "There is something tough about this school": "The authors are convinced that the 'something tough' is the 'Peabody spirit'—the warm feeling of association in the quest for excellence in education."

SOURCES

The Past is Prologue —Peabody Demonstration School 1915-1970, 1969-70 American Problems Class (L. Johnson, ed.), 1970.

J. Allen, R. Norris, and I.L. Rogers, *Design for the Future —A Report From the Select Committee on Peabody's Second Century to President John Dunworth and the Board of Trustees*, August 24, 1974. Appendix C: "Rationale for the Recommendation to Close the Peabody Demonstration School" was used for this article.

The Role of the Peabody Demonstration School: A Study Report, Division of Surveys and Field Services (George Peabody College for Teachers), May 1973. Files from archive box number 2095, Vanderbilt University Special Collections. Files quoted from include: John Dunworth to Mrs. J. W. Hays, May 16, 1974; L. Edward Pratt, *Report to The President of George Peabody College*, December 19, 1973.

"The Transition: PDS to USN"

CAROLINE PIGOTT
Class of 2006

The ultimate decision to close Peabody Demonstration School may have come as an unpleasant surprise on August 29, 1974, but the context surrounding this announcement had been developing over the past decade. In the years preceding the closing of PDS, the importance of laboratory schools was called into question across the country, and PDS was no exception. Six years before, on September 30, 1968, John M. Claunch sent his "Memorandum" to the Peabody faculty under the subject heading: "The Role of the Demonstration School." He addressed the difficulty in maintaining a demonstration school amidst the growing consensus that they are not needed. He said, "the high cost of living is making it increasingly difficult for private colleges to maintain such schools." And, thus, he asked for the assistance of the PDS faculty members in helping him search for the justifications of keeping the Demonstration School alive. Among the responses, a general opinion regarding the decline of demonstration schools pointed toward a failure in communication between the demonstration school faculties and college faculties.[1]

A Demonstration School's purpose is to synthesize "observation, practice teaching, and experimentation into a single entity." Just as the Demonstration School had trouble finding its own voice amid the college campus, the school continued to experience controversy over supporting its belief in its practices. Since 1915, its first year as an institution, PDS experienced "a continuing healthy conflict over the purposes of the school," requiring "constant self-examination and constant renewal."[2] Every two to three years, from about 1959 to 1974, a feasibility study was conducted looking at the function of the Dem School. In addition to this period of self-reflection, the decline of the Dem School also has its roots in outside influences. In 1963, the city government and metro merged to produce new options for teachers. Peabody College and metro came up with two centers: a secondary track practice teaching and an elementary track practice teaching. This new system eventually led to the decrease in the number of practice teachers coming to PDS, for it was "more realistic than a private school" and lab schools across the nation were losing recognition and closing.[3]

As PDS struggled to define itself in the context of a true "demonstration" school, different teaching methods and overall purposes of the school conflicted. For instance, the question of "student teaching and observation vs. experimental research and theory development . . . " created an "almost impossible burden of multiple purposes." In 1972, the Peabody Board of Trustees voted that the Division of Surveys and Field Services prepare a report that examines the role of PDS. Objectives for the report include determining the role of PDS, identifying possible alternatives to the role, and assessing fully the possible roles. The report noted a significant enrollment increase in the 1971-1972 school year. This increase led to problems in which questions arose: "Can the school continue to serve both the 'demonstration purposes' for the college and the desires of an increased clientele without alienating the clientele on whose support the school now depends?" The report cited that 75% of college departments and 85% of college faculty sampled made little or no use of the Dem School.[4]

The report's ultimate findings and conclusions state that, for the most part, the role of the school was buried. At this point, during the '72-'73 school year, the school served primarily as a college preparatory school in which the lab role was secondary. In closing, the report offers alternative roles for the schools: 1) to serve as a private college prep school. 2) to establish the lab function as the school's primary role. However, the authors believe that switching the foremost role of the school to that of a lab would not be feasible with all the financial pressures on the college. They say that the most justifiable and practicable role is to 1)meet the educational needs of the paying clientele and 2)provide the broadest services to the college program "without adversely affecting the compatibility of the two purposes." However, instead of consequently suggesting its closing, the report concluded that PDS should work more to serve the college in order to justify the relationship between the two.[5]

In 1974, John Dunworth was sworn into the position of Peabody College president, and after a short time, commissioned the report "Design for the Future" to examine the future role of the college. The group of three faculty members chosen to write the report, making up the Select Committee included Professors Jack Allen, Raymond C. Norris, and Ida Long Rogers. The report suggested that the college make multiple improvements, including the cutting or trimming of specific departments. The committee ultimately came to the conclusion that the Dem School close, citing their reasons in the article under Appendix C entitled *Rationale for the Recommendation to Close the Peabody Demonstration School*. This article very much reflects the finding of the aforementioned Field Services report, explaining the "conflicting goals" of the school which ultimately creates an "almost impossible burden of multiple purposes."[6] The Rationale report cites the Field Studies report, saying, in regard to the 1972-1973 school year, the school "must be described primarily as a private college preparatory school, providing only limited laboratory functions which do not interfere with its major function." The final word from the Select Committee:

> *Inasmuch as the Peabody Demonstration School cannot assume a*
> *major laboratory school role for the college and cannot become a fiscally*
> *independent, high quality private school under a comprehensive program of*
> *cost accounting, the Peabody Demonstration School should be closed.*

On August 29, 1974, the Board approved the report's recommendation. After the upcoming '74-'75 school year, PDS would close.

Over at PDS the same day, Registration Day was already under way. PDS Director Dr. L. Edward Pratt called an emergency meeting for faculty in the library to deliver the news. Shock waves were sent out over the entire PDS community. As the school had been on the decline financially and philosophically, Dr. Ida Long Rogers asserts that the school "should have seen it coming."[7] Nonetheless, reactions generally involved great surprise and confusion. Heber Rogers says he acted "like a bombshell had been dropped."[8] USN College Counseling Director Janet Schneider, then Janet Carney, was getting through her first day when she received the news. Upon hearing the news, she was convinced she was out of the job.

The following day, August 30th, 1974, Peabody College President John Dunworth sent a letter to Dem School patrons, assuring them of the possibility for the school's continuance. Dunworth stated that the Board of Trustees of the college "empowered its Executive Committee to 'negotiate with officials of any corporation which may be created to consider the continued operation of the Demonstration School under another name and under contractual relationships . . . ." He goes on to say that he and his staff would be willing to meet at any time with a "representative committee of parents to review this option." Lastly, as the school would officially cease operation in May of 1975, he mentions possible negotiations to operate courses in consideration of students graduating in May of 1976.[9] Instead of stepping back and letting the shock wash over, the PDS community wasted no time in galvanize everyone to address their present situation.

Less than a week after Dr. Pratt's somber announcement, over 900 PDS community members, including parents, students, teachers, and administrators, met in Vanderbilt's Neely Auditorium to discuss the fate of the Dem School. The entire community agreed that every possible maneuver be made to continue the school. Dr. James W. Hays announced that it was not a time to panic but to get the school started and assure the students that they would have a school the following year. Passed unanimously, a "basic Transition Committee" formed that night, chaired by Bernard Werthan, Jr. As the school was not yet paid for through the '75-'75 school year, the meeting included discussions over alternative facilities, notably the Blair School of Music campus.[10] Ultimately, though, moving the campus was decidedly too difficult. Operating under the PDS Patrons, Inc., several sub committees formed as well. One of these was the Liaison Committee, chaired by Dr. Hays. In subsequent weeks, Dr. Hays negotiated with the Peabody Board of Trustees to operate facilities through the 1976 school year. He was willing to pay rent of $80,000 (approximately $0.90 per square foot).[11] Eventually, Mr. Werthan negotiated the buildings for $86,000.[12]

At the initial meeting on September 4, Transition Committee member Laura Knox expressed an optimistic view of the matter when she stated that everyone could choose to see this as an opportunity to build a school more exciting and more educational than before.[13] This was merely the beginning of financial woes and struggles to keep the institution afloat.

With the goal of establishing an independent and stable institution, the various sub committees met as many as three times a week throughout the first years of

USN's existence. Immediately following the Neely Auditorium meeting, the PDS community hurried to raise as much money as possible to ensure the school's continuation. Former faculty member Leland Johnson asserts that had the school relied on alumni, they would not have survived, for a majority of the alumni were teachers. Furthermore, the school could not get enough grants.[14] Raising money became a task in which the whole school invested itself. In a PDS Board Meeting just a few weeks after the committees formed, the progress report sounded promising, as a school-wide effort to raise money was made. Student Cathy Fraser, alongside the Student Council and PTA, was organizing a spaghetti supper, from which all the proceeds would go to the PDS Patrons, Inc. Other events were organized, and soon it was decided that all proceeds go to the PDS Patrons, Inc. At the same board meeting that September day, Peggy Hays announced the need of a historian to keep records, save newspaper clippings, and track changes in the new school. No one volunteered.[15]

Although the students, for the most part, were protected from the politics of the transition, they proved an integral part in raising funds and, most importantly, keeping the spirit of the school alive. In an early October '74 issue of the school newspaper, a few articles dedicated to uncovering the transition process were published. An interview with Student Council representatives emphasized the need for student involvement in helping their school assume independence. In two students' "Report on Transition Committee," they reported a tuition increase that added up to less than $100, still significantly below other schools. The same report cites head of fundraising Mrs. Suzie Morris sending pledge cards to parents in hopes of donating ten or twenty dollars per month for a few years.[16] Student involvement proved crucial in the naming of the new school. Not long after the newspaper article was issued, the list of suggested names was reduced to five on which students could vote: University Center School, Winthrop School, Nashville University School, University School of Nashville, and Nashville Community School.[17]

The several sub-committees that formed under the Transition Committee include Building and Grounds, Mission and Purpose, Public Relations, Finance, and Planning and Development. All the committees dedicated themselves to establishing a stable structure for the new school, meeting several times a week and even on weekends. Some committees' tasks required little time, and thus, ceased existence after a while, such as the Mission and Purpose Committee. This group, in particular, created a statement foreseeing the school's policies and philosophies:

" . . . Interest in learning is fostered in an informal relaxed atmosphere of mutual respect on the part of the faculty, administration, and students . . . ."

In April of 1975, the first officers of USN's Board of Directors were elected, including James Hays, President; Bernard Werthan, Jr., Vice President; Alfred Galloway, Treasurer; and Georgette Hardman, Secretary. The new Board of Directors kept the remaining committees afloat and assumed leadership of the Transition Committee's purposes, as most of its members were now on the Board. The Board, along with all the other committee, meetings welcomed any interested students. Sophomore and Student Council Treasurer Martha Tanner was one of the few students who took an active role in the transition, as she represented her fellow classmates at the initial Neely Auditorium meeting and dozens of meetings the rest of the school year. Proving notably ambitious compared to her peers, she served on the Transition Committee and Board of Directors, dedicating long hours and multiple Saturday-morning meetings in Board President Dr. Hays's office. She says that most students didn't take an interest in the naissance of the school because, "By and large, it felt like it was being handled." The Transition Committee even spread the word about PDS's transition, while conveying the solidity that underlined the new school, by distributing bumper stickers reading: "PDS is now US." However, not every student felt as secure with the school as hoped. Tanner recalls peers leaving for other schools or graduating early. She herself, on the other hand, was excited about the challenge and enthusiastic about her role in the process, as she says she was able to witness "history in the making."[18]

A memo sent out during the '74-'75 school year specifies that although other educational institutions provided useful references, USN wanted its own unique "conceptual model for governance."[19] The "Statement of Principle" in 1974 sums up USN's goals in declaring itself a unique institution apart from the college: "students are regarded as individuals . . . who are encouraged and expected to exercise an increasingly large measure of initiative and self-discipline." It goes on to say: "students . . . represent the varied racial and religious composition of the [Metropolitan Nashville] area."[20] After severing ties with the college, students no longer roamed the Peabody College campus, for all classes now resided at the PDS/USN campus. This caused a problem of close quarters, for teachers reached a point when they were forced to use any space available. Martha Tanner recalls taking a math course in the school's basement.[21]

Even though USN slowly but surely materialized as a successful, independent institution itself, sources of ambiguity emerged in the years following the '74-'75 school year, as leaders quickly came and left. Tanner even went as far as to say that the school years of 1977 to 1981 seemed more unstable than the first years of the actual transition of the school.

The 1976-1977 school year was a time slated for change and inherent uncertainty. As planned, Dr. Pratt would resign from the director's position in the spring of 1977. When explaining Pratt's time at the school and subsequent resignation, many define him by his lack of involvement in the school. At the time, his office was located in a gray house on the school's campus in which he spent most of his time, rarely emerging to observe and experience the school itself. He had a very strong secretary, Thelma Felton, who, according to witnesses, took over the spotlight and ran things for him. USN was still a young institution and didn't have the autonomy it aspired to, and Pratt had to deal with the college telling him what he should do. Janet Schneider, formerly Carney, sees the difficulty in Pratt's position, for he was concerned not only with solving the problems of USN but also with pleasing the college. Pratt was not a very thorough director, not even bothering to look at Schneider's credentials upon hiring her. Furthermore, as the transition progressed, the Transition Committee overshadowed Pratt, proving the more powerful source of leadership. Most agree that Pratt was a lame duck.[22] The school was in a position to accept and utilize any help it could get. At a September 1976 Board meeting, an announcement was made regarding the arrival of a member of the Educational Consultants in Nashville in the coming weeks, and that he would speak with Board members, faculty, students, and parents.

Simultaneously, a Search Committee set off to find Dr Pratt's replacement.[23] A member of the committee, Schneider recalls the search for a young, dynamic man to take over as director. By mid-December, the committee reported significant progress in narrowing down candidates, and by mid-January, reported the decision to offer Dr. Harold Snedcof an Administrative Contract. Around the same time, the Board announced the inception of a Transition Committee to "work with Snedcof during the transitional period of the administration."[24] The USN community was glad to welcome a new leader to accelerate the path to establishing itself as a respected, autonomous institution, and Snedcof fit the description. He was charismatic and seemed to have the right ideas for the school's future. It was difficult to perceive the shame which he would bring upon himself in the coming '77-'78 school year. Schneider was one of the Search Committee members who really pulled for Snedcof, and she considered herself very close to him at the time. Later she figured out that his charming façade merely was an act to mask his scheming, bitter approach.[25] In a school newspaper article entitled, "Headmaster Pleas for Student Respect," featuring an interview with the director, he exhibited a sour attitude toward student behavior, saying that respect was a significant problem: " . . . I was surprised with the rudeness and sloppiness for this building and institution."[26] In the first months of 1978, USN community members met to discuss Snedcof's position and his negative influence on the school. Consequently, he was asked to resign and did so on April 18th, 1977 after spending less than a year at USN.

After Harold Snedcof resigned, USN found a capable and reliable person in Heber Rogers to help get the school back on its feet. Rogers had been part of the PDS/USN community since his practice teaching days in the summer of 1954. He had been serving as assistant director since 1971 and was now being asked to serve as the interim director until USN could find a new director. Rogers recalls meeting with the Board of Directors following Snedcof's resignation. Because of the increased uncertainty of the school, resulting from Snedcof's resignation, they told Rogers to work on restoring stability and calming things down. Rogers felt the uncertainty himself after having discovered his name on a list of faculty members found on Snedcof's desk. The list implied who would be fired had Snedcof continued as director. Rogers recalls the frequent visits of faculty members in the following school year, asking whether his or her name appeared on the list. Rogers persevered beautifully, acknowledging the Board's instruction to maintain the school's solidarity and refrain from making major changes.[27]

In the fall of 1977, another Search Committee set off to find a new director and found that Harvey Sperling was the man for the job. Sperling admits that upon his being hired, he didn't realize how dire the school's actual situation was. There was a great lack of resources, namely financial, and no sheer vision as to where the school was going. Thus, the situation proved precarious and scary. However, he soon began making significant decisions and changes that would ultimately define USN. Sperling remembers the inherent chaos that comes with setting an institution's foundation, as other school administrators would ask him to tell stories of the school's handling ambiguous issues for entertainment. Proving to be the strongest, most influential director since the closing of PDS, Sperling worked hard and succeeded in propelling the school forward into the future. He is quick to point out, though, that the school's changes and success was a result of, not one person, but a consortium of people, saying that you "can't accomplish things the first five years," and that you "have to build a school with great leaders." He wholeheartedly attributes the school's stability to the USN community and outside helpers, which include the faculty members, a strong succession of Board members, and a "kitchen cabinet" that includes people from Vanderbilt. He knew that it would take much patience and determination in order to accomplish his goals. He compares USN's beginnings with a young America, noting that you can *say* you are independent but that uncertainty soon follows. Sperling, alongside many other hard-working people, fought to counter this uncertainty and manifest the school's visions. Most agree that USN's history began with Sperling, for he led the movement to achieving a steady foundation and beginnings of a new school. Although Sperling is humble in his acknowledgment for his impact on the school and is happy with its state at present, he wants to stress that to maintain greatness, you must constantly strive to do better: "If you don't go beyond us, it's nothing."[28]

ENDNOTES

1 Claunch, John M. "Memorandum: The Role of the Demonstration School." September 30, 1968.

2 *The Past Is Prologue*, pg. 102. 1970.

3 Interview with Heber Rogers. September 14, 2005.

4 "The Role of the Peabody Demonstration School: A Study Report," Division of Surveys and Field Services (George Peabody College for Teachers), May 1973.

5 "The Role of the Peabody Demonstration School: A Study Report."

6 J. Allen, R. Norris, and I.L. Rogers, *Design for the Future — A Report From the Select Committee on Peabody's Second Century to President John Dunworth and the Board of Trustees*, August 24, 1974. Appendix C: "Rationale for the Recommendation to Close the Peabody Demonstration School."

7 Historical Method Class of 2002. Interview with Dr. Ida Long Rogers.

8 Historical Method Class of 2002. Interview with Heber Rogers.

9 John Dunworth. "Letter to Demonstration School Patrons." August 30, 1974.

10 "Transition Notebook." Notes from September 4, 1974 meeting.

11 "P.T.A. NEWSLETTER–P.T.A. September 1974."

12 Gillmor, Matthew. "PDS Becomes USN."

13 "Transition Notebook."

14 Interview with Lealand Johnson, 2005.

15 PDS Board Meeting. September 27, 1974.

16 *Tiger's Eye*, Volume1, No. 1. October 4, 1974.

17 Culpepper, Connie. How the Dem School Became USN.

18 Interview with Martha Tanner. December 12, 2005.

19 "Memo" from "Transition Notebook."

20 Culpepper.

21 Martha Tanner interview.

22 Interview with Janet Schneider. January 5, 2006.

23 Board of Directors–Minutes. September 7, 1976. December 6, 1976. January 18, 1977.

24 Board of Directors–Minutes. January 18, 1976.

25 Schneider.

26 Volume 1, No. 9. "Headmaster Pleas for Student Respect." February 17, 1978.

27 Interview with Heber Rogers. October 6, 2005.

28 Interview with Harvey Sperling. September 29, 2005.

From "Demographics, Diversity, and Desegregation"
BRYAN HEARN
Class of 2005

From the INTRODUCTION

What kind of school are we trying to be? Who should go to the school? Are we representative of the Nashville community? Along with philosophical educational issues, such questions may reside in the heads of administrators, directors, teachers, parents, and students of the past and present. USN is known for academics, attention to the individual, great faculty, and diversity, according to a detailed survey of parents.[1] Whether you define diversity by race, beliefs, religious preference, or socioeconomic status, USN has tried to maintain such differences in its community. Many have come to think of the school as a "bubble" where differences were accepted and welcomed, and racial matters were not even an afterthought in the judgment of character.

African-American graduates such as [Cassandra] Teague-Walker '67, [Joy] Sims '72, and [Midori] Lockett ['78] contributed to a new image for PDS. Their desegregation policy was considered progressive, and it was not by any means forced. McCharen's voluntary and successful desegregation changed PDS for the better. Word began to spread regarding PDS' values and their intention to be different. "Percentages of persons here who were Jewish already knew what it meant to be different, so there was an intentionality here about addressing differences," Reverend Sonnye Dixon '70 recalled in a September, 2004 Desegregation Symposium at USN. And while many turned to the "white flight" private Christian schools, many, both black and white, turned to PDS. Many parents saw the world their children would grow up in as being very different from the one that they grew up in, citing a belief that the world would be *diversified* and different.[2] They saw the value of diversity, and the value of education. They saw that PDS provided walls that excluded racism and embraced differences in race, religious and sexual preference, and socioeconomic status. "The reason our parents were willing and we were willing to come here is that we knew a change had to come," Dixon said.[3]

With the busing order upsetting both white and black families, many parents enrolled their kids at PDS/USN because they saw its commitment to the "new world." As African-American students were transitioning from all-black schools and all-black neighborhoods into PDS/USN, they began to feel welcomed. The consistent opinion from African-American alums is that, while students were aware and curious of differences, their questions were never derogatory.[4] Students formed friendships and established camaraderie with one another.

The African-American students at PDS/USN had idealistic goals that the school could help them reach: "[We] knew . . . that education was the key to access the American dream," Teague-Walker said. PDS/USN knew that it was becoming a school that allows students to achieve the dream.

School desegregation alone does not guarantee a curriculum, an environment, respectful students, or intermingling of races that is welcoming or diverse.[5] The spirit of PDS makes this promise. Interviews of both white and black administrators reveal that little racial bias is remembered inside the walls of PDS/USN.[6] An accepting environment contributed to a graceful and smooth transition to an integrated school. Although racism surely could be found underneath in the minds of students due to societal norms, it wasn't displayed outwardly in PDS (as it was in the Nashville society). This environment consisted of individuals at PDS that preached tolerance and welcomed differences, both values that help you achieve the American Dream.

From PLANTING THE SEED OF TOLERANCE: POST-DESEGREGATION

PDS had firmly established their commitment to diversity, but they still were behind. Inside PDS, various problems arose and motives were questioned. Yet, the biggest concern was the double-lives that African-Americans were living: the differences between PDS' environment and Nashville were profuse. What African-American students experienced outside PDS' walls was different than inside, and that was detrimental to achieving tolerance and acceptance inside.

Dr. McCharen's process was a bit mathematical: he wanted at least two African-Americans in every class so they could go to the dances together.[7] His purpose was to have PDS be a comfortable environment for students of all races. Interracial dating, although it did not occur often until the late 70s, has always been accepted at PDS/USN.

It was anticipated, however, that when African-American students left the comfortable environment of PDS, they would experience prejudice and racism. The African-American students, such as Teague-Walker '67, were living in two different worlds. Teague-Walker's parents were college administrators and teachers. But when she left her parents' and the PDS environments, people called her "nigger" and slammed doors in her face. Her parents wouldn't let her go to the movies because they didn't want her to have to go up to the back stairs and sit in the balcony. The outside world was very different, as one could find more prejudice and racism in Nashville society than inside the walls of PDS.

....

From RACIAL RELATIONS AND PROGRESSION: THE 1970s

Seven years after Ms. Teague-Walker graduated in 1967, and PDS had a new director: Dr. Edward L. Pratt. The integration of the school was not going as smoothly as possible. A couple of parents wrote to the school, withdrawing their children due to racism, discrimination in hiring, and admissions practices. Many believed that racism was present at the school, just as it was everywhere else in the South.

But as the 1970s progressed in terms of racial relations, so did USN. After the transition from PDS to USN in 1975, some thought of USN as "a little shell where kids felt good about diversity," where they were "treating people as people." As students graduated, they became more aware of different cultures, and were thankful for the diversity that USN provided.[8] One aspect of USN that many admired was the fact that people were not separated as to race or socioeconomic background. Many claimed that the school "was a prototype of what a school should be" in terms of progressiveness in racial relations.[9]

When he first desegregated the school, Dr. McCharen wanted to have PDS graduates to contribute not only through diversity, but also through academic reputation. And as African-American students graduated in the top ten percent of their class and went on to study at Ivy League schools, this goal was certainly being accomplished.[10]

From TRANSITION INTO THE NORM: THE 1980s

The 1980s continued to raise awareness and acceptance. A "bubble" or an "oasis" was being formed, and differences were not questioned as much—diversity became the norm. USN was one of the only viable options for African-Americans who desired independent schooling, as MBA and Harpeth Hall did not desegregate as fast as USN. Therefore, more and more African-American families sent their children to USN, and families became very comfortable with the way that USN welcomed diversity.

Diversity numbers then were much lower than they are today, and therefore African-American students found that interaction between blacks was often limited, according to Jana Chandler Adesegun '81.[11] Adesegun did not find any outward animosity in the USN environment.

....

Adesegun's experience at PDS was affected by the large Jewish representation at the school, who knew how it felt to be in the minority.[12] There certainly was a large Jewish population at the school. An article titled "*University School maintains rep as diverse, picky place*" in the October 7, 1980 issue of *The Vanderbilt Hustler* noted that 30 percent of USN students are Jewish. The validity of this statistic, however, is questioned. Regardless of the actual number, the percentage of Jewish students at USN is still disproportionately larger than the percentage of Jews in the Nashville community. Also in the issue, it was said that at the time, minority enrollment was at 18 percent, 15 percent black. It claimed that USN "is the only private school in Nashville that actively seeks to racially integrate its student body." [13]

While integrating its student body, USN still had one consistent goal: achievement through support and respect. The USN basketball team might experience racial prejudice when they went on the road. But according to Wendell Foster '81, that created a bond. It didn't create any added pressure; the only pressure Foster felt at USN was the pressure to succeed. [14]

Pressures and conflicts were not openly found. "USN was not touched by many of the racially motivated conflicts that public schools suffer from. But there is always some tension present in schools: at USN, it came from misplaced feelings of superiority. It was never violent or overt but noticeable," [15] Melissa Irvin '96 said.

From HAVE WE PROGRESSED? (1990s - PRESENT): AN EVALUATION AND LOOK INTO THE FUTURE

The central question on USN's diversity is: are we representative of the Nashville community? Answering such a complex question is a difficult and complicated task. One must keep in mind the word "relativity," and the complexity of diversity in education. A school with a 23.5% minority population in a city with a 34.1% minority population is relatively diverse.

Talk is cheap: free speech isn't, a saying goes. After the birth of USN, Mrs. Robert Eisenstein (Ann Fensterwald) '37 wrote: "Now incorporated as the University School of Nashville, it is the only independent school in this area that truly reflects the ethnic and religious diversity of Metropolitan Nashville." [16] In 1982, college counseling began to include in their school profiles the statement that USN's "fully integrated student body is representative of the diverse population of the Nashville area." [17] What do these vague sentences mean? Can we really be representative of the Nashville area when most of the Nashville population can't afford a USN education?

Although prejudice may have been found inside the school from time to time, on paper, significant progress was made in diversity. In 1973 with 179 students in the 4th grade and below, 140 were white and 39 were black.[18] In 1985-1986 the senior class was 17% of color. Ten years later, in 1995-1996, the senior class was 18% of color. In 2004-2005, the senior class was 24% of color and 16% of international background.[19]

Diversity in Senior Classes

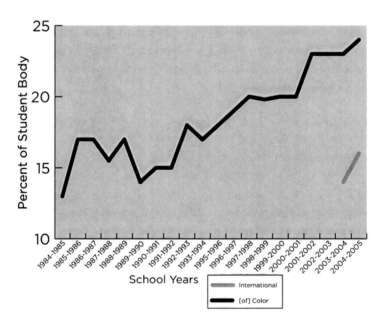

The chart shows that significant progress is being made in terms of diversity at USN. A strong linear, upward trend can be found as time progresses. International students' numbers began to be recorded in 2003, and even a small increase can be found from the 2003-2004 school year to the 2004-2005 school year.

Today for USN as a whole, we have 108 African-American students, 64 Asian students, 13 Middle Eastern Students, 2 Hispanic students, and 50 biracial students, a total of 237 out of 1006 students. That is 23.5% minority enrollment in 2004-2005.[20] 132 of our students are international students; highest totals were 17 from China and 33 from India, combining for 13.1% of our student body in 2004-2005.

USN vs. Nashville Diversity

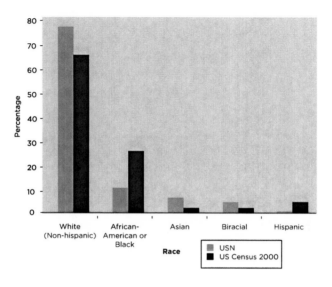

The chart above documents USN's racial diversity relative to the population of Nashville.

One may see that we have a disproportionate percentage of white students, and our African-American students' statistics are well below the Nashville population. In terms of Asians and biracial students, however, we are above the Nashville population. As the Nashville Hispanic population is rapidly growing, the number of Hispanic students at USN stays relatively small. On the whole it is evident that USN is doing its best to answer the question, "Are we representative of the Nashville population?"

Racial diversity is one thing, but economic diversity is a more difficult challenge to achieve, as USN is a private, independent, and nondenominational school that costs a certain amount of money each year, making it hard for many families to afford. Also, keep in mind that one cannot directly connect economic diversity with racial diversity: one cannot buy diversity. In terms of economic diversity, however, we have increased dramatically in the amount of financial aid awarded. The need-based aid category was just implemented in the mid-1980s, as soon as USN reached economic stability. Because of an increase in funds, the amount of financial aid awarded has increased from $111,413 in 1993 to $641,850 in 2004.[21]

This has allowed those who cannot afford a USN education an opportunity, likely increasing the socioeconomic diversity at the school.

Those individuals who get access to diversity policies (i.e., people of color, women, people of different socioeconomic status levels, and people otherwise "disadvantaged") benefit through more traditionally privileged schools, who *may* provide superior educational experiences and outcomes. Less obvious, but important, are the arguments around the benefits of diversity *itself*, qua diversity, for white and other students. These arguments focus on three themes. First, students can learn more from each other academically, but more importantly civically and socially. The outcomes from that real-life education are life-long. Diverse school experiences increase students' level of understanding of the world and its different points of view, and it also enhances their desire to interact with people of different backgrounds in the future.[22] Second, campuses are more vibrant, productive, and successful as organizations and communities when they are diverse, because more opportunities, values, and beliefs are presented. Third, societies benefit when there is no cookie-cutter mentality, especially among young people growing into citizenship and adulthood: tolerance, civic participation, and political engagement appear to grow after exposure to diversity. USN is committed to those values.

Obviously, in certain aspects (Hispanic students, arguably)[23], we have a long way to go. But one thing cannot be argued: USN has always tried to be a school that not only tolerated but accepted differences. It all comes back to those brave few from 1964 and the ones who followed. "We did our best as the 'love and peace' generation to rise to the challenge of loving and accepting people for who they are," Cason said.[24] And in such a "melting pot," we are aiming towards the common goal: an education. Besides solving algebraic formulas and addressing questions like who won what battle in the Civil War, what the significance is of Robert Frost's *The Road Not Taken*, and what the chemical formula is for sulfuric acid, USN students and faculty are pursuing very significant real-life goals, for USN has always tried to prepare and excel in more ways than one. "USN never stopped trying to educate people in as many ways as possible. And there is no greater foe to prejudice than understanding. And understanding comes from learning. As long as USN continues to provide a high level of education, I think the school will continue to create accepting and open-minded students,"[25] Melissa Irvin '96 said.

ENDNOTES

1 Interview with Juliet Douglas, November 8, 2004.

2 Interview with Dolores Nicholson, December 9, 2004.

3 Desegregation Symposium September 10, 2004: Rev. Sonnye Dixon '70, Joy Sims '72, Cassandra Teague-Walker '67, Heber Rogers, and Florence Kidd.

4 Email correspondence with Midori Lockett '78, January 25, 2005.

5 "The Impact of Racial and Ethnic Diversity on Educational Outcomes: Cambridge MA School District" by Michael Kurlaender and John T. Yun, January 29, 2002.

6 Interview with Lynn Lewis '71 on December 9, 2004.

7 Desegregation Symposium.

8 Interview with Dee Hicks, October 4, 2004.

9 Interview with Janet Schneider, September 30, 2004.

10 Email correspondence with Midori Lockett '78, January 25, 2005.

11 Email correspondence with Jana Chandler Adesegun '81, January 24, 2005.

12 Ibid.

13 "University School Maintains rep as diverse, picky place" by Steven Way, *Vanderbilt Hustler*, October 7, 1980.

14 Email correspondence with Wendell Foster '81, January 24, 2005.

15 Email correspondence with Melissa Irvin '96, January 27, 2005.

16 Letter from Mrs. Robert Eisenstein (Ann Fensterwald '37) to PDS graduates, class unrecorded.

17 1982-83 University School of Nashville Profile.

18 Writing by Basak Kizilisik '04.

19 1985-86, 1995-96, and 2004-05 School Profiles.

20 Director of Admissions' Juliet Douglas report to the Board of Trustees, September 2004.

21 Interview with Juliet Douglas, November 8, 2004.

22 Kurlaender and Yun, 2002.

23 Interview with Juliet Douglas, November 8, 2004.

24 Alumni magazine correspondence, Peggy Parker Cason '72.

25 Email correspondence with Melissa Irvin, January 27, 2005.

From "The More Things Change, the More Things Stay the Same:
Curriculum At a Glance"
JAMIE NEDELMAN
Class of 2005

It's around eight o'clock and the bell rings. You either arrive early enough in time to participate in the backgammon tournament up on the third floor, or just in time to quiz your friends for the test you have first period.[1] As some scatter quickly to class, others lounge around, take their time, and stroll into the classroom.

These two scenes provide something significant to remember from these two separate decades of life at University School of Nashville. If you went to school in the seventies you would probably take the leisurely approach, since it didn't matter if you were late to class. You could stroll in and say "here" when your name was called, but then walk right back out into the hall.[2]

In the eighties things were a little different. Although you might arrive early and play backgammon (a fad back then), you would be on time to class.[3] You know those students that always dread the long, boring, math class? Not in the seventies Mr. Kammerud.[4] Dots tournaments were going on in the back of the room and students would rotate and play one another until a winner was proclaimed. This is just a glimpse of how University School used to be, although things may physically appear to be the same to some extent. How things have changed.

University School of Nashville's curriculum raises certain questions: How are we different from Peabody Demonstration School? Have we become more challenging or less strenuous compared to past years? And the biggest of all, are we leaning towards a more traditional or progressive academic outlook when it comes to the way the administration governs the school?

Peabody Demonstration School was considered the "laboratory school" of George Peabody College for Teachers in the early 1970s.[5] This relationship helped define the curriculum at PDS. The Peabody Demonstration School's curriculum was geared towards the needs of the particular students who wanted to continue their formal education into college. The school was eager to mold students into "educational specialists".[6] Oddly enough, with these "high" expectations, only eighteen credits were required to graduate[7] Fourteen units came from the English, Foreign Language, Mathematics, Science, or Social Studies departments, while four other units came from the arts category.[8] These four units could be fulfilled through participating in art, chorus, music understanding, orchestra, photography, typing, or physical education.[9] During this time curriculum requirements were minimum, what the state required and nothing more.[10] Although University School students were supposed to be distinguished as talented, hard-working, and bright, many were not. Mrs. Janet Schneider began working at Peabody Demonstration School in 1974, only two weeks before classes actually began. "There were holes in the curriculum, there were classes being taught that weren't really necessary," Mrs. Schneider revealed, " . . . people could graduate in three years—some left too early, when some people weren't emotionally ready, or physically ready for college."

Seniors at Peabody Demonstration School had to maintain a minimum class load of four subjects for both semesters.[11] Along with the remaining high school students, they had to have eighteen credits to graduate; however, if they were qualified to take courses at either Peabody College or Vanderbilt University, they were allowed to do so.[12]

During the 1974-1975 school year, Peabody Demonstration was in a state of unrest: rumors of the schools close swarmed the campus. Some of the faculty was nervous because they had just begun their teaching careers, and if the school closed, they would have nowhere to explore their careers.[13] Contagious insecurity regarding the fate of the school spread quickly among the faculty. With much of the administration focused on this conflict at hand, the teaching efforts failed to meet high standards.

Despite the numerous distractions present on campus, kids still proved to develop into strong young adults. "Kids were always doing amazing things," comments Mrs. Janet Schneider. An alum said, "students were allowed to think, solve problems, discuss issues, take the opposite point of view- turn it around, and still get an A."[14]

PDS alum, and now a teacher at University School, Mrs. Dee Hicks comments that, "here they took a different approach for learning. You could tell people were interested, and students had a voice in class." This is perhaps where the famous *PDS/USN Spirit* originated that helped create the unique academic atmosphere still present today.

When headmaster Dr. Ed Pratt hired Mrs. Hicks in 1971 the margins on teaching were lenient or even non-existent. Although the curriculum and many of the books were given to teachers, they were able to go about teaching it however they pleased.[15]

As University School progressed into the 1980's, both the curriculum and class structure grew for the better. USN had an average of fifteen to twenty students in every class.[16] Within each class, students could speak freely with one another without being reprimanded. They were encouraged to use class time to digress with one another and talk about ideas relevant to the class. The USN class atmosphere was and still is one of a kind. Interaction and discussion were strongly suggested, and a lot of teachers planned class time around discussion. University School has a special "classroom aura" unlike any other school.[17]

Harvey Sperling, USN's first real director who came in 1979, paved the way for many important adjustments to the school atmosphere. The fall season of the 1979 school year brought with it six new courses and a schedule of eight class periods a day.[18] The *Life Skills* class, open to only freshman and sophomores, offered experiential learning in developing self-sufficiency.[19] It was supposed to teach the younger students how to "appreciate [one's] own uniqueness." The school felt that a course like this was important and crucial to lower classmen in order to prepare them for their future endeavors. Secondly, the *20th Century Europe* class helped students grasp a "better understanding of Europe today."[20] Problems in Science taught students about the current scientific issues facing society.[21] Another course, *Drama and Acting*, split the year into two sections: the first half of the year focused on the history of dramatics, while the second half focused on the actual practice of acting.[22] The other two courses added were *Business and Management* and *Fundamentalism in Design*.[23] These courses didn't just pop out of nowhere, Mr. Sperling was interested in making school leadership a real option for those students who wanted to get involved. Not only was leadership important, but he wanted to allow students to pursue their interests and have more freedom.

1975–1976	5 Class Periods
1976–1977	6 Class Periods
1977–1978	7 Class Periods
1978–1979	8 Class Periods

A partial history of past daily schedules.

Despite the fact that there were opinions on both sides, most students found that eight periods a day was a positive change.[24] Eight periods allowed students to have "the freedom to go study, go to the student center, and to interact with colleagues."[25] Ironically enough, the eight period schedules allowed a greater allowed a greater flexibility in course selection for students.[26] Not only did most students enjoy the change, but the faculty took pleasure in it as well. Teachers liked the new schedule because now students had more time to complete assignments; and with more time, they could be completed with the best effort.[27]

As a decade, the 1980s represent a liberated approach towards teaching. Teachers could design their own classes. According to Mrs. Linda Wallis, the current Academic Dean who began working at University School in 1982, "Teachers could pretty much do whatever they wanted to do."[28] There was not structure when it came to the composition or behavior of a class.

In 1986 the school experienced problems with cheating and dishonesty among students.[29] The school proposed instituting an honor code in attempt to help this problem.

Dr. Ann Wheeler led the Academic Integrity Committee.[30] Together the students and teachers worked together to develop a "Declaration of Values" that stated a specific philosophy in attempt to guide actions.[31] After much hard work, the code was installed during the 1986-1987 school year.[32]

By 1986 the administration put forth a concentrated effort in order to improve the standards and public perception of the school (the wall). Now, University School demanded twenty-three credits, five more than requisite in 1972.[33] Freshmen were required to take one semester of a computer tools and applications course, a music listening and literature course, or an introductory course to art history. It was argued for some time that freshman students had a "heavier load" according to the *USNews* newspaper of 1986. One reason the school decided to increase the workload was because of academic demands from colleges.[34] Freshmen were taken aback by this change, and didn't like the increase in workload in the least bit. The common feeling among the students was that they were "hit hard."[35]

Juniors also experienced an astonishing adjustment to academic life. Amusing activities such as Winterim were cancelled.[36] Winterim was a two-week period after Winter Break between the Fall and Spring semesters where students could take trips and/or do internships to chase interests outside of the curriculum. In conjunction with this, more academic requirements were necessary.[37] The junior class began to feel overwhelmed and felt that they were being put under too much pressure.[38]

When Sperling was the headmaster of the school, many old customs that helped the school earn its "slacker-hippy" reputation were exterminated. "The wall" was seen as the public image of the school. Adults, parents, and anyone who drove down Edgehill Avenue saw kids on the wall smoking. Though smoking was allowed in the seventies, Harvey Sperling didn't approve of the image it gave the school.

He outlawed smoking during school hours causing many students to go ballistic: many students began to say, "We're turning into an MBA."[39]

Contrary to the trend towards more structure in the eighties, there were a few "slip-ups" here and there. The general trend does prove that compared to the seventies, the eighties was a definite step towards more control but it's almost impossible to run a faultless school. When these events are reported curiosity tends to rise; so we ask ourselves, "Why did these things happen?" Could the answer possibly be that Mr. Sperling was simply placing too much structure on the school? It's difficult to say for sure, but the changes that Mr. Sperling imposed were great and deviated a lot from how the school used to run.

The "Sperling era" represents a crucial transition period within University School. Harvey Sperling felt that a more structured school was the way to achieve excellence on a greater level. "Harvey Sperling was really trying to make the school stronger in all areas but particularly in academics," says Dr. Ann Wheeler. The 1970s were a time of reconstruction and much hard work for Mr. Sperling. He worked for hours on ideas of how to improve the school as a whole.

Sperling arrived at University School when it was in a state of disorder. It was not academically rigorous, students were sloppy, and there wasn't structure within the school; Mr. Sperling was there to clean up the school and transform it into an organized and exciting atmosphere.[40] The school had structure yet students still wanted to come, which is how a school should be. "We didn't have a functional school," Sperling said. University School was a place where everyone wanted a voice, not just any voice but an equal voice, and it's hard to run a school that's like this.[41] Many people would agree that USN started to look more conservative when Harvey Sperling came.[42]

Prohibiting smoking was only one of many changes Mr. Sperling brought with him as headmaster. Occasionally girls would lie out in their bathing suits on the wall and sunbathe, but not anymore after Mr. Sperling came.[43]

Mr. Sperling felt that the actions of the school and students in the school weren't accurately representing the style of USN. One of the hardest conflicts to solve was the issue of power in the school. Where did the power reside? With the students, teachers, Peabody College, the parents, or somewhere else? Mr. Sperling decided that the board held the power. In past years the school board was *elected*; usually the brightest, most successful men and women represented the board. Mr. Sperling didn't want an elected board he wanted an *appointed* board.[44] He didn't want all businessmen on board because they didn't know a single thing about education, but he wanted enough businessmen so that school could start to raise funds. It was important to Mr. Sperling however, that the board keep in mind that they were running a school and not an industry.

When asked what the biggest difference in the school today is compared to what it used to be, many people would talk about academic rigor, the increase in requirements, or the tremendous amount of structure that's present.[45] Due to Harvey Sperling's devotion and love for University School, we have the wonderful school that is standing today.

After Mr. Sperling left in 1989, Edward Costello took the position as the new head of the school. When Mr. Costello came to USN he found that most of the students were "goal oriented, generally bright, and working very hard to make sure people knew USN was not like MBA." Mr. Sperling had surely set the stage for only greater accomplishments from USN: "I am prideful enough to say that the public thought we were one of the best schools in town, maybe with the highest academic standards."[46]According to Costello there were still those who oriented USN with "sex, drugs, and Rock and Roll, most particularly the drug part." Mr. Costello took it upon himself as the head of the school to change the drug and alcohol policy due to these views. Not only would this new policy help change the opinions of the school, but it would also help "promote better decision-making among the students."[47]

MOVING TO THE PRESENT

Looking back on the past thirty-five years of University School's history, one extreme change stands out. As the school progressed from a laid back "hippie school" in the seventies, to a more focused academic institution in the eighties, to a prestigious kindergarten through twelfth grade school in the nineties, to a well-respected, eminent school as the millennium came and passed, we can detect major structural changes in the actual organization of the school. Whether it's the class options, schedule, or broad focus, University School has only improved immensely.

While University School has a prescribed core of courses that students must take, a myriad of additional courses are available. Student and faculty interest have led to new courses.[48] For example, *Biomedical Physics* is not a course that you would normally see offered in a High School, but because we have a qualified teacher who enjoys teaching the course, we offer it. Another faculty interest proclaimed recently was a Psychological approach to the Holocaust. University School offers *Social Conscience* because we have a teacher who wants to teach it.

The faculty at University School is unique in that the student-teacher relationships formed are one of a kind. Both students and teachers are comfortable with one another, which allows for amusing classes and outside of school friendships. The school is extremely lucky to have such a number of teachers that are so excited to teach and want to make their knowledge available to students. Their love and interest in specific educational fields is passed through them to the students, and through their work we see positive results.

Some students decide to not follow the "AP language path" but still want a grasp on the language they've learned for the past four years, this is why we do what we do. The school has recently created language electives in order to meet specific student interests. For example, *French Cinema and Culture* is an academic elective taught by Mrs. Woo. This course allows students to continue learning French, but in a more relaxed atmosphere. Students watch French movies and then follow up viewing the movie with a group discussion. Along with watching movies, students learn about French culture and customs. As a school we try to accommodate student interest as well as allowing these interests to count for credit; we want to "allow students to pursue a passion."[49]

Despite the minor changes in scheduling that occurred in the late 1970s, University School decided to take a large leap, beginning in the 2002-2003 school year, when USN introduced the block schedule. After much thought and planning, Mrs. Linda Wallis and Mr. George Flatau designed the new schedule. The schedule was made for a number of reasons. One reason was to alleviate stress; now that students wouldn't have every class every day, there wasn't as much homework to complete in one night.[50] The rotation of the schedule also helped with athletics. Instead of students having to leave early from the same class on game days, students didn't take time away from one single class.[51] The longer class periods allowed teachers to become more creative with their class time.[52] English and science teachers seem to benefit the most from this schedule.[53] English teachers have made their classes more active, planning activities that might take longer than they would have been able to do on a normal day. For science teachers it is now easier to complete labs and demonstrations.

WHEN IS ENOUGH, ENOUGH?

Diane Sacks, an alum from the class of 1981, remembers not having tons of homework: "I did homework, and then I was done. I was an average student and that was okay." In her eyes the curriculum is harder today, expectations are higher, and the workload is different compared to what it used to be. When Dr. Ann Wheeler was asked if the homework load was heavier today she said, "that seems to me to be true . . . there was so much less back then."

After going to school during the day, students are assigned homework. Has it ever been any different? Students' homework load has fluctuated up and down. Seth Eskind, a graduate from the class of 1976, remembers being able to get through the homework pretty fast. It's important to keep in mind that kids could be C students if they wanted to be or they could be A students if they wanted to be, it was solely up to the students.[54] Students were expected to be self-motivated. Contradictory to what Mr. Eskind felt, Ronnie Steine (class of 1974) felt that the academics at USN were challenging and that most people would have trouble sliding. Both alumni from the seventies had different views, which lead to the conclusion that some students simply didn't put in as much effort as others, which was acceptable and in a way not apt for penalty.

Today the workload and work effort are still the same to some extent. Surely it's the students' choice whether they want to put an effort forward, however, if they choose to not work hard there *are* consequences. Sometimes teachers send progress reports home; schedule a meeting with the parents, or a conference with the student, their parents, and the respective teachers.

The truth is that most people will acknowledge and accept that University School pushes and challenges its students to their full potential. "Academically, everything is moving much faster now. Our work was nothing like you guys have now, especially in High School."[55]

....

Despite what has changed at University School, several aspects remain the same. Some comment on the excellence and the level of energy in classes.[56] Contradictory to what some say, people claim to always see students eager to learn and excited about doing either experiments or even creative writing. University School is a place that lets you be you. When you walk into the school, you become a part of it, "you are a part of something . . . it's hard to explain. You feel like you make a difference here."[57] "I loved the High School atmosphere," comments Mr. O'Hara, former Head of the High School, "there was always high energy, lots of good students. Making them feel comfortable and at ease in their surroundings allows students to be themselves."

....

In the eyes of some of the women who still work at University School, the school "hasn't really changed philosophically."[58] The times have changed, and with that, the school continues to mold into "a little something new, not anything big."[59] Overall they believe that the Mission Statement has never changed much: "USN fosters each student's intellectual, artistic and athletic potential, valuing and inspiring integrity, creative expression, a love of learning, and the pursuit of excellence." University School attempts to create a diverse environment, and within that environment encourage an original, one of a kind atmosphere for learning where students can excel. The school has a particular *USN Spirit*. This spirit embodies many of the distinctive assets that are only relevant to University School that have been discussed: the collegiate atmosphere when you walk into a classroom, the comfort that students feel in their classes, the student-faculty relationships, or the devotion and excitement that you sense from teachers as they teach a classroom full of students. USN has and always will foster these special attributes; they are fixations that will never be lost.

After examining the composure, construction, and life of the school it's essential to think about what *kind* of school University School of Nashville is: the underlying question is whether we're traditional or progressive. According to *Webster's New World Dictionary* "progressive" is defined as: "moving forward; continuing by successive steps; of or favoring progress or reform." University School can be considered as a progressive school because instead of paddling or making our students come in on the weekends to "pay" for their mistakes, we take action in the form of asking students to write letters of apology or do community service for the well-being of the school. With the help of our Disciplinary Board and Judicial Board, University School favors dissimilar forms of punishment. Some schools in Nashville support the demerit system and oblige their students to come in on the weekend to fulfill their Saturday Detention, not University School. In the 1990s USN was, "definitely seen as challenging though not as 'traditional' as Harpeth Hall or MBA, for instance—more 'hands on', more discussion based than lecture-based."[60] Today University School supports a modified/reformed judicial approach.

A progressive institution is experimental. University School is indeed experimental when it comes to not only the behavior of the school but also the opportunities at the school. University School allows study halls and free periods for high school students. Depending on the courses a student takes, they may also have "late mornings" as many call it. Opportunities at USN are diverse, with independent studies, which allow students to pursue their own fervor in the academic realm. Students not only decide on what their study is about but they also design their personal curriculum. Students also have the option of spending a class period in the school Administration offices, the Health Room, or being a personal aide to Lower School classrooms. These are opportunities that you don't normally see at other schools.

Rick O'Hara argues that the school was indeed a, "diverse, pluralistic and progressive school." USN was definitely a place where students were allowed to be themselves, and each and every personality was reflected in the school body. "There were students who enjoyed the individuality and freedom of expression the school allowed them . . . ." says O'Hara.

Conversely, University School could be considered as a traditional institution. Sure, the school has some different opportunities, but in the broad sense we are what every school is: a place for learning. A school must have challenging aspects, homework, and academic periods, which is what USN has, but it's beginning to lean a little more towards the progressive lifestyle.

University School's curriculum is more traditional while the teaching style is progressive. The curriculum fulfills credit requirements and leaves each student with the basic skill that he/she needs for college. The teaching style is progressive because not every class is merely students sitting in desks in front of a teacher that's lecturing. Our classes are planned with interactive behaviors, project planning and working time, separate time to work on individual assignments, and sometimes even games.

Sometimes it's easier to assess a school over time. Looking back to the 1970s up to the present school year, 2005, it's only obvious what University School has become.

"We're much more traditional now compared to what we used to be."[61] USN used to be the "easy-going, relaxed, hippie school" where kids would skip class and spend their time out on the wall. Today there is a significant amount of structure to the school: there are requirements to fill, tests to take, and presentations to plan, which seem to occur quite frequently for most students. A great deal of the structure comes from societal changes. "People don't know how to relax anymore," says Bobbie Grubb.

Some look at University School as a school that's trying to go back to being progressive but just hasn't crossed the line yet. Through the incorporation of numerous seminar English courses, electives, and independent studies, the school is trying to create distinctive learning opportunities that students can't find anywhere else on a High School level.

Truthfully it is difficult to say whether University School is strictly progressive or traditional. It's safe to say that compared to what it used to be it's traditional, but compared to other High Schools today it 's progressive. Although many mechanical aspects at USN have changed, the mission statement has preserved. The alteration in the performance of the school has only helped the school preserve its purpose and goal, and with that it's been able to shape the lives of many young students.

ENDNOTES

1 Sacks, Diane. December 16, 2004.

2 Eskind, Seth. December 2, 2004.

3 Lubow, Sara. December 16, 2004.

4 Ekind, Seth. December 2, 2004.

5 *University School High School Handbook*, 1972-1973, page 8.

6 *University School High School Handbook*, 1972-1973, page 8.

7 *University School High School Handbook*, 1972-1973, page 8/9.

8 *University School High School Handbook*, 1972-1973, page 9.

9 *University School High School Handbook*, 1972-1973, page 9.

10 Wallis, Linda. November 19, 2004.

11 *University School High School Handbook*, 1972-1973, page 9.

12 *University School High School Handbook*, 1972-1973, page 9.

13 Schneider, Janet. September 30, 2004.

14 Hicks, Dee. October 4, 2004.

15 Wallis, Linda. November 19, 2004.

16 *The Paper*. "Notoh Observes Classes At USN." November 6, 1979.

17 Wallis, Linda. November 19, 2004.

18 *The Paper*. "USN Adds Six Courses," "Positive Reactions To Eight Periods." September 21, 1979.

19 *The Paper*. "USN Adds Six Courses." September 21, 1979.

20 *The Paper*. "USN Adds Six Courses." September 21, 1979.

21 *The Paper*. "USN Adds Six Courses." September 21, 1979.

22 *The Paper*. "USN Adds Six Courses." September 21, 1979.

23 *The Paper*. "USN Adds Six Courses." September 21, 1979.

24 *The Paper*. "Positive Reactions To Eight Periods." September 21, 1979.

25 *The Paper*. "Positive Reactions To Eight Periods." September 21, 1979.

26 Wallis, Linda. November 19, 2004.

27 Wallis, Linda. November 19, 2004.

28 *The Paper*. "Administrators Need to Create Effective Teaching Environment." May 26, 1983.

29 1986 *USNews*. "High School Plans Honor Code."

30 Wheeler, Dr. Ann. November 19, 2004.

31 Wheeler, Dr. Ann. November 19, 2004.

32 *The Paper*. "Administrators Need to Create Effective Teaching Environment." May 26, 1983.

33 1986 *USNews*. "Freshmen Have Heavier Load."

34 1986 *USNews*. "Freshmen Have Heavier Load."

35 1986 *USNews*. "Freshmen Have Heavier Load."

36 1986 *USNews*. "Juniors Agonize Over Term Paper."

37 1986 *USNews*. "Juniors Agonize Over Term Paper."

38 1986 *USNews*. "Juniors Agonize Over Term Paper."

39 Hicks, Dee. October 1, 2004.

40 May, Jack. Maier, Hal. Meador, Dr. Cliff. October 12, 2004.

41 Sperling, Harvey. October 15, 2004.

42 Hicks, Dee. October 4, 2004.

43 Grubb, Bobbie. September 24, 2004.

44 Sperling, Harvey. October 15, 2004.

45 Wallis, Linda. November 19, 2004.

46 Costello, Edward. February 3, 2005.

47 Costello, Edward.

48 Wallis, Linda. November 19, 2004.

49 Wallis, Linda. November 19, 2004.

50 Wallis, Linda. November 19, 2004.

51 Wallis, Linda. November 19, 2004.

52 Wallis, Linda. November 19, 2004.

53 Wallis, Linda. November 19, 2004.

54 Eskind, Seth. December 2, 2004.

55 Strupp, Dana. December 20, 2004.

56 Wallis, Linda. November 19, 2004.

57 Sacks, Diane. December 16, 2004.

58 Grubb, Bobbie. Miller, Norma. Schneider. Janet. November 11, 2004.

59 Grubb, Bobbie. November 11, 2004.

60 O'Hara, Richard. February 7, 2005.

61 Steine, Ronnie. December 2, 2004.

From "Administration"
SHEA SULKIN
Class of 2003

Once Mr. Sperling received the title of headmaster, there were many changes that he set out to make. Although only a small detail, he first changed the title of headmaster to director. This showed that Sperling would not lead as the dictator-like Snedcof had, but would act as a guide to lead the school to more stable ground. After settling into the new school, he was immediately hit with issues that quickly needed solutions. USN had a $1.5 million debt, no endowment, and the Board of Directors, who should have been working to solve this financial problem, was not good at raising money or sturdy enough to push themselves out of debt. The Board was attempting to run the school, rather than the director managing the school and the Board hiring and firing the Director based on his performance. Also, the Board was elected by the school community, which meant anyone could run and be a part of the Board. This approach allowed for the Board to be inconsistent and the school to be unstable. Once Sperling changed the system (the Director runs the school and the Board hires/fires him), he then was able to raise money and stability within the school. Where teachers and the school community had once been paranoid about the safety of the school and their jobs, Sperling was allowing faculty, students and parents to regain balance and confidence in the school's management and future.

Sperling's next obstacle was to increase graduation requirements, tighten the curriculum, and create more administrative structure. Compared to former headmasters, Sperling's directing style was considered much more conservative and structured, but after many years of chaos and turmoil, structure was just what the school needed. He assembled curriculum guides, department chairs, and level coordinators (lower, middle and high school). This management structure helped each teacher have a better understanding of what the students should be learning. It also forced the teachers within each department to work together to coordinate and balance the material they were teaching, and for each section of the school (lower, middle and high school) to be more organized and on track. Regarding the students, Sperling instituted a higher level of discipline. This discipline included taking attendance at each class (and keeping students for the full length of class time), no longer allowing high school students to drive off campus during the school day, and stopping all smoking on the infamous "wall."

Although many students felt they were losing their freedom, USN was in dire need of stability and a more positive reputation. Enrollment had slowly been decreasing during the late seventies and early eighties, due greatly to the loose, grungy reputation the school had gained in the seventies. Class size was down to an average of 40 or 50 students per graduating class, whereas, in earlier years, the class size was closer to 70 students. The school needed more students to raise money and push the school further out of dept. By 1985, Sperling felt stability had been achieved. No longer in debt, with a more challenging curriculum, no more smoking on the wall, and stability within the school's administration, Sperling was able to reach his goal of increased enrollment and a better reputation for USN.

Once a feeling of stability had been reached, Sperling was able to focus on improving the future of University School. After nearly a decade as director of USN, Harvey Sperling had accomplished the stability and positive reputation he pushed the school to have, and raised the money to build two additions to the original building to house the school's increased student population. Although enrollment had increased over the mid-eighties, USN was still functioning in the original buildings the school had bought from Peabody College. There was a major lack of space, but with the school's new fund-raising abilities, Sperling provided the leadership to allow the school to expand. In 1986, the school built the west wing to house new classrooms, a kindergarten area, and music and art rooms for the Lower School. Then, in September of 1989, a new space opened including the new gym, a cafeteria, locker rooms, and a chorus and dance room. This was fittingly titled the Harvey Sperling Center. This capital campaign was Sperling's final contribution to USN's thriving educational community. In January of 1990, Sperling resigned after accepting the position of Head of University School of Milwaukee.

After four directors, and over a decade of struggle, the school was finally able to stand strong. While speaking about the directors of USN, Heber Rogers stated that it is "a constant refining process." With each successive director, the school was able to find more stability and growth. USN's community and reputation continues to grow stronger because of the leadership these directors provided.

From "School Facilities"
BOBBY PERRY
Class of 2003

Our school's facilities have a much more interesting history than most people would ever imagine. Who knew that the same group of architects that designed our main building in the early 1920s also designed several buildings for Columbia University's Teachers College? Or what about how our auditorium caught on fire at the beginning of June 1954? And what about how PDS high school students used to take classes on Peabody's main campus? The USN student of today knows very little about the history of our facilities, and the story is a lot more intriguing than most would perceive. Let's dive in.

Our main building was finished in 1925, when our school was just 10 years old.

....

However, by the early 1970s this architectural masterpiece had succumbed to Peabody College's neglect when it came to the Dem School's upkeep. The rumors about our school having trouble passing zoning examinations are valid. There were also over-crowding problems that were beginning to become more and more prevalent. In 1973, the Demonstration School had an enrollment of 830 students; that is just 169 students less than today, but we've got nearly 200% of the classroom space now. Several high school classes were held on Peabody's Campus. In a report to the President of Peabody, Edward Pratt, the director of the Dem School, said: "A total of thirty high school classes are held in space formerly assigned to college classes. The space that was freed in the Dem School has been assigned to Middle School classes." Other classrooms were split by teachers, and classes were even held in the basement of the school's annexes.

From "A Social History of the Wall"
STEVEN VENICK
Class of 2003

The USN of the 1970s and early 1980s came to its present form under the guidance and leadership of Mr. Sperling. The freedom and egalitarianism of USN was what attracted Mr. Sperling, and it was also what Mr. Sperling recognized would bring USN's doom. He saw his mission and his chief problem as trying to preserve the former environment of USN and still ensure its future. His mantra perfectly expresses the new goals of USN and foreshadowed the current USN: a disciplined mind is a free mind.

Currently at USN, administration abounds. There are now independent heads of the lower, middle, and high school. There are heads of each independent academic department under which the faculty are organized. Fellow teachers, administrators, and even students evaluate teachers often. Graduation requirements have become more comprehensive and rigorous. And of course, roll is taken, and students have to go to class.

CPSIA information can be obtained at www.ICGtesting.com
Printed in the USA
LVOW11s0547260814

399717LV00005B/1/P